1003493028

	DATE DUE	
OCT 17 2002		
		OCT 30 2003
OCT 31 2002		NOV 24 2003
		DEC 4 2003
NOV 21 2002		MAR 4 2004
DEC 13 2002		
FEB 18 2003		MAR 25 2004
		DEC 10 2004
APR 15 2003		DEC 5 2005

LEARNING RESOURCE
CENTRE
GRANT MacEWAN
COMMUNITY COLLEGE

STRESS MANAGEMENT FOR LAW ENFORCEMENT
(Behind the Shield: Combating Trauma)

by

Peter J. Pranzo, Ret. Lt., NYPD
and
Rachela Pranzo

GOULD PUBLICATIONS, INC.

INDEX, LAYOUT, PAGE MAKE-UP,
DESIGN AND TYPESETTING
COPYRIGHT © 1999
by J. & B. Gould
Printed in the U.S.A.

Published by
GOULD PUBLICATIONS, INC.
1333 North US Highway 17-92
Longwood, Florida 32750-3724
(407) 695-9500
World Wide Web—http://www.gouldlaw.com
E-mail—info@gouldlaw.com
ISBN 0-87526-532-4

All rights reserved. No part of this book may be used or reproduced in any manner whatsoever without the written permission of the publisher except in the case of brief quotations embodied in critical articles and reviews.

The views and instructions expressed herein are those of the author.

Every attempt has been made to ensure the accuracy and the completeness of the material contained herein. No express or implied guarantees or warranties are made.

Since procedures change very often and vary from jurisdiction to jurisdiction, it is very important to check the timeliness and applicability of the procedures contained herein. Always consult with your supervisor before changing or modifying an existing procedure.

FOREWORD

In many law enforcement agencies across the country, the "shield" is the official term for an officer's badge. With the nominal meaning of "shield" being a protective barrier, the subtitle of this book, *Behind the Shield*, signifies a look past the thin blue line and deep into the heart of the law enforcement officer.

Today, stress and trauma in law enforcement are more prevalent than ever before. Stress and trauma are produced not only from events in the field that police officers across the country face, but also from internal departmental events and policies that are actually responsible for the officer's employment and well-being. Law enforcement men and women face daily challenges that most American citizens could not fathom. It is during and after such challenging events that over-scrutinizing of officers and lack of support may be so prevalent and damaging.

Excessive supervision, second guessing, and internal investigations, coupled with the specters of death and despair, eat away at the very physical and psychological foundation of the officer. The mental health of law enforcement personnel should be of the highest priority as it directly affects the quality of service and protection citizens receive and often demand.

Readers of this book will learn what law enforcement officers really experience on a daily basis, including:

- How officers actually feel, from the inside out, while coping with the enemy within;

- How, in some departments, police suicides actually outnumber line-of-duty police killings, and why;

- How police families are torn apart from the results of stress and trauma; and

- How a spouse lives with the burdens of loneliness and fear of the loss of his or her loved one.

This book discusses the analogy of a breaking point that comes from the many stress and trauma factors inherent throughout police work. Personal experiences and reflections gleaned through honest responses to questions posed reveal officers' states of mind. Finally, this book explores the coping mechanisms, supervisory goals and behaviors, and rehabilitation programs presently in place that enable the police officer to continue functioning as a public servant and protector.

For as many heroes as are in law enforcement, there are those standing behind them ready to catch them as they fall victim and succumb to the tribulations within their profession. They are the families, peers, psychologists and psychiatrists, and other mental health professionals who are dedicated to restoring the mental well-being of the officers they represent. Many of these people, profiled in this book, today offer their professional services within established programs by working in support units such as critical incident debriefing teams, or volunteering as peer counselors.

When the young adults, sometimes family members or neighbors, enter into the world of law enforcement, they are entitled to support, for they are the part of society that is sent forward to serve and protect. This service comes with a heavy price. These men and women are asked by society to lay down their lives so that others may live, work and play in peace, free from the harmful elements that detract from a safe environment.

ABOUT THE AUTHORS

Peter and Rachela Pranzo, husband and wife, have been married for thirty years. They have raised two children, Anthony and Lorinda, now adults, who are pursuing careers of their own.

Peter J. Pranzo is a retired New York City Police Department Lieutenant with over 21 years of service. He has received over 60 awards, Department commendations and community awards, including some of the Police Department's highest: the Police Combat Cross, the Award for Valor, and the Honor Legion Medal for Valor. In the 32nd Precinct of Harlem, where he supervised a narcotics team as a Sergeant for 8 years, his unit made the more than 8,000 arrests that kicked off the Operation Drug Campaign that spread citywide.

Retired Lieutenant Pranzo has written for 12 police and law enforcement magazines from across the United States. Additionally, he has done technical consulting and advising for various court testimonies and TV shows, as well as given lectures and seminars. Peter's final assignment was to the New York City Police Department's Street Crime Unit. There, he supervised, daily, plainclothes/undercover police who made use of various impersonations such as cab drivers or street persons while they made arrests for violent street crimes in progress. This Unit achieved a rate of between two and three thousand felony arrests per year. Today he enjoys retirement at home with his wife, Rachela.

Rachela Pranzo, after a career as assistant to the vice-president of a large engineering corporation and raising a family, now manages her own business designing home-study courses for career and promotional advancement. She has also written for many years and specializes in poetry.

ACKNOWLEDGMENTS

We wish to thank the following men and women for their valued support and contributions to this book.

Boston Police Department
P.O. Michael O'Sullivan

Chicago Police Department
Lt. William Powers

Cleveland Police Department
Carolyn M. Tenerowicz, Ph.D.

Erie County
Dr. Grady Bray
Cynthia L. Goss

FBI - San Antonio
Dr. Nancy Davis
Dr. Dickson Diamond
FBI Director Louie Freeh
SSA Chuck McCormick
SA Vincent McNally

Fraternal Order of Police
Jerry W. Atnip
Andrew Bittner
Gilbert G. Gallegos

Las Vegas Metropolitan Police Department
Det. Michael Bryant
Sgt. Thomas G. Harmon
Lt. Edward H. Jensen
Sheriff Jerry Keller

Los Angeles Police Department
Det. Walter J. DeCuir, Jr.
Debra F. Glasser, Ph.D.

Metropolitan Dade Police
Scott W. Allen, Ph.D.

The National Institute of Justice

**New York City
Police Department**
Sergeant Janet Greco
Carol McKenny
Michael W. Popp, Ph.D.
Dr. Martin Symonds

Oklahoma City Police Department
Diane Leonard
Dr. Jack Poe, Chaplin

San Diego Police Department
Steve Albrecht, Police Officer, Res.
Jolee J. Brunton, Ph.D.
Robert Burgess, Ph.D.
Dennis A. Davis, Ph.D.
Mark Marvin, Ph.D.
Trudy Slater, Ph.D.
Launi Treece, Ph.D.
Steven G. White, Ph.D.
Lourdes Perez-Williams, Ph.D.

San Francisco Police Department
Capt. Allen Benner, Ph.D.
Sgt. Forrest Fulton, Ph.D.
Sgt. Lynette Hogue
Chief of Police Fred Lau
Sgt. Vicki Quinn
P.O. Mick Shea
P.O. David W. Tussey
Deputy Chief William Welch

DEDICATION

There are literally thousands of different police functions being performed daily, including some that end in tragedy and death. We dedicate this book to the men and women in law enforcement agencies across America, who in their heroic daily chores, have concluded their tour of duty by serious injury or death. Many law enforcement officers have sacrificed their own existence in order that others may live and work in peace.

This is our way to say thanks to an exceptional group of people who have the powers of decision and responsibility to either snuff the life of a villain, or to bring life itself into the world. We should never forget the achievement, bravery, responsibility, and heart of the police officer.

It is here we also acknowledge those men and women who work behind the scenes by lending valued support for our law enforcement officers. These are the doctors, psychiatrists, psychologists, health professionals, counselors, family members, and peers.

And, above all, let us never forget those police officers who have taken their own lives after incurring large doses of stress and trauma that are almost beyond comprehension. They, too, are our heroes.

TABLE OF CONTENTS

	Page
FOREWORD	iii
ABOUT THE AUTHORS	v
ACKNOWLEDGMENTS	vi
DEDICATION	viii
INTRODUCTION	xiii

CHAPTER 1. PERSONAL REFLECTIONS 1
    A. A Cop Out of Control 2
    B. Portrait of a Friend 3
    C. "Catch a Falling Star" 6

CHAPTER 2. ON THE JOB—FROM STRESS TO BURNOUT 9
    A. Stress in Everday Life 10
    B. The Real World of Police Work 11
    C. Sources of Stress 11
        1. Living with Extremes 11
        2. Oppressive Schedules 11
        3. High Crime Time 12
        4. Fear of Injury or Death 12
    D. Stress From Within the Department 13
        1. Discipline 13
        2. Promotion Process 14
        3. Fear and Mistrust 17
        4. Allegations of Police Brutality 18
        5. Women in Law Enforcement 19
    E. Police Officers Speak Out 20
        1. Personnel Survey 20
        2. Personnel Comments 21

CHAPTER 3. CRACKS IN THE SHIELD 23
    A. Masked Suicides 24
    B. Emotional Hardening—A Dangerous Defense 24
        1. Personnel Interviews 25
    C. Stress-Related Problems 29
        1. Combat Team Syndrome 29
        2. Substance Abuse 30
        3. Stress upon Spouse and Family 30

CHAPTER 4. STRESS AND TRAUMA—AN OFFICER'S INSIGHTS 33
    A. "Running Out of Gas: Compassion & Fatigue" 34
    B. "The Police Officer's Companion: Pain & Grief" 37
    C. "Keeping It In Balance" 40

CHAPTER 5. COPING WITH STRESS 43

    A. Preventive Measures 44
        1. Training and Supervision. 44
        2. Psychological Services and Research 45
        3. Helpline 46
        4. General Warning Signs of Depression 46
    B. Stress Management, Dr. Jolee Brunton, Ph.D. 47
        1. Valuing Skills 47
        2. Personal Planning 48
        3. Commitment 49
        4. Time Use 49
        5. Pacing 49
        6. Sleep Management 50
        7. Communication Skills 51
        8. Effective Stress Management 52
        9. Anger Management. 54
        10. Thirteen Styles of Distorted Thinking 55
        11. Golden Rules for Coping with Panic 56
        12. Alcoholic Thinking 57
        13. Assertiveness Training 58
        14. Marriage and the Affair. 63
        15. Burnout 65
        16. Relationships 69

CHAPTER 6. POST TRAUMA 73

    A. "The Morning After". 74
    B. Trauma and Neurosis 74
    C. Traumatic Incidents 75

CHAPTER 7. POST TRAUMA—TREATMENT AND REHABILITATION PROGRAMS 79

    A. The McMains Study—Findings and Recommendations . . . 80
    B. Post-Shooting/Combat Stress Reactions 82
        1. Post-Shooting Stress Reactions. 82
        2. Combat Stress Reactions 82
        3. Conclusion 83
    C. Principles of Managing Trauma 83
    D. Professional and Peer Support System 84
        1. Debriefing and Counseling Program Applied 84
        2. Dr. Martin Symonds—Counseling with Compassion . . 86

CHAPTER 8. POST TRAUMA—RESPONSES AND HEALING 89

    A. The Trauma Response. 90
        1. Building a Wall Around Pain 90
        2. Common Responses to Traumatic Events 90
        3. Getting Over the Trauma Response 92
    B. The Healing Process. 92
        1. Caring For Physical Health. 92
        2. Moving Through the Healing Process 93
    C. Finding Meaning in Trauma 94

D. Family Support 95
E. Co-worker Support 96

**CHAPTER 9. SPECIALIZED FIELD AND
              TESTING UNITS** 99

A. Critical Incident Debriefing Teams 100
B. Peer Support Units. 101
C. Psychological Testing Units 104
   1. Psychological Testing of Police Recruits. 104
   2. Functions of Screening 105
   3. How Tests Work 105
   4. The Assessment Center 105

CLOSING 107

GLOSSARY 109

**APPENDIX
LAW ENFORCEMENT STRESS AND TRAUMA
MANAGEMENT PROGRAMS, SOLUTIONS,
AND PERSONNEL** 111

A. **NEW YORK CITY POLICE DEPARTMENT/NYPD** 111

   1. Trauma Counseling and Response Program 112
   2. Trauma Counseling Team. 113

B. **LOS ANGELES POLICE DEPARTMENT/LAPD** 113

   1. LAPD Behavioral Sciences Services/Scope of Services . 113
   2. LAPD Mental Evaluation Unit and System Wide
      Mental Assessment Response Team 115

C. **CLEVELAND POLICE DEPARTMENT** 115

   1. Officer Profile 115
   2. Dr. Tenerowicz's Program. 116

D. **SAN FRANCISCO POLICE DEPARTMENT/SFPD** 117

   1. Behavioral Science Unit. 117
   2. Behavioral Science Unit Programs Profiled 119

E. **LAS VEGAS METROPOLITAN
   POLICE DEPARTMENT/LVMPD** 121

   1. Officer Profiles. 121
   2. LVMPD Police Employee Assistance
      Program (PEAP). 124
   3. LVMPD Supervisor's Guide to Employee
      Job Performance and Assistance under the
      Police Employee Assistance Program 125

F. **CHICAGO POLICE DEPARTMENT** 135
   1. Personnel Concerns Program 135
   2. Personnel Division. 138
   3. Behavioral Intervention System (BIS) 138
   4. Professional Counseling Service/Employee
      Assistance Program 139
   5. Professional Counseling Service 139
   6. Alcoholism and Other Addictions Services Unit 140
   7. Traumatic Incident Debriefing Program 140
   8. Department Referrals to the Professional
      Counseling Service 141

G. **BOSTON POLICE DEPARTMENT**. 141
   1. Officer Profile 141
   2. Boston Police Critical Incident Support Team 141

H. **OKLAHOMA CITY POLICE DEPARTMENT** 142
   1. Officer Profiles. 142
   2. Critical Incident Workshops—A Pathway To Peace .. 144

I. **SAN DIEGO POLICE DEPARTMENT/SDPD** 146
   1. FOCUS Psychological Services Program 146
   2. FOCUS Personnel 147
   3. FOCUS Program Description 151
   4. FOCUS—Trauma Treatment and Crisis Intervention . 154
   5. FOCUS Psychological Services
      Supervisor/Management Guide. 162

J. **CATCH A FALLING STAR LAW ENFORCEMENT
    ASSISTANCE PROGRAM FOR OFFICERS AND
    THEIR FAMILIES, INC.**. 170
   1. "Catch a Falling Star" 171

K. **METRO DADE POLICE DEPARTMENT
    COMPREHENSIVE PSYCHOLOGICAL SERVICES
    MIAMI, FLORIDA** 176
   1. Personal Profile 176
   2. Comprehensive Psychological Services Program 178
   3. Psychological Screening and Testing Regulations ... 178
   4. Psychological Services Program. 180
   5. Intradepartmental Stress or Performance-Related
      Programs 185

L. **FEDERAL BUREAU OF INVESTIGATION** 186
   1. Background 186
   2. Program Progression 188
   3. Programs 189

INTRODUCTION

During the past 15 years, the New York Police Department (NYPD) lost more than 100 police officers, not through shoot-outs with or stabbings by violent perpetrators, but because they took their own lives; they committed suicide. This continuing bloody, shocking, and alarming pattern has left a trail of torment and desperation for police brass, fellow officers, and surviving members of those officers' families. Although the numbers vary from city to city, America's police officers take their lives at roughly triple the national average of 13 suicides per 100,000 population, and on average, police suicides are double the number of line-of-duty killings.

These facts strongly suggest a need to examine the causes of such an event. What would make a police officer take his or her life? Could the suicide have been prevented? Looking inside the mind of the police officer, let's see how some cops really feel.

This page intentionally left blank.

CHAPTER 1

PERSONAL REFLECTIONS

A. A COP OUT OF CONTROL

A few years back my whole world seemed to fall apart. It just seemed like everything I did turned out wrong. I was on an emotional roller coaster. One minute I was up and the next minute I was down. I lost all control over my life. I felt completely alone. I felt like no one understood or even remotely cared about me. My marriage fell apart even though I thought I was trying as hard as I could. I did everything I was supposed to do and nothing turned out right. I tried to talk to my wife about the job. She really didn't understand what being a cop is all about. There's a lot of pressure out there on the street; you bring a lot of other people's problems home. People look to cops when they need help. Where does a cop go? After a while my wife stopped talking to me. If we did talk, it was a battle. My own home was a battlefield. There were times I just drove around so I didn't have to go home. I was physically and emotionally exhausted. I lived on coffee and cigarettes most of the time. I drank too often and too much. I can remember the night I decided to end all the pain. There was no elaborate plan. I've held that gun hundreds of times before. But that night it felt different—it was so heavy. It was fully loaded, like I was expecting to fire more than one shot.

You know, I once asked a friend of mine where it was best to shoot yourself and he gave me this lecture about the temple versus the mouth. Pretty crazy? But you know, I listened to every word. I at least wanted to kill myself right.

You have these people who ask, "What about your family? Don't you know how hurt they'll be?" Well, I just didn't care about anyone else at that point. I was completely out of control. How could I be expected to think about someone else?

It was almost like watching a movie that night. I'm sitting in my bedroom with my gun in my hand trying to remember if I should put the damn thing in my ear or my mouth. I'm trying to imagine my family's reaction when they find my body. Like I was going to be there to see it.

It was a strange, warped way of thinking, but at the time it made perfect sense to me. I thought that at some point I would jump out of the closet and say, "Surprise, I'm not really dead! But didn't you feel bad that you thought I was?"

So here I am, pointing a loaded gun straight at myself. Think about it. If a guy was pointing a gun at you in the street what would you do? And here I am holding myself hostage. It was insane. Nothing could be more scary.

I don't know what made me stop. I think it was that I was angry too. I remember throwing the gun across the bedroom. It hit the wall so hard, I thought it might misfire. I sat there for a long time. I couldn't believe I had come so close to death.

The preceding account was an interview conducted by Sergeant Janet Greco, NYPD, from the NYPD's department magazine, Spring 3100. Although it might sadden or shock many, this reality is a facet of police work that has remained hidden for too long. This officer was one of the fortunate ones. He underwent treatment and continued to serve the department. Many others have not been so fortunate.

B. PORTRAIT OF A FRIEND
Interview by: Lt. Peter J. Pranzo, NYPD

Some years ago, I met with Carol McKenny, the widow of Jim McKenny, an NYPD Police Officer who took his own life on April 15, 1984, at the age of 42. Jim was a good friend and a great cop. To many of us at the 32nd Precinct, he was a hero. That old saying, "a cop's cop," must be used again in Jim's case. He managed to win the respect of the community he served, his fellow officers, and bosses. We called him by his nickname—"Choo-Choo." He was always on the go, bubbly, outgoing, and fun; but above all, he was very serious about his police work. During 17 years on the job, he received numerous medals and awards. Jim not only saved the lives of many innocent persons, but, on more than one occasion, was involved in serious shootings. He was religious, family oriented, and involved in many of the department organizations. As I talked with his widow, Carol, she spoke about her feelings, then and now.

We sat and spoke at her dining room table while sipping coffee. As we began discussing Jim, Carol's eyes quickly filled with tears, but she continued on in such style, with a warmth and compassion that I have never before experienced. Carol told me she met Jim in September of 1958 at a local parish, The Good Shepherd, at a teenage church dance. She married Jim in that same church six years later, and ironically held Jim's funeral mass there as well. They were married for 19 years, and were blessed with two children, Jim and Carol.

Carol spoke of her relationship with Jim. She said it was warm and understanding. "We were always in each other's pockets, never apart. We would walk on the beach, holding hands, and always exclaim how fortunate we were to have each other." Carol took a couple of slow breaths, sighed a little, and began to speak about Jim. She said he loved to laugh, was outgoing, and had a keen sense of fairness. He loved cops, loved the job, loved New York City, and was very positive about living there, in the Bronx. He felt close to the community he served. Carol said Jim was very fond of children, especially the unfortunate ones—the disabled. He always had a warm heart for the mentally retarded. On his

Portrait of a Friend   Reflections

own time, he would help out and personally visit mentally retarded persons who resided nearby his Bronx apartment.

When it came to talking about police work and the job, and its relationship with Jim, Carol started to beam. Her face glowed from within as she expressed how proud she was of her husband. She knew that the job meant everything to him; it was his life.

Jim cherished the challenge of police work and loved the people he worked with, as well as the public. She said he greatly admired police bosses who would stand up for their officers, because it gave those officers the courage and strength to continue to perform at their best and the ability to render those serious decisions every day. He loved to help cops, especially throughout the years he spent in the 32nd Precinct. They were busy years—it was a violent precinct. Jim's biggest thrill was his assignment to the department's Emergency Service Unit. Carol said it was there that his talents, dedication, strength, and job knowledge fully blossomed. She stated that Jim stopped at nothing to complete his rescues and support his fellow officers. He felt his unit was the backbone and strength of the department.

I asked Carol what disturbed Jim the most about his job, or police work in general. She paused, took about two minutes to think about it, and, surprisingly enough, her answers were brief. She said Jim's beliefs, as he often discussed them with her, were that the judicial system was just not appropriate to handle the crime problem within the city, that the city was being cheated, and that communities were suffering because of these problems. He also believed that police officers being personally held liable for all their actions, and lawsuits, or the threat of lawsuits, hindered them from performing good, aggressive patrol.

Jim believed in steady work hours. Shift rotations often bothered him because, on occasion, they would keep him from attending important family events, especially with the children. He felt steady posts or areas were good, because it gave the public personal contact with the police.

Carol said Jim was disappointed when, on occasion, he encountered supervisors who would not support their officers. He felt hindered by them. He was steadfast on the point that job knowledge, ability, and performance should be the main criteria in promotion, instead of written exams and seniority alone.

Carol stated that Jim always wished the department would offer more time and assistance to the officers and their families who experienced traumatic incidents, whether on the job or off. I explained to her about today's new approach to traumatic incidents, with response teams, medical professionals, and other expanded programs.

Reflections   **Portrait of a Friend**

The saddest part of the interview I had with Carol McKenny came when we began to discuss the last period of time, maybe 10 days or so, before Jim took his life. Carol's eyes began to fill with tears again, and as she spoke, I was careful not to interrupt; not to make her lose her train of thought, and to make sure that, if I did say something, my voice wouldn't crack. I really tried to hold back my emotions, not letting her know that I was hurting inside.

She said that Jim was on multiple medications for an infection, and that the medications might have been a contributing factor that led to his depression. She did take him back and forth to the doctors for help. She questioned Jim about his mood, and why he was feeling so down. Jim answered flatly, "I don't know, I just don't feel right—sluggish, tired." Carol said that he appeared to have a kind of tunnel vision, in which he was not able to turn left or right, not able to separate himself from easy tasks or problems, and not able to handle them. It seemed that he was losing the psychological protective barrier that a police officer must have to fend off any bad, ugly, or traumatic incidents, in order to leave them at work, and not bring them home.

On the day before he died, when questioned by her again, Jim just said, "I don't feel like a cop anymore. I don't feel like I can make any more decisions." The next day, on April 15, 1984, it was over. Police Officer Jim McKenny did take his own life, the life of a protector, father, husband, and above all, "hero cop."

Carol repeated to me more than a few times, "If only I could have known, or someone else would have understood the signs before it was too late." If only someone could have explained to Jim that it's all right to have such feelings. Police officers are not machines. They do have emotions and have every right to express them openly.

Immediately after learning of the incident, Carol said she experienced a rush of different feelings; shock, disbelief, numbness, and confusion. For at least a year she felt as if she was floating on a raft, going in no set direction, and having no anchor. She said, "My anchor was gone; Jim was my anchor. I lived in a world of silence; that person, that human being I communicated so openly with, was gone."

To regain her stability it took four years of constant support from family, friends, private therapy, and tremendous assistance from a group known as Survivors of Suicide(SOS). "Recover completely? Not really," said Carol, "Never forgetting—one thousand unanswered questions—something unfinished. That stigma about suicide is very difficult to handle. But, I've finally realized that a suicide death is a disease death, like heart failure or cancer. I've gone on with my life, working and caring for my family." She now manages three businesses, a long day for sure.

Carol and I talked for almost three hours, non-stop. We both vented a little. I knew our interview was ending. She was drained, but content. Her last statement was a quick remembrance of reading Jim's 8th grade yearbook, where he wrote that some day he wanted to be a police officer. "You know, Pete," Carol said, "on his cemetery headstone I didn't know if it was appropriate, circumstances and all, but I had them put: 'Jim McKenny—A Cop's Cop.'" I said, "Carol, you're blessed. You did right."

I shook her hand, kissed her on the cheek, and thanked her a number of times. As I left and went down on the elevator, I made the sign of the cross, and said to myself, "I hope I did O.K. for you."

I lost other close friends on the job, especially in the early '70's, a time when violence was all too prevalent, and police officers were frequently targets of assassinations. These losses saddened me, but the loss of Jim had a special impact on myself and my fellow officers. I'll never forget Jim McKenny. I'm sure that somewhere he's looking down upon us, and, as he did on so many other occasions, is looking out for us, protecting us, and reminding us of those dangers that may befall us. May God Bless you, Jim.

Not all stress and trauma related problems experienced by police officers need end in suicide or attempted suicide. As this book will demonstrate, help is available. The following is an example of one person's insight and courage to confront the problem head-on.

C. "CATCH A FALLING STAR"

I recently had the pleasure of speaking with Cynthia L. Goss, founder and president of "Catch A Falling Star," a law enforcement assistance program for officers and their families. The following is a short story she related to me which tells of how she started helping law enforcement officers.

Back in 1987, Ms. Goss was hired by the County of Erie to reorganize their Employee Assistance Program (EAP) for approximately 10,000 employees to include both blue and white collar workers. The Employee Assistance Program included family members as well. Within her jurisdiction was the County's Sheriff's Department and Correctional Facility. She was doing very well with all departments except the law enforcement agencies. The law enforcement agencies were not sending referrals, so she made an appointment to visit the Sheriff and his executive staff. They discussed the EAP program and what it could do for their department. After her orientation, the Sheriff informed her that they did not need an EAP because they did not have problems in the Sheriff's Department! Of course, there were deputies being suspended and terminated for substance abuse and suicide attempts, among other reasons. But, they didn't have problems. So Ms. Goss let it be for then.

Approximately six months later, a deputy got into trouble. He showed up for court for someone he arrested for DWI. The problem was the deputy's Blood Alcohol Count (BAC) was higher than that of the guy he arrested. His brother took him to a local alcohol treatment facility located in Buffalo for detoxification and treatment. Within a few hours of his admission, he phoned Ms. Goss, screaming to get him the hell out of there. He stated that he recognized another patient whom he had arrested by putting a shotgun to his head just a week earlier in a drug raid.

The officer was right. You cannot integrate a police officer within his or her own community because not only may cover and confidentiality be violated, but it can impose a real serious threat to the officer's safety as well.

In this instance, this patient paid $15,000 cash for his treatment, while the deputy did not have the adequate coverage for inpatient treatment. In fact, two-thirds of police officers in New York State do not have adequate coverage if they fall prey to a stress- related disorder. Cynthia Goss was fortunate to find an out-of- state treatment facility that offered him help, and today he is still working and has been promoted.

Approximately three months after that incident, there was a line of duty death of one of the deputies. The Sheriff requested Ms. Goss' assistance to do a debriefing, because he thought that is what she did to help the officers. He called a debriefing for the next morning that was attended by more than 40 officers, including the Sheriff and Undersheriff. Cynthia was relieved that her role was to observe and listen because she had limited experience with this process. She said to herself, "What's this debriefing stuff anyway?"

She learned soon enough. As each officer spoke on how they felt about this incident, much of their feelings remained suppressed to some point. One officer talked about how he felt guilty because he called in sick that day and he could have been the one killed. Another officer who was the training officer spoke on how he may not have trained the officers properly and that it was his fault. All officers were able to express their feelings, including the Sheriff, who went last. He called the debriefing to help his men, but when he started to speak he broke down and literally cried his eyes out. He thought maybe he was to blame because he was the Sheriff and he did something wrong. After he spoke of this situation, he started to talk about another deputy killed in the line of duty two years prior, and then, after that, all of the other officers he had known who were taken in the line of duty. When he was done, he expressed being embarrassed and ashamed for losing it in front of his men, and asked them what do they think of him now? They responded that not only did they respect him more, but he allowed for them to express their feelings as well. The Sheriff never realized the impact of holding in all those feelings for so many years.

After experiencing this incredible debriefing, Cynthia Goss realized that something needed to be done. What was working for everyone else, did not work for officers. She learned a lot of mental health professionals did not know how to handle police officers, nor were they in touch with the hazards of the police profession. For example, one deputy who was involved in a shooting and witnessed the killing of his partner shared with Cynthia his horror story. He had agreed to attend a debriefing his training officer set up with a psychologist from the County Medical Center. There were probably 10 to 12 officers who attended. Twenty minutes into the debriefing, the psychologist stopped to ask, "Which one of you officers was the one who got his partner killed?" End of debriefing.

Something had to be done. With the cooperation of the Sheriff's Department, Ms. Goss began to develop a specialized Law Enforcement Assistance Program for all law enforcement personnel in Western New York. She referred only to those professionals and agencies who were trained to work with law enforcement officers. She developed a critical incident stress debriefing team along with a peer support officers program. Within five years, her program became a model for other law enforcement agencies in the United States and Canada.

Her program, Catch A Falling Star Law Enforcement Assistance Program, is now a non-profit organization and is tax exempt. The logo, "Catch a Falling Star" came out of a question she was often asked; "How do you save these guys?" Her response was, "You have to catch them before they fall." The star signifies every law enforcement officer's badge. The goal is to catch them before they get into trouble or kill themselves.

CHAPTER 2

ON THE JOB—
FROM STRESS TO BURNOUT

A. STRESS IN EVERYDAY LIFE

Emotions, whether pleasant or unpleasant, usually come and go quickly, leaving no lasting impact. However, sometimes emotional states may be of sufficient intensity and duration that they produce physiological and psychological effects known as stress. According to Hans Selye, a Canadian physiologist, some amount of stress is normal, and even beneficial. In fact, he called the complete lack of stress, death (Selye 1974).

Any changes in a person's life, whether seen as negative or positive, can be sources of stress. The following is a list of life events that are either major or minor sources of stress. These are general events that may be encountered in the normal course of life.

Marital and Family

- Death of a spouse
- Divorce
- Separation
- Death of a close family member
- Marriage
- Pregnancy
- Child custody battles
- Extra-marital relations
- Household disruptions

Personal

- Major injury
- Sickness
- Failed relationships
- Sexual difficulties
- Death of a friend
- Alcohol/drug abuse
- Change of assignment
- Promotion
- Change in eating habits

Career

- Firing
- Retirement
- Change of assignment
- Trouble with the boss

Financial

- Change in financial status
- Foreclosure on house

The police officer lives with all of the stresses that the civilian meets and deals with in the normal course of life. In addition, an officer experiences situations of an intensity and duration not commonly experienced by most people. Situations involving personal disaster and calamity are routine in the world of the cop. Let's enter that world.

B. THE REAL WORLD OF POLICE WORK

Entering the world of law enforcement is like beginning life anew, without knowing what lies ahead, or what the future, if any, holds. The ability or inability to adapt can mean either a life of gratification or destruction. Shortly after starting a career, possibly after only a few days on patrol, a young officer gets the picture. This is not like TV, where the work is clean and heroic, and where good guys win and bad guys lose. Police work might be completely different than a rookie could have ever imagined. The reality cannot be transmitted through a television or movie screen.

The young officer begins not only a career, but possibly decades of being subjected to that condition called stress. He or she learns how to cope with stress, or loses the struggle to survive mentally and physically, drowning in a sea of relentless turmoil, confusion, and depression. In either case, the young police officer will be forever changed by the sources of stress encountered on the job.

C. SOURCES OF STRESS

1. LIVING WITH EXTREMES

In general, police work maintains certain conditions not found in most civilian careers, one of which is a constant roller coaster of adrenaline surges. Routine patrol may, in an instant, transgress into a blazing gun battle. A simple arrest situation can turn into a long, tense radio-monitored car chase or an exhausting foot pursuit. Time spent listening to chirping birds and watching children play on a beautiful Sunday morning might, in a moment, be pierced by the sounds of small children screaming while trapped inside a burning car. A seemingly routine canvas of one's patrol post can uncover a decapitated body, or a newborn infant concealed within a plastic garbage bag, motionless from death. Quietness and tranquillity can suddenly turn into fear, confusion, and horror. The intensity and randomness of such events creates pronounced stress reactions, both physiologically and psychologically (Benjamin, Hopkins & Nation, 1987).

2. OPPRESSIVE SCHEDULES

Working hours and shift rotation can also have a disastrous effect on a police officer's life, creating fatigue through poor eating and sleeping habits. The ability to perform on the job and think clearly surely becomes hampered by an ever-changing daily work schedule. Constant change coupled with poor health maintenance will damage the physical body by weakening its immune system, thereby making the police officer more susceptible to disease(Jemmott & Locke, 1984).

For a police officer, the disappointment of spending a holiday in the station house separated from family just cannot be expressed. Missing a child's most important game of the year because a change of tours could not be arranged, or because of sheer exhaustion following a midnight shift, creates pent-up feelings ready for expression. Not seeing his or her children for days on end because of awakening after they have begun their day and getting home after they are already asleep just doesn't seem fair. The police officer takes it in stride, or so it seems. However, once the officer stops to think about how abnormal this really is, his or her routine becomes engulfed with feelings of resentment.

3. HIGH CRIME TIME

Another important source of stress that needs attention by both police officers and administrators is too much "high crime time" for police officers. Many of our men and women have spent too many years working in tough and heavily combative neighborhoods. Studies have proven that these officers may transform from quiet spoken, well-adjusted rookies, into gruff, overworked, over-stressed and possibly bitter members of a department.

A new program started in New York City guarantees a general rotation of all police officers. This ensures that an officer does not overstay to the point that leads to sudden tragedy.

4. FEAR OF INJURY OR DEATH

Lurking behind confrontations with extreme events on a near daily basis is the fear of death or serious physical injury. The thought of being shot, stabbed, or beaten to death does not please the officer. Once involved in a very volatile, life threatening situation, an officer might never release the memory of the event from his mind. The officer's fear of death might be heightened to such a degree that he or she avoids dangerous encounters or freezes in a tactical situation. Fitful nights of sleep may be punctuated by nightmares about the event. An officer who loses a comrade or partner in the line of duty may experience doubt and guilt and ask, "What am I doing here?" and "Why him, and not me?" An officer exhibiting a debilitating fear of death is a danger to him or herself and to his or her partner. Unfortunately, a standard stress reaction like emotional hardening, while necessary, presents its own problems.

D. STRESS FROM WITHIN THE DEPARTMENT

Patroling the beat, engaging in gunfights, and arresting offenders are not the only or necessarily the most stressful activities of police work. The operation, administration, and policies of a department regarding discipline and promotion, along with the possibility of internal investigation and lawsuit, are sources of great stress on the officer. In addition, with the integration of women into law enforcement field work, problems of expectation and behavior affect both men and women.

1. DISCIPLINE

Of course discipline in today's police departments is an essential management tool necessary for the proper function and good order of any organization. Without it, failure is a certainty.

Although it is thought of as punishment or penalty, discipline actually should consist of instructing, training, or teaching. Its main purposes are to facilitate coordination of effort, develop self-control and character, and foster orderliness and efficiency. One of the primary measures of the level of discipline within any department is the orderliness with which it operates. The degree of this orderliness is directly related to the conduct of the employees, which, in turn, is largely dependent upon how well the supervisor performs his or her duties.

Retired Inspector Iannone from the Los Angeles Police Department, author and instructor, classifies the various forms of discipline as either positive or negative. Positive discipline is that form of training and attitudinal conditioning which is used to correct deficiencies without invoking punishment. It is constructive in nature. Its influence engenders an habitual or conditioned reaction from within the individual to the established values of the organization, its customs, and traditions. It is present when employees willingly follow the directions of their supervisors and adhere to the standards of conduct prevalent in the organization.

A well-disciplined organization is one that is highly trained. It follows that an effective, efficient organization is a well-disciplined one in which the principles of positive discipline have been recognized and practiced. The members have the same individual objectives as those of the group. Such a state can only be achieved, however, when the group objectives are made known to the members and they adopt these objectives as their own.

If supervisors are thoroughly indoctrinated in their responsibilities; if they are expert planners, trainers, and leaders; if they assist their subordinates by demonstrating, guiding, and counseling; and if they set a good example by their conduct, positive discipline will prevail and the need for punitive discipline (a prime stress factor) will be lessened. Indeed, the skill with which supervisors use this positive tool to a large

Stress From Within the Department   On the Job

extent determines the quality of their leadership and the effectiveness of the organization. Iannone stated: "An organization may be considered to have been brought into the ideal state when there exists a maximum of efficiency and satisfaction of its members generated by techniques of positive discipline, with a minimum use of the punitive or negative discipline."

Negative discipline is that style of discipline which takes the form of punishment or chastisement. Even in departments which have good discipline, there are times when negative disciplinary action must be exercised in order to achieve conformity when accepted methods of positive discipline fail. Over- supervision, or a department that is riddled with negative discipline to an extreme military/autocratic style of discipline, is a prime stress factor.

Superiors should always use the positive (training) approach first and most frequent. When disciplining, they should never display outbursts of temper. Remaining calm and professional, even in the most serious situations, is of utmost importance. An unstable boss will quickly lose his or her authority and leadership. They should expect from subordinates only the effort or image that they personally portray to them. Consistency in a mode of supervision is mandatory. Creditability, morale, disposition, and allegiance to a department will be imitated and repeated. Over-supervision in petty situations should be avoided. This is a common fault among newly appointed sergeants or first-line supervisors. Praise and acknowledgment of good work should vastly overpower criticism. Finally, when mediating punishment, a cooling off period should be allowed, and one should never play on personalities or favorites. All facts must be taken into account.

Although proper control or restraint in relation to discipline is necessary, modern day police departments and all supervisors should never forget that they are working with human beings who require and are entitled to certain needs and considerations. This will avoid the stress that comes from improperly administered discipline.

2. PROMOTION PROCESS

Promotional opportunities and selection can be the catalyst for either enhancing or reducing stress. Perhaps no other management tool comes close to the effect that the promotional opportunities and selection process can have on police departments, both large and small. It can dramatically increase or decrease both morale and organization efficiency, thus either increasing or decreasing an overall aura of stress. On pages 14 to 17 of this book, O.W. Wilson, co-author of *Police Administration* (4th ed.), describes the pros and cons of actions taken in the promotion process.

Promotion in police service ordinarily means advancement to a position of leadership. The officer's first promotion is normally to a supervisory position (from patrol officer to sergeant). In the original

On the Job   Stress From Within the Department

selection of a patrol officer, assuming the department adheres to the traditional rank structure and promotional pattern, qualities of leadership over and above those needed for the performance of the usual patrol tasks should be sought. When patrol officers are promoted to the rank of sergeant, it is essential to choose those who possess the greatest potential qualities of leadership, together with those who have displayed the greatest proficiency in their duties as patrol officers. From among the group of sergeants will subsequently be drawn those for advancement to higher responsibilities of command, unless lateral entry becomes a reality. It is extremely important for the department to have at each level in the chain of command an adequate number of officers who are well qualified for advancement to higher positions.

Selection for promotion presents greater difficulties than selection of recruits. It is also more important. In spite of the firsthand knowledge that supervisory and command officers may have of the characteristics of promotional candidates, the present methods for detecting and accurately measuring the necessary qualities of leadership sometimes do fall short.

Seniority or length of service should not in itself be a prime factor in the selection for promotion. However, this factor should not be overlooked in the promotional potential and oral board evaluations, since by its very nature, it will have either increased or lowered leadership potential. In the first instance, a long period of service may have given the candidate better judgment, greater self-confidence and decisiveness, greater knowledge, and an improved ability to get along with people. In the second instance, it may have resulted in diminished energy, initiative, enthusiasm, interest in work, and willingness to accept responsibility. So, the factor of length of service should be carefully considered and integrated into the evaluation process that is most suitable for each department.

As a general rule, police departments, especially the larger ones and those under the influence of a central personnel agency, rely heavily on written tests of knowledge in selection for promotion. The popularity of the written test for this purpose arises from a sincere desire to select personnel on the basis of merit, free of outside or departmental favoritism. The test is easily administered, it provides a numerical score, and it seems fair in that candidates can blame only themselves for unsatisfactory results. Suitable tools and procedures for evaluating other desirable qualifications have been slow to develop, so it is not surprising that the use of the written test is so widespread.

In the promotion to sergeant, supervisory content should be stressed in the written examination. A good balance of subject matter should provide material on supervision, principles of administration, departmental procedures, criminal law and procedure, and police investigations and procedures. Written examinations for higher supervisory positions should stress supervisory and administrative matters by devoting more than half the content to this subject. The central personnel agency should refer to training-course content, written directives, statutes, current professional literature, and textbooks for test materials.

Some intangible characteristics cannot be measured by written examinations. In the absence of a well-developed promotion-rating system, another logical way these qualities can be evaluated is through the oral interview. Many agencies use an oral board composed of senior supervisors, while some departments use persons from other police agencies to avoid the charge of favoritism. The board may be assisted by a non-voting member who may act as moderator and coordinator. Usually, but not always, those candidates who pass the written test will be given the oral interview, and the scoring or weighting varies. This process has been spreading rapidly throughout the country.

The evaluation made by an oral board in the relatively short time at its disposal cannot be as accurate as a composite evaluation made by all the supervising officers who have observed the work of the candidate over a period of time. There is also the danger in oral-board review that favoritism or other factors of personal acquaintance may influence the rating of the candidate. In the case of promotions, a rating scale should be prepared by the candidate's supervisors. Here again, techniques of rating need continuous study, and any refinements or changes should be evaluated for possible use.

In the first promotional step, from patrol officer to sergeant, it is often not possible to judge the candidates on the basis of achievement of operational objectives. Although superior officers may be selected partly on the basis of written examination, personal qualities, service ratings, and the like, their performance should be rated primarily in terms of accomplishment of departmental goals. They may also be rated in terms of their judgment and control of subordinates, including: their ratings of their own subordinates, their aggressiveness in taking and reporting needed corrective measures and of their willingness to criticize, and their ability to communicate departmental policies and objectives to subordinates. A critical analysis of all these factors will enable the rating officers to rank candidates in a relative order of merit and with a reasonable degree of accuracy.

Probationary service in higher ranks has not been as successful as probation at the entrance level because of the problem of what to do with the higher ranked supervisor who fails the probationary period. Getting supervisors and administrators to embrace the concept of probation as part of the selection process is difficult enough, but it is easy when compared with getting them to accept the idea of meaningful probation at higher levels. Nevertheless, during the supervisor's probationary period, the administrator can use probationary status as leverage to encourage the new supervisor to carry out activities which might seem unpopular, particularly to the new first-line supervisor. Once the new supervisor begins to mature in the role and realizes that it is possible to make constructive but sometimes unpopular decisions without losing respect, attitudes that can persist for the rest of his or her career may be solidified in a healthy way. (Wilson O.W., McLaren R.C., *Police Administration* (4th ed.), McGraw-Hill Book Company, New York, 1963, pp. 274-278.)

A source of controversy in the promotional process has been the establishment and use of the quota system to aid minority candidates to enter supervisory positions. There probably has been no other stress factor that has stirred such an emotional and sometimes physical upheaval towards administrations and departments. This undermines any semblance of prestige and self-esteem for all supervisors, including minorities, especially those who have previously been promoted without the assistance of judges rendering unpalatable decisions. Although there is not enough minority supervisory representation within many departments, and many minority candidates have possibly not been afforded ample educational opportunities, it still does not rationalize a promotional system of selection, whereby one candidate is placed over the next, based upon his or her ethnic background. Wherever this system has been used, there has followed a pervasive climate of internal stress plus an internal collapse of morale, job performance, and departmental efficiency. This is just the opposite of the goals and objectives of a proper functioning promotional selection process. To offset any imbalance of minority representation, a far improved educational and tutorial system should be given and maintained by the department itself. This would preclude any source of favoritism or discrimination, and eliminate one stress factor.

3. FEAR AND MISTRUST

The National Safety Council and the private sector have long understood that managing stress is a necessary part of increasing productivity, and numerous programs to diagnose and treat serious problems are employed routinely and without penalty. In the case of police officers, there is an instinct to survive within a system they perceive as punitive. Many believe seeking help may permanently isolate them in the department and effectively end their careers. Officers fear that the mere mention of an emotional problem may result in the removal of their firearm and assignment of a stigma of weakness that will remain with the them the rest of their careers. This stigma is dreaded by all officers and, as a result, they do not seek professional help nor avail themselves of the counseling services within the department. These are obstacles that are both difficult, if not impossible, to overcome.

A mistrust in the system prevails among police officers despite any police department's efforts to the contrary. This lack of trust is the single greatest obstacle to treatment. Before anyone can begin to use clinical skills to treat police officers, a climate of trust must be in place. Given this environment and assurance in a resource outside the department, officers will more readily seek help for personal and job-related problems when they are afflicted, thereby reducing suffering and suicides among police.

4. ALLEGATIONS OF POLICE BRUTALITY

Looming allegations of police brutality upon law enforcement agencies, can be a long standing, hidden stress factor for all officers, even to those in departments not directly involved. Today, many large city police departments find themselves amidst turmoil with widespread allegations of police brutality. These accusations are simply an ongoing process of a segment of our modern day society that never seems to be satisfied. Left- and right-wingers alike will either be for total strict law enforcement up until death penalties, or support a "slap on the wrist" with rehabilitation for armed robbers, murderers, and rapists. The melee falls nothing short of political gamesmanship, swinging forward and backward, twisting and bending towards the most favorable public opinion. It might hinge on upcoming elections or appointments, reflecting the mood of the majority of voters. The configuration of a city administration can change overnight by one mistake, by one police officer involved in a single incident. A hero one day might be sacrificed the next, if circumstances necessitate calming an angry neighborhood misled by a quick selling media.

Where does this leave local cops on the beat? What feelings go through their minds as they are vigilantly watched by a scrutinizing public, as well as an unforgiving department or agency who employs them. This underlying dose of stress eats away at the very fabric which initially brought them into the occupation of law enforcement itself.

Only on TV does law enforcement look so easy. In real life situations, criminals do not wish to be arrested. They do not put their hands out, waiting to be handcuffed. These felons run, fight, and kill, just to avoid apprehension. Some instigate police reactions, telling the police officer to kill them, exclaiming they'll never give up! Most have nothing to lose. Prison is not new to them. Crime is their way of life. Video cameras and lawsuits have added a new dimension. A cop never knows what type of criminal he or she is dealing with. Criminals could be first-time offenders, first time being caught, or firsthand killers. Many have rap sheets that are taller than themselves. Police officers must apprehend these criminals to protect the public. No one is there to see what a challenge this is or the level of stress it delivers. No one knows the strength necessary to overtake someone who has been caught disobeying the law and resisting arrest. Everyone feels a gun in the holster should be enough to keep perpetrators at bay. Police officers today know how untrue that statement is.

Each criminal is an individual, as is each person. What is necessary force for one to be apprehended certainly may not be enough for the next. Who is the judge of this? Who has the right to say what "should" have transpired during an arrest? That decision is left up to the police, and now, after their job is done, they may be told, "It could have been done differently." How does this affect their attitude on their next tour of duty? Should they use different methods, debug their mind of all they've been taught, leave their lives hanging on the line with a person who may have nothing to lose by killing them while they try to persuade him to come calmly? These are things to which the public cannot relate. This is what law enforcement officers across the country carry with them throughout their entire career.

At times, the police frequently arrest persons who have been injured in fights or as the result of accidents. Prisoners are sometimes injured in jail as a result of fights with other prisoners or falls due to intoxication, fainting, or epileptic attacks. Also true, police often use physical force to subdue a person in order to effect an arrest, and injuries may result.

The public is inclined to look upon the injury and illness of prisoners with suspicion and believe it is evidence of police brutality. Because of this attitude, today, it is doubly important that the police give careful attention to injured or ill prisoners and detain no one in jail who is in critical condition. Police officers are not trained to judge the extent of an injury or seriousness of an illness, thus they must be sure that the prisoner is examined by a physician. The commanding officer and other superiors should be informed when injured and ill prisoners are brought to police precincts, courts, booking centers, or headquarters. Necessary steps should be taken to safeguard the life and health of such prisoners. They should be sent to a hospital or examined by a physician, and should not be held in jail except on the written consent of the physician. A suitable injured-prisoner report should be filed, protecting the prisoner, as well as the police by recording the physician's approval of the prisoner's incarceration, showing an examination was made and necessary treatment given.

Who judges police incidents whereby an allegation of police brutality has been put forth? Civilian complaint review boards have failed to satisfy police departments, as well as the public. Police officers may have to make a life or death decision in a matter of seconds. To use deadly physical force or not? To hit or not? To use a baton or night stick or not? No matter what an officer's decision, he or she stands to be criticized, penalized, fired, or even jailed by people who have days or months to decide if a cop overreacted or used a little too much force, possibly to save his or her own life. While others are trying to analyze the situation, public sympathy is leaning towards the criminal. Due to press releases and one-sided news coverage, malice spills towards the cop who only did his or her job of serving the public.

5. WOMEN IN LAW ENFORCEMENT
Women and stress in law enforcement go hand in hand. Police work today in general is still a male dominated occupation. As such, women officers today face a double challenge. First, there is the challenge of police work itself; and second, they must prove on a continuing basis

that as women, they can withstand the constant scrutinizing and judging as to whether they "can do the job." What an enormous amount of stress this brings to bear down on the shoulders of each and every woman in law enforcement today. It has been proven many times over, day after day, they can do the job.

Women supervisors face still one more stress factor. Today, basic management principles are as applicable to women supervisors as to their male counterparts. However, women police supervisors have found that some modifications or adjustments have been necessary in the manner in which they apply such principles in supervising some of their male subordinates. This is because a small percentage of male police officers find it difficult to accept women in authority or to submit to their direction and control. Since most men have grown up in a culture of male dominance, a few may unfairly demand better performance from women than from male supervisors performing similar duties.

A woman supervisor is often required to prove herself over and over. She finds that she is expected to be more circumspect in her personal conduct and performance than the male supervisor because an inordinate amount of attention is focused on her. This condition may be totally unjustified, but does exist, and since it does, she must dispel it as soon as possible to reduce resistance to her supervisory efforts. The solution is to prepare herself technically for her position and to avoid the commonly recognized leadership weaknesses in any supervisor of indulgence of wrongdoing or misconduct, vacillation in the decision-making process, and unfairness. If any of these characteristics are observed in a woman, they may only serve to fortify the myth and stereotyped opinions of those who contend that women are not good leaders. (Iannone N. F., *Supervision of Police Personnel* (3rd ed.), Prentice-Hall, Inc., Englewood Cliffs, N.J., 1980, pp. 4-5.) Female police supervisors have not only overcome this stress factor, but have added a more humanistic, compassionate, and self-motivating approach in their role as managers.

E. POLICE OFFICERS SPEAK OUT

1. PERSONNEL SURVEY

An informal survey of 250 NYPD police officers identifying sources of the stress they experience gave the following results listed below, in order of priority.

1. Internal investigations/civilian complaint review board actions/fear of job loss/stringent rules and regulations

2. Poor promotional opportunities—including biased or special allowance or consideration

3. Too little pay/compensation

4. Fear of death or serious injury

5. Poor working hours/shift rotation/working holidays

6. Failing or restrictive judicial system

7. Marital and family disharmony from job related factors

8. Poor equipment/vehicles/etc.

9. Police relationships and personal dealings with the public

10. Co-worker relationships

11. Death/violence/traumatic incidents—too frequently experienced

12. Too much high-crime/combative violent neighborhoods

13. Peer pressure

14. Poor precinct facilities/cleanliness/orderliness/etc.

15. Narcotics/alcohol

2. PERSONNEL COMMENTS

The following are some personal write-in comments quoted from the same survey.

"Frustration caused by the Department constantly yielding to different political pressure groups. Assignments not to fight crime, but to placate political groups or special factions of the public. This is done without considering a cop's needs."

"I feel no one really cares, but just always second guesses my actions as I work."

"No support from the Brass. They are too worried about how they look politically. They are unrealistic about their decisions relating to day-to-day police work."

"Unfair promotional system. Priorities are wrong. Job complains about officers who use force to protect themselves."

"Poor management training; job forces people to avoid conflict for the sake of public acceptance. Officers cannot effectively do what their hearts and oath dictate."

"Bosses who fail to back up their men when they need support or get involved."

Officers Speak Out   On the Job

"Incompetent supervisors who are more interested in promotion than helping their officers or the public."

"Stress in dealing with Bosses."

"Poor management training for Bosses."

"Alcohol abuse by fellow officers."

"Bosses that fail to back up their people. Too liberal. They are not supervisors, but puppets for a non-appreciative public."

"Favoritism, quota systems, preferential treatment for certain groups."

"Mayor and Police Commissioner and job does not back you up."

"Lack of knowledge by superior officers in making decisions."

For the police officer, the amount of violence encountered in one busy evening's work could overwhelmingly outnumber the average private citizen's encounters with violence during an entire lifetime. Add in lawsuits, internal investigations, departmental discipline and punishment, peer pressure, poor promotional opportunities, including unfair, biased selections and the misuse of the quota system, and just imagine the pressure. Combining some or even all of these stimuli can eventually lead to the final collapse of morale, motivation, and work performance; simply stated—"burnout!"

CHAPTER 3

CRACKS IN THE SHIELD

A. MASKED SUICIDES

Suicide among police officers is not confined to any one geographical area, any one department, or any one type of officer. The best research shows that internal organization stressors are a major cause of this tragedy. Occupational stress in police work is a fact of life. No police department is immune; no police officer is immune.

A recent interview with Michael W. Popp, Ph.D., Program Director of the Lower Hudson Valley Employee Assistance Program and decorated retired New York City police officer, reveals some enlightening, but disturbing facts about police suicides. In 1994 and 1995 at least 21 New York City police officers tragically took their lives, and the onslaught of such high numbers continues to date. The words "at least" are used because only the obvious suicides, usually those in which officers end their lives with guns, are known. No one knows how many other apparently accidental deaths of police officers—car accidents, accidental shootings, fatal falls, etc.—were suicides.

A study released in an article that appeared in the November 2, 1995 edition of *The New York Times* has brought to light that the suicide rate among New York City police officers is nearly two and one-half times greater than that of the general population. In recent years, police officers have taken their own lives much more often than criminals have killed them. In addition, "The Samaritans," an international suicide and prevention organization, points out that suicide statistics do not take into account homicides and accidental deaths of people who voluntarily and recklessly put themselves in dangerous situations. A thought that emerges with this statement is that a despondent police officer can easily put him or herself in this type of situation.

The police officer who has not succumbed to suicide still feels and deals with stress and trauma. Effects on behavior can range from excessive absenteeism to violence, corruption, and apathy. Whatever negative behavior arises, underneath lies a view of stress as an embarrassing weakness which must be denied. The "macho" shield that keeps officers brave in the face of danger often forces them to internalize growing personal problems until they can no longer bear the pain.

B. EMOTIONAL HARDENING—A DANGEROUS DEFENSE

Witnessing so much violence and death on a repetitive basis can subconsciously set off serious behavioral changes. Police work in general encompasses a negative faction within our society. Citizens do not call the police during happy occasions. The highest percentage of service requests pertains to either personal disaster or calamity.

Cracks in the Shield   **Emotional Hardening**

In New York City, high experience precincts are precincts inundated with crime and calls for service. They are the precincts found in ghetto and crime ridden neighborhoods. Most police officers in New York City get placed in these precincts after graduating from the police academy and can remain there too long. After enough stressful experiences they may become emotionally hardened, affecting both their work and personal lives.

Basically, emotional hardening is a reduction in the capacity to experience emotions. It is an adaptive process which helps resolve conflict and allows a person to maintain psychological equilibrium in highly stressful situations. If the situation is a permanent one, this defensiveness or hardening becomes incorporated into the person's character and remains a part of his or her life. It may result in changes of a person's attitudes, feelings, values, ideals, and motivations. An emotionally hardened person may appear cynical, hostile, or apathetic—all qualities that, in a police officer, pose a danger to his or her career, life, and to the safety of the public.

The following sample interviews clearly illustrate the attitudes of police officers who have become emotionally hardened. Pay careful attention to changes in their attitudes toward death, personal feelings, and perception of the public. Also note any self-contradictory responses.

1. PERSONNEL INTERVIEWS

This is just a sample of the many interviews that were conducted of police officers that had worked in high crime areas for some period of time. The responders are simply listed as police officers A, B, and C. These officers maintain a symptomatic condition frequently known as emotional hardening; a reflexive, defensive condition often found necessary for mental and physical survival.

In these selected protocols of segments of each of the interviews, each question is followed by three different answers, each from separate interviews of police officer A, police officer B, and police officer C. The responses, as listed below, are all near or exact quotes.

Question: How many years have you worked on patrol in a high experience or high crime precinct?

Answers

    A. 11 years.

    B. 7 years.

    C. 10 years.

Emotional Hardening   Cracks in the Shield

Question: Why did you become a police officer?

Answers

    A. Because of the pay and retirement benefits and I wanted to help people.

    B. To help people.

    C. To do good. To help people.

Question: What were your values, thoughts, and ideals about life, death, family, and love before you became a police officer?

Answers

    A. Death scared the hell out of me. Having a family and kids were important to me. I believed in honesty, that most people and the police department were on the level, and it was a good job.

    B. Death didn't bother me. I spent two years in Viet Nam. I was used to seeing it. Having a family was important to me. I wanted a big family. I believed in the goodness of people.

    C. I had a good outlook on life. I was a pretty happy-go-lucky fella. I felt uneasy about death. Family relations were most important to me.

Question: What are some of your values, thoughts, and ideals about life, death, family, and love now?

Answers

    A. Death doesn't scare me now. If it happens, it happens. Love, I can live without it. I just don't need it. (I ask, "Why's that?") I've withdrawn into a shell of my own, and I just don't need it. The kids and family are there; I have it. It doesn't mean as much; it's just there. On honesty, no one's honest. Everyone is full of bull—this job, the people.

    B. Death still doesn't bother me, but it's so much more brutal. It's for stupid reasons. The only death that bothers me is [that] of a young child. Family is still important to me, and I still have the same ideals about marriage and children that I did, but now I go see other women on the side, especially one. Maybe that's an escape, but I don't let it affect my family life.

    C. Family is still most important to me. They're the only ones you could turn to when things are bad, but I feel sometimes I have too many responsibilities. Death makes me nervous.

Cracks in the Shield — Emotional Hardening

Question: Have you seen any changes in yourself emotionally or in your attitudes, either positive or negative, after being on the job, and if so, what are they?

Answers

A. Oh, sure. I'm a lot harder. A lot of things that would of affected me before would never affect me now, like sickness, death, [and] injuries to people. After spending 11 years in Harlem, it doesn't bother me—even with robberies and muggings. I just don't feel sympathetic towards people anymore. Then again, I'm more easygoing at home. Things used to bother me, and now I don't care. I'm also short tempered where I wasn't before.

B. First my sense of humor has increased; probably as a defense mechanism. I've become more cold-blooded. I'm very cynical about people and the job, and what they want you to do. I don't drink as much as I used to because I see so many other police officers drink. Drinking is their escape, and I didn't want to be like that. I saw how many guys got screwed up by it. Also, emotionally, I don't get excited or surprised anymore. Nothing seems to phase me. Like if my wife buys me a gift it's nice, but I don't get excited. I don't show a great deal of emotion towards kindness to me.

C. I dislike many minorities because they're always committing all the crimes. I didn't think I'd be this prejudiced, because I wasn't before I came on the job. I'm a little bitter, not as happy-go-lucky as I used to be. I feel more stress. Emotionally, I feel harder, but it depends on the situations and people. I am nice when people are nice. I feel I made a mistake by coming on this job; its not what I thought it would be. People don't want to be helped, it seems.

Question: Where do these changes affect you?

Answers

A. On the job and at home—in my life.

B. In my whole life.

C. On the job. I try not to let it affect my private life. I've been around too many cops and saw what it did when they brought things home and how it affected their lives.

Question: These changes, what do you attribute them to?

Emotional Hardening　　　　　　　　　**Cracks in the Shield**

Answers

   A. This job—working with mutts—lousy people. These people don't care about themselves, so why the hell should I?

   B. Well, the job doesn't cause it, it's the conditions they (the job) put you into. In a ghetto precinct, you see human life has no value. A pack of cigarettes means more to these people. Plus, you're dealing with people who call you "mother..." all day, and it rubs off on you. You start talking to people the same way.

   C. Being in a precinct with all minorities having too many rights according[sic] to them, and they take advantage of their rights.

Question: Can you try and pinpoint when these changes took place?

Answers

   A. About a year after I got on the job while I was in the 28 in Harlem.

   B. Only a year after I was on the job, and I was in Queens then. It only enforces[sic] it after you go to a ghetto precinct and you find out there are two sets of laws; one for whites and one for minorities.

   C. After 4 years on the job.

Question: What kind of person would you describe yourself as now?

Answers

   A. Cynical.

   B. I understand better [the] reasons why things happen.

   C. Honest, emotional, and understanding.

Question: Is there anything you or I haven't mentioned that you feel is important? Is there anything I overlooked or that we haven't covered?

Answers

   A. Anger. You go to work angry at the people in the street. I feel I bring that anger home sometimes.

   B. No matter who the cop is, after 3 or 4 years in a ghetto precinct, he'll change. There's no cop that can say he's the same person as when he went in there. It just changes your mind. You're surrounded by brutality. To change is the only way to survive there. A lot of guys can't survive—they go chronic sick or drink, or have their wives call up on them. You have to be crazy if it doesn't affect you. You'd be nuts already if it doesn't.

C. No.

C. STRESS-RELATED PROBLEMS

The unceasing aforementioned stress factors coupled with the adaptive mechanism of emotional hardening can push a police officer "over the edge." Prior to that moment, the officer may develop other problematic ways of coping that involve escape or redefinition of the situation. In addition, the officer's spouse and family suffer indirectly from the conditions of the job and directly from changes in the officer's behavior. Fortunately, police officers, their spouses and families, and the departments can work to alleviate these problems and learn to cope.

1. COMBAT TEAM SYNDROME

Police work is often considered a service oriented occupation, and the men and women officers as servants, protectors, and guardians of communities. However, due to stress, some officers crossover the line that separates protectors from predators. Those so affected are often small select groups of law enforcement personnel usually assigned to arrest teams. Arrest teams fight crime by making arrests, hundreds or even thousands per year, per team.

In order to make the stress of the job more acceptable, these teams can easily turn themselves into combat units. Highly trained, tough, and frequently the users of physical force, and on occasion, deadly physical force, some of these officers can be led or become self-motivated to drive themselves into too much combat by conducting violent arrest operations. They may play the numbers game, prompted by the crime-reducing, high-volume arrest expectations of their police department.

These officers can sometimes go beyond good, tough, aggressive police arrest work, by becoming an over-zealous group of officers making invalid arrests, abusing their authority, and actually committing criminal acts. The various teams can actually separate themselves from their departments and begin playing by their own rules. They could possibly be driven by department recognition, awards, promotions, or even monetary overtime. Competition amongst various arrest units is all right, unless it is pushed too far. The officers involved may become blind to their wrongdoing, and may eventually find themselves seriously injured or the subject of internal police investigations, or worse yet, the target of criminal investigations.

To avoid this pitfall in law enforcement, arrest teams within police commands should be closely monitored to alleviate overly aggressive behavior. Personnel should be continuously evaluated to assure that no officer or team of officers has extended themselves beyond the boundaries of departmental regulations or their local criminal laws. The ultimate responsibility for the allowance of such behavior rests with the department itself. The department owes an allegiance to the public, as well as to the officers who have sworn to uphold the law.

2. SUBSTANCE ABUSE

Today, probably the most dangerous of all the stress-related problems and the number one concern of top police administrators is drug abuse by its department's members. Never in the history of any police department has one single factor caused such a stir. To rationalize a police officer using narcotics is impossible. Remember, the morals and lifestyles of the society which is rearing young police recruits is completely different than the one which produced the recruits of 10, 20, or 30 years ago. Whereas, years ago, alcohol was the drug of choice of teenagers and parents, today, unfortunately, narcotics is their choice! It is a common fact that as many civilian youngsters now are using narcotics as were using alcohol in an earlier era. "From drinking to drugs" is the phrase that stimulates so much turmoil and anguish at all police headquarters around the country. Psychiatrists and psychologists working closely with the upper echelon of departments are scrutinizing the causes of drug abuse and searching for answers. Many of these same people overwhelmingly label mandatory drug testing as the overall solution to the intrapolice department drug problem.

But, there is a catch; a legal one. Many of the police unions are presently battling mandatory drug testing as a denial of one's privacy as not only a police officer, but as a U.S. citizen as well. Another snag is that specific drug testing has not yet been proven to give 100% accurate results. Think of the damage to an individual officer, his or her family, and the department that would result from being labeled incorrectly as a drug user. It would be devastating. Scientists and doctors are now striving to devise tests that are error free. Only then should it be used on a department-wide basis. If a recruit realizes that periodically and without notice he or she will undergo testing for narcotic usage, it might certainly alter the recruit's behavior in connection with drugs, and could even alter his or her entire lifestyle. The thin line that separates a department from allowing itself to exist with a lingering rumor of drug abuse, and one that declares itself morally and physically pure of all narcotics, might be drawn by a department drug testing unit.

3. STRESS UPON SPOUSE AND FAMILY

Lifestyle Issues

The spouse and family of an officer must deal with many domestic and lifestyle issues forced upon them by the demands of police training and work. The police officer's husband or wife has to make up his or her mind that shift work is simply a part of the job. In many instances, the officer has absolutely no control over the particular shift that he or she works. In fact, shift work in many departments includes a regular rotation. The officer will most likely have to take a turn at all shifts. There are usually three basic shifts per day, 8 a.m. to 4 p.m., 4 p.m. to midnight, and midnight to 8 a.m. In all actuality, shifts run at all times of the day and night, depending on the various needs of each department. A spouse can accept the shift work and learn to work around the problems it can create or go completely against the concept of shift rotation which, of course, can cause serious family and marital problems.

Today, there are many police officers and their spouses who actually enjoy shift work, either steady or rotation. It can give husbands and wives a chance to be together while the children are in school. It gives the officer and his or her spouse time to do mid-week chores and enjoy forms of recreation, without the hustle and bustle of the weekend. In many instances, it can give the officer a chance to get a second job. It can give his or her spouse the opportunity to work in or out of the home while the officer can maintain a watch over the children. This can save the family some of the expense of baby-sitters, nannies, or child care. Ultimately many spouses not only have adjusted to rotating shift schedules, but also have integrated the schedules into a positive family structure. If a spouse is not ready to accept this particular portion of their husband's or wife's occupation, they are probably setting themselves up for a never-ending battle. The bottom line is that the police officer and the spouse should work together in turning what appears to be a negative factor of the job, into a positive one.

Another family stress issue in law enforcement is that of the holidays. This involves the absence of the law enforcement officer on a particular holiday. Family traditions can run deep. Mothers, fathers, and other relatives can add a great amount of stress and turmoil to the officer and family by not accepting his or her job requirement of having to work on the holiday. Care should be used in discussing this problem with family and relatives so that provisions can be properly made whereby family visits and celebrations can be a bit off schedule in order not to interfere with an officer's schedule. There is certainly no need to forego celebration and happiness that comes with any holiday.

Danger on the job is another stress to the relationship between a police officer and spouse and family, which may include young children. Care should be used when explaining this facet of police work, especially to young ones. Family members should be reassured of the actual camaraderie amongst officers, and the safety precautions they take on a daily basis.

Phases of Police Life

The stresses that a family encounters are likely to be different in each phase of police life. In the recruit and rookie years, the police academies can bring a great amount of stress to bear on the officer, as well as on the spouse and family. The amount of work to be accomplished, including homework, can be overwhelming. Besides the instructional portion, there are also the physical requirements, which include combat training, self-defense, and an in-depth firearms program. Remember, there is a new visitor in the home—a gun. This should be openly discussed with both spouse and children. Each officer has the responsibility to instruct his family accordingly as to the proper safeguards of a weapon.

During the academy years, a spouse or family will have to deal with the same type of problems that anyone would have to deal with when someone is attending a serious educational program. Some departments realize the pressure a police academy can put on home life, and to avoid many problems, they send the recruit away from home during the educational process, and allow visits only on special occasions. This is similar to a military style of life. It is essential during these beginning months and years of an officer's career that the people who are part of his or her home life give 100% support. One of the most important ways to gain support from family members is to keep an open line of communication, and to keep family members informed of daily situations and accomplishments. No spouse wishes to be kept in the dark. Sharing is also a good form of release for the officer.

Following the rookie years, an officer may fall into a deep pattern of job involvement which may include many tumultuous situations daily. This may, at some point, distance the officer from spouse and family, as the officer does not wish to bring home the morbid side of police work. A spouse may recognize personality changes in the officer. He or she may notice moodiness and cynicism, or even racism and sexism. An officer who never drank or caroused may begin to do so. The officer may cling more closely to work partners than to spouse and family. Civilian friends may be pushed aside. It is imperative that the spouse or a family member be cognizant of these changes and reach out to the officer. In more serious situations, a spouse should seek assistance within the officer's department. Remember, a life or lives may be at stake.

Toward the end of an officer's career, he or she may experience a calming. This is considered to be a development of maturity and wisdom acquired over the years. It is essentially a good thing. This will, in many instances, extend to the family as well. The officer realizes that career and family are the most important things in his or her life. It is at this point that an officer may begin to plan his or her retirement or separation from the department. It is the spouse's responsibility to assist and be part of the planning. Retirement and job separation are also stressful events and should be handled with the same care and concern as when entering the law enforcement profession.

CHAPTER 4

*STRESS AND TRAUMA—
AN OFFICER'S INSIGHTS*

A well-known author and tenured police officer, Steve Albrecht, has been with the San Diego Police Department since 1984, both as a regular officer and now as a reserve sergeant. He is nationally known for his accomplishments in workplace violence prevention. He has written eleven books, including: *Fear and Violence on the Job: Prevention Solutions for the Dangerous Workplace*, and *Ticking Bombs*.

Steve Albrecht has contributed the following three articles that deal with stress and trauma in law enforcement. He gives us insight on the stressors of law enforcement, as well as a personal look behind the actual traumatic events themselves. Suggestions for coping with stress and trauma, covered more fully later, are also given.

A. RUNNING OUT OF GAS: POLICE OFFICERS AND COMPASSION FATIGUE
Article by: Steve Albrecht, SDPD

The subject of stress is no stranger to law enforcement. The subject worries me professionally (for my partners and colleagues), and personally (for myself and my police officer wife). We know police officers and stress go together like mobile homes and hurricanes. Our knowledge of this subject comes from some on-going study of how people react to high-intensity stress in public safety/public health jobs (cops, firefighters, paramedics, emergency room personnel, etc.), and mental health positions (crisis counselors, social workers, child protective personnel, etc.).

Most of us are familiar with the concept of "post-traumatic stress disorder" or "PTSD." In lay terms, it's the mind and body's re-occurring psychological and physical responses to a highly stressful event from the recent or distant past. After World War I, soldiers were said to suffer from "shell shock" and the term has evolved into PTSD as a way to categorize the ways many people feel after being exposed to life-threatening events.

Police officers who have had to shoot someone or otherwise inflict serious or fatal injuries on a suspect (or a victim or a bystander) know PTSD quite intimately. It surfaces in their daydreams and nightmares, or what is correctly called their "intrusive thoughts." In other words, although the event may have happened months, years, or decades ago, they still can replay every detail.

While the clinical definition of the actual "disorder" portion of PTSD is more than a bit complicated, it's safe to say that those who have experienced the impact of past exposure to violence and death know it when they feel it. The physical and psychological feelings can range from mild and irritating to severe and incapacitating.

At this point, if you were expecting the news to get much better, I'm sorry. The fact is not only are we in law enforcement more susceptible to the impact of PTSD in ourselves, because of our own life-threatening, life-protecting activities, but we are also vulnerable to the traumatic events of others.

Another form of PTSD is called "compassion stress" and it occurs when we are exposed to the trauma experienced by others with whom we come into close contact. As Dr. Charles Figley, a psychologist and researcher from Florida State University had defined it, compassion stress comes from

> "the natural behaviors and emotions that arise from knowing about a traumatizing event experienced by another person and the stress resulting from helping or wanting to help a traumatized person."

In other words, just because you did not personally experience a physical assault like a rape, gun shot wound, or a debilitating car accident, you can, by coming into close contact with the victim(s), feel many of the same physical and psychological "pains."

This is a difficult concept to discuss or explore in ourselves. We are trained to respond to the terrible life situations of others with calm, emotionally-controlled professionalism. Some officers have come from work backgrounds that include significant work in military, medical, or service careers that have already exposed them to trauma. And related to this is the fact that many people who go into law enforcement have exactly the right temperament for effectively dealing with other people's pain. In other words, from a pre-employment screening perspective, the fact that you are doing this job indicates that you have the emotional stability and coping skills to survive in highly difficult environments. But, as the old sages always say, "Knowing about something in advance doesn't always mean you'll be able to fix it up right."

And, the fact that we choose a law enforcement career means we have at least a propensity for wanting to help people. After all, we know from street experience that we do more helping than crime-fighting, more serving than protecting. So it is from within this unique position of "police officer as 'helper'" (just like a physician, nurse, paramedic, firefighter, psychiatrist, psychologist, social worker, or counselor) that we can experience burnout, emotional and physical exhaustion, and a disturbing concept known as "countertransference."

According to the definition, feelings of countertransference "occur when the wounds of the helper are triggered by the victims they are trying to help, by similarities between the victim and the helper, or by recent traumas in the life of the helper."

This can occur along two levels, sort of like a sliding scale. At one end, you respond to the trauma of another person by becoming overly detached—using a "Just the Facts, Please" approach that serves to distance you from the person and what happened to him or her. You may also seek to minimize the traumatic event as "not that big of a deal," express "bystander's guilt," as if you could have prevented the act by driving faster, arriving sooner, or being in the right place at the right time. At the other end of the spectrum in this mode, you may feel partially or completely overwhelmed by the severity or details of the victim's traumatic event, or numbed or horrified so much so that you're unable to respond "normally" as a law enforcement officer.

Events that will trigger either of these responses can take you quickly out of the mode of the helper and into thought processes, actions, and feelings that seem almost as if you're experiencing the same event as the first victim. In effect, you can become a second victim.

Most of us become hardened to the painful reality that some human beings have a sickening knack for injuring, maiming, or murdering others in unique ways. And still others of us have figured out various positive (and perhaps not so good) methods for coping with a certain specific range of "acceptable" crimes or traumatic events, as long as they don't cross our own personal boundaries. What might horrify the average civilian with no experience or knowledge of this city's traumatic events, *i.e.*, the presence of a dead body in their neighborhood, a neighbor injured in a car accident, or a robbery that happened at their local branch or favorite convenience store, does not usually invoke a traumatic response in the average police officer.

But other events that can take us out of our training and experience-created comfort zones include the brutal rape of a young child, the murder of a person who reminds us of a family member or close friend, a multi-car accident involving people we know, or a mass murder event, or any multiple-victim homicide scene. In these cases, the sheer size and immense pain of these traumas can cause us to doubt our once rock-solid belief systems that we can cope with any thing, any time, any place.

Other less severe examples might include the officer who responds to the battered woman with inappropriate feelings that she should "fix her own problems" or at the other extreme, that he or she will go out of his or her way to get her life back in order by helping to "get" or "punish" the abuser. Or, the officers who have an alcoholic or drug abusing family member and can't separate their feelings of anger or anxiety toward this relative when forced to deal with similar people in the field.

Countertransference symptoms can appear as rage, dread, horror, revulsion, shame, grief, "mourning"-like responses to death, over-attachment or inappropriate "bonding" between the victim and the officer, and a sense that the officer wants to be or take on the role of "liberator" or "hero" for the victim. It seems highly unlikely that any of these responses will help the situation for either the officer or the victim.

Look at possible solutions to feelings of countertransference, if you feel them to any degree in yourself, in a family member, or with a close colleague who has expressed some signs or mentioned some symptoms, as prelude to increasing problems. The first and best solution is one that therapists, counselors, social workers, and other mental health caregivers use themselves: they get immediate counseling help from other caregivers who know about post-traumatic stress disorder, countertransference, and the related feelings of loss of control.

Many police agencies have access to excellent psychological services for police department members and their families, available on a confidential, immediate, and 24-hour basis. Make the call when you feel you need to talk to someone who is sympathetic, empathetic, and qualified to help you cope more effectively with the demands of this job.

Besides some therapy sessions, other helpful intervention techniques might include more and varied physical exercise; more contact with friends and family who live and work outside law enforcement; and taking reasonable and timely breaks from your work (up to and including changing assignments, divisions, shifts, partners, or squads). Personally, you might want to find new hobbies or interests outside police work: write down some of your feelings for later re-reading; get involved with religious services in your neighborhood; adjust your eating and sleeping habits to maximize the rejuvenating benefits from each; monitor your energy level throughout the day; and finally, know your limitations with certain "hot button" subjects, events, suspects, or victims.

We're all human. Feelings of post-traumatic stress disorder and countertransference are entirely normal and given the right kinds of qualified, professional help, very treatable. Because you're currently subject to the demands of so much physical and emotional trauma in the lives of others, it's possible to see these events impact many parts of your life as well. Recognizing these feelings is an important first step toward feeling better about them.

B. THE POLICE OFFICER'S COMPANION: PAIN AND GRIEF
Article by: Steve Albrecht, SDPD

After attending the funeral of a fallen officer, I was too choked by tears and sadness to even walk to my car. My drive home was filled with the usual thoughts that accompany someone who has attended the funeral of a good friend or relative who died tragically, or as in this officer's case (who died of a sudden heart attack), far too young. The word "Why?" dominated my internal conversation, as in "Why him?" "Why now?" and "Why do good people leave us early and why do evil people seem to live forever?"

I was certainly not alone with my emotions or my feelings of sorrow and grief. Before, during, and after the funeral, there wasn't a dry eye in the room. And, crying in general is tough for cops, because we are schooled to "deal with it" from the time we sign on until we leave.

Phrases like, "The tougher it gets, the cooler you should get" or "Deal with the situation now, grieve about it later." In truth, this is the reality of the job; it can be full of one horrifying or grief-inducing event after another. And, we are expected, as members of this difficult profession, to show a non-stop stiff upper lip while we work. But as people who have been in highly stressful, distressing, life-threatening, or more correctly life-changing events will attest, how do you cope when the lights are off and you're lying in bed replaying these events behind your eyeballs, over and over and over.

The uncomfortable truth about this job is that a highly traumatic event can appear before you during the first hour of your first day in the field. And while you may have been able to cope with the first one, the tenth one, and the 100th bad scene, as the numbers get higher, your internal defensive mechanisms can begin to shred. To put it in Star Trek terms, your laser shields have failed and the burning hot beams are penetrating. Things that used to bounce off may now get through and eat at your inner self. And perhaps what makes all of this so difficult is that the cumulative effects of so much grief and pain may not catch up to you for years and years. You can surmise by now that all of this stress cannot be good for your heart, your stomach, or your psyche.

And perhaps this is part of the reasons why police funerals hit all of us so hard. When bad things come upon us with a hard rush, it's tough not to feel as if the whole world is off its axis. How can so much bad happen so quickly and to our thin blue line?

In his best-selling self-help book *When Bad Things Happen to Good People*, author and Rabbi Harold Kushner says that in times of grief and sorrow, it's hard for all of us not to feel like life has no purpose, that our creator has allowed bad things to happen in order to punish us for some past failing, or that there is no justice. In truth, he says, bad things don't happen for some as yet unexplained reason, to punish us, or to prove that for every good person, place, or event there must be an evil one to match. This is just not so; bad things happen because that is the way of the world. There is no hidden cosmic book which keeps track of these things; they just happen.

And it is the cumulative effects of so many bad things we see, experience, and are forced by the nature of our profession to deal with—the murder or rape of a child, an attack on an elderly woman who is left dazed and bleeding in the street, a family killed in a car crash, a dead officer—that can make it hard to cope with the rest of our lives even after we unpin our badges.

When faced with what seems like one terrible event after another, some officers turn to alcohol, drinking after work in an effort to forget the day and drinking on their days off in an effort to forget their week. Others turn to too many cigarettes, feel-good junk foods, or other self-destructive habits to help themselves cope. But above all of this, most cops internalize their feelings of sadness, rage, anger, guilt, fear, or anxiety, until their inner selves are filled to the brim. And this is what leads to the bad hearts, aching bellies, and other stress-induced ailments that can serve to end our lives before we've got full use of them.

What psychologists tell us is that we deal with our feelings of grief, pain, sorrow, and horror about some of the terrible things we see, hear about, or experience firsthand, by talking about them. While it may be in our nature to hold things in, don't expose our feelings to the cold light of day (where, as many of us believe, they might be subject to ridicule), the better approach is to get them out, not bottle them up.

This is not to say that you should go about blurting out horror stories to your unsuspecting friends and family, but that under the right circumstances, these people can be good sounding boards. And your police partners, police friends, and other law enforcement colleagues can serve a similar role, just as you can do for them. And finally, your department offers confidential psychological services which are available whenever you need them.

Using your spouse or partner as means to vent your feelings can be a powerful asset for your mental health, but only if you follow certain ground rules. A trusted colleague, who has suffered through too many of this world's evil people and evil visions, gave me good advice:

- Try very hard and avoid the temptation to talk about bad things, bad people, or other highly-disturbing events while lying in bed together.

Beds are for sleeping, snacking, reading, lovemaking, and talking of many things, all except for negative police events. The bedroom and your bed should be a sanctuary for each of you, a place where you share good things and good times. It should not be the place where one person unloads his or her problems upon the other, so much that it becomes psychologically troublesome for the person who has to listen.

As my friend suggests, if you have the need to talk about something disturbing, like a frightening police event, get up and go into another room, like the kitchen. There needs to be a safe physical and psychological distance between bad things and the bedroom. Create the right geographical boundaries to keep this room protected.

- Prepare your spouse or partner for the arrival of sad, frightening, or disturbing news.

When we're upset by something we've had to carry around all day, all week, or all month, there is a tendency to want to blurt it out all at once and get it over with. If you've ever been on the receiving end of disturbing news which you heard without warning or time to put up your own defensive shields, you know how shocking it can be. Instead of helping the other person to deal with what he or she has experienced, you may be too stunned by the news to cope with your own feelings.

Preface a piece of disturbing news with the sentence, "I want to talk about something I experienced that has been bothering me a lot. Is now a good time for me to talk with you about it? Is there some place we can go where we can talk and you can help me feel a little better?"

- Develop your own self-coping mechanisms as a supplement to talking about your feelings, emotions, anxieties, or fears.

This can include taking a shower as soon as you get home from a particularly difficult patrol shift (this can serve as a physical and psychological "cleansing" process, as you clean the "dirt" from the streets off more than just your body). It can also include a winding down ritual as you drive home, a quick workout after your shift, or even spending some time with your partners or police friends just rehashing the events of the day.

The pastor presiding over my colleague's funeral made a good point: It's okay for tough cops to cry. We're all human and we should be able to express our feelings when things upset us more than usual. Create your own coping rituals, find friends and loved ones who will help you share your heavy load. Do the same for them when they need it, too.

C. KEEPING IT IN BALANCE
Article by: Steve Albrecht, SDPD

If you were to look at your life like it was a large scale—not unlike the so-called "Scales of Justice"—you can see that when you put too much effort into one area of concern, the scale becomes unbalanced. Too much of one thing throws the other side into turmoil. People who focus their attention and energies on one area to the exclusion of other pursuits, can find themselves feeling stressed, apprehensive, or frustrated about their lives.

Take a look at some of the areas that affect your life and see if your personal scale balances properly. Ask and answer these questions as they relate to you:

Physical Health—How is your overall health? Do you feel energetic, illness and pain-free most of the time? Are you relying on drugs, alcohol, cigarettes, or excessive caffeine to mask physical or mental pain symptoms?

Mental Health—How is your attitude? Positive or negative? Do you feel happy and content with your life, at least most of the time? Do you experience any lingering feelings of apprehension, fear, or anxiety with regard to the other balance factors that are a part of your life?

Family Relationships—Do you have a strong family bond with the members of your immediate family? Do you feel happy and safe in your home? Do you receive love and support from the people who are closest to you?

Love Relationship—Are you involved in a love relationship with someone? Does this person help to make you feel better about yourself? Are you content in this relationship?

Professional Life—Are you happy with your present career position? Do you feel satisfied that your job will give you the chance to grow and develop, both as a person and professionally? Do you get along well with your supervisors, colleagues and peers? Do you like most of the work tasks you do each day? When you tell people what you do, is it with a sense of pride?

Social Relationships—Do you have a few close friends who you can rely upon? Are you able to share your thoughts and feelings with these close associates? Are you able to make friends easily and establish social relationships on various levels?

Notice how far down the list your job appears? There's a good reason: Ask yourself if you "work to live" or "live to work?" If your honest answer is that you only live to go to your job, then you need to rethink your life priorities. As you scan this list of life balance points, notice in yourself or others that if certain areas become obsessively important, each of the remaining ones suffer from neglect.

Stop and look at your life as a whole. "All things in moderation" as the old proverb tells us. Do what you like to do, enjoy life as you want, but keep things in balance by devoting your energies and attention to your physical, mental, family, love, professional, and social areas. Careful attention to each of these factors can help satisfy you in so many ways that your work life will thrive and your professional goals will become real.

This page intentionally left blank.

CHAPTER 5

COPING WITH STRESS

A. PREVENTIVE MEASURES

There is no better way to prevent police officers from committing suicide than through early diagnosis and quick response to the symptoms associated with stress and traumatic experiences. Prevention of suicide is the responsibility of everyone involved in law enforcement. As discussed below, recruits can learn the nature of their new job; supervisors can defuse stressful situations within the department; researchers can acquire and disseminate knowledge; hotline workers can listen and counsel; and co-workers can spot signs of depression among their comrades. Through these efforts and many others, law enforcement personnel can learn to cope.

1. TRAINING AND SUPERVISION

Learning to cope with the unremitting stress of police work should begin early on during academy training of the police recruit. If an officer knows verbatim the stress-producing factors, he or she will undoubtedly be able to overcome not only the causes and symptoms, but the final effects as well. Teaching "by the book" is fine for enabling the officer to properly handle all the types of police presented, including those very factors that lead to stress. Both the positive and negative sides of law enforcement should be disclosed. No instruction is complete that does not include an in-depth course on how to personally deal with stress. An officer should also have a broad knowledge of the inner workings of the department in relation to his or her career potential. Career development and enhancement is the officer's highest priority, but no one may ever openly discuss how and when to accomplish such goals as promotion or special assignments. We must not allow an officer to become stagnant, gaining in seniority, but decreasing in his or her productivity and morale.

A multitude of tenured senior officers throughout police departments across this nation have been grossly under-utilized. Administrators have often discarded these members and knowingly sentenced them to unproductive, low morale, reclusive finishes to their careers. They have been exiled to the far corners of the precinct station houses and allowed to deteriorate. Strength and knowledge come from these people. They should be revitalized, used as advisors, and included in daily operations. Even younger, less aggressive officers should be returned to a path of achievement and productivity if they are found to be faltering. By finding their strong points and capabilities, administrators can develop them into self-motivated and contributing members of the team.

Also, experienced and highly trained supervisors should be cognizant and knowledgeable in all aspects of diagnosing a subordinate's problem. Once discovered, the supervisor should have many alternatives at his immediate disposal. A change of assignment to a more suitable atmosphere, non-enforcement in nature, may ease the problem. A change of supervisor may be necessary if the boss is responsible for undue stress coming in the form of a severe personality conflict or excessive favoritism. Steady hours instead of shift rotation could also aid in a good recovery.

Proper referral and counseling are probably the most important and efficient means of correcting the most serious problems. Many departments today utilize professional counseling programs with highly trained and experienced police officers mentally equipped to handle the worst of crises. Counseling can help an officer confront and overcome interpersonal problems that he or she might otherwise avoid or mask. These sessions can be conducted on a one-on-one basis, or as group sessions. Self-appraisal and participation is essential. All lectures or threats must be avoided. Counselors should be well educated and experienced in police work. Before an officer returns to the environment that contributed to his or her fall, the officer should be ready and able to cope. The officer should understand that all personal dealings with the counselor are confidential and will not affect future assignments or promotional opportunities.

Please keep in mind that police supervisors and top ranking managers are responsible for the well-being of subordinates. They have both a commitment to the community and to their fellow officers. Each and every officer deserves full attention. Supervisors must watch for signs of animosity or severe changes in the police officer's regular behavior. They must be ready to approach him or her with compassion and understanding. Guidance is of the utmost importance to putting the officer back on the right track. Police supervisors must find the cause of the officer's downfall and take the proper steps to help him achieve dignity once more. They must be sure that those who are functioning properly continue to do so, while watching for a change in even the best officer. Total collapse that leads to suicide begins somewhere, and it is up to the supervisor to detect the warning signs in their early stages.

2. PSYCHOLOGICAL SERVICES AND RESEARCH

The NYPD's Psychological Services Unit devotes its time, administratively and personally, to seeing police officers who have been seriously injured, involved in traumatic incidents, or suffering from stress, and helps them to return to a sense of well-being, as well as back to full duty, if possible. Early contact and debriefing lets the officer know that they are there to help. The successful debriefer tries to be responsive to the individual, and not to what happened. This personal interaction on a one-to-one basis is the key to a successful debriefing.

In order to overcome the suicide problem, the NYPD has established a division called the Suicide Investigations Unit (S.I.U.). This group consists of highly trained officers working with psychologists and psychiatrists in conducting profiles on suicide deaths. This procedure is known as a psychological autopsy. They look for common denominators, causes, and preventions by carefully interviewing families and co-workers of those who took their own lives. The Psychological Services Unit, including the S.I.U. team, is the most experienced in the world. Their task is awesome, handling about 30,000 people who undergo high levels of daily stress.

3. HELPLINE

In response to the alarming increase in the number of police suicides in recent years, the NYPD, along with many other police departments across the country, has established a 24-hour, 7-day-a-week hotline for members of the service struggling for emotional survival. These HELPLINES are staffed by specially trained police officers and civilians, who, as dedicated professionals, are there to help, whatever the nature of a caller's emotional distress. They are prepared to listen and provide guidance and direction. All calls are completely confidential, and referrals to mental health care specialists are provided without the caller having to identify him or herself.

Numerous phone calls are received from police department employees in emotional turmoil. Their problems run the gamut. Many suffer from severe depression. Some are trying to cope with marital difficulties or losing a loved one. Others are struggling with alcohol abuse or problems related to alcohol abuse. Some callers even discuss committing suicide. In all cases, HELPLINE teams are there to listen and counsel.

4. GENERAL WARNING SIGNS OF DEPRESSION

The advice given below deals with spotting the warning signs of clinical depression. Early recognition of the symptoms and timely action can help save a life. If a friend or colleague displays symptoms of depression, encourage him or her to seek professional help as soon as possible.

- Don't ignore people who say they are depressed and are thinking about killing themselves. Take them seriously! They are crying out for help.

- Tune in to any friend or co-worker who appears more restless, irritable, or depressed than usual. Be aware that he or she might need help with a personal problem.

- Notice any significant increase in alcohol use. It is a telling warning sign. Alcohol is a depressant, and its use will make already depressed individuals more at odds with themselves.

- Keep an eye on friends who have suffered a major loss, such as a failed marriage or the death of a close family member. They are prime candidates for serious, perhaps dangerous, levels of depression.

Physical damage may be readily noticeable, but mental fatigue and the effects of stress may remain hidden, even into an officer's retirement years. Learning about stress and models of supervision sensitive to the effects of stress will go a long way toward ensuring that no psychological impairment or illness in a police officer will go unnoticed and untreated. Hopefully, officers and their families will be spared the devastating loss of suicide.

So far, this book has detailed the kinds of situations encountered by police officers, both within the department and out in the field, that create high levels of stress and how police officers react and deal with stress within the context of the job. Now it is time to look at what you, the police officer, can do on a personal level to cope with and relieve the accumulation of stress in your life. The remainder of this chapter presents behavioral information on managing stress that you can use both on and off the job. This information is adapted from the text of FOCUS Psychological Services by Dr. Jolee J. Brunton, Ph.D., Chief Psychologist of the San Diego Police Department.

B. STRESS MANAGEMENT

How you interact with your environment can reduce your stress level. If you want to manage your stress by making better use of your time and energy, you can use the skills of: Valuing, Personal Planning, Commitment, Time Use, and Pacing.

There are 24 hours in everyone's day, 365 days a year. Then, why do some people always seem to have plenty of time to get their work done, to play, visit friends, care for their homes and relax, while others race frantically against the clock, never quite able to catch up? Watch how they budget their time and energy, and you'll have the answer. Whether your stress is the result of a stressful profession like law enforcement, or from events beyond your control, or your failure to take charge of your life, personal management skills can help. They can reduce your stress by helping you learn to spend your time and energy more efficiently and effectively.

1. VALUING SKILLS

Look at the racks of clothes in a clothing store. The choices seem endless. None of the clothing is right or wrong, although a choice of clothing may be right or wrong for you. So it is with life. Choosing is stressful. What's worth spending your time on? Your energy? That depends on what is important to you. Valuing skills can help you identify what's important to you so you can spend your time and energy wisely. Develop your valuing skills by trying the following activity.

WHAT'S REALLY IMPORTANT?

Start by doing nothing. Sit quietly for 5 minutes with no agenda. Wait until your mind feels clear and you feel calm.

Make notes on what's important to you. List the things you like to do, the things you don't, what you wish you could do, qualities you admire in your heroes and friends, attributes you dislike in people around you, ways you'd like to be like your parents, and ways to be different from them.

Look at your day. What did you spend your time on yesterday? How much time? If someone looked at your list, what would he or she think you valued most? Our values are what we spend our time, money, and energy on. Do you see any conflict between your values and the way you spend your time?

2. PERSONAL PLANNING

Do you spend your days acting or reacting? If you want to be the captain of your own ship and you're clear about where you want to go, planning skills can help you get there. Personal planning, through the art of setting goals, lets you turn your values into action plans. It's more than lists (a good start) of jobs to be done. Once you've got the lists, you need to rank each item in order of its importance to you. Then, group them according to:

(a) those items ranked most essential or most desired,

(b) those items which could be put off for a while, but which are still important, and

(c) those items which could easily be put off indefinitely with no harm done, so they can be tackled efficiently.

Try this activity to help you clarify and attain your goals.

REACHING YOUR GOALS

Clarify your life goals. What do you want to do with the rest of your life? Where do you want to be in 5 years? What do you want to make happen in the next 6 months? What specific goal will you achieve next week? You have to know what target you're aiming at before you can hit it. Update every 3 months, or you'll end up shooting at targets you're not even interested in hitting anymore.

Divide and conquer. Break your big life goals into smaller chunks that can be done in 5-10 minutes a day to give you incentive.

Make a daily plan. List all the tasks needing attention today, rank them in importance, and estimate how long they will take to accomplish. Start with the first task and move down the list.

Coping with Stress — Stress Management

3. COMMITMENT

Commitment is the courageous act of choosing to pursue certain goals and letting others go. It gives you incentive to make your plans work. Both under and overcommitted people have not made up their minds, instead they hold all their options open.

So, make a commitment! Get involved. Take the risk. Build a sense of personal history. Put down roots. Invest yourself in your community. You'll build a sense of belonging that will yield great rewards over the long haul and will help you maintain a perspective on your life.

4. TIME USE

Where did the day go? Where did my vacation go? My youth? Your use of small scraps of time becomes very significant when you realize that by age 70 you'll have slept 23 years; spent 11 years working; 8 years playing; 6 years eating; 5 years grooming; 3 years being educated; 6 years talking and reading; and 7 years on odds and ends. If you can cut out just 20 minutes per day of wasted time, by the time you are 70, you'll have gained a year. When you say "I've no time," you are really saying you aren't managing your time well. Try the following activity to improve your time management skills.

MANAGING YOUR TIME

Name your time wasters. Are they: Procrastination? Trivia first? Jumping from task to task? Give them pet names and laugh at them when they start to control you.

Night or day person? When are you most alert and creative? Do your priority life goals then, and save important and trivial goals for other times during the day.

Be satisfied with doing a partial job. One expert says 80% of your best work is done during the first 20% of the time you spend. Blast away at your top priorities and let some of the lesser tasks fall by the wayside.

Stop running late. Set your watch 5 minutes fast. Practice being a little early. Check yourself and adjust to match your values, goals, and commitments.

---

5. PACING

When you stomp on the accelerator for drag racing starts and stand on the brakes for screeching stops, you waste fuel and your car wears out faster. When you work in sudden bursts of frantic activity, you waste energy and cause yourself distress. Pacing is the skill of taking on no more and no less than you can handle and work on steadily. It allows your mind and body to relax, since they know what to expect. As law enforcement personnel fully recognize, when you are surrounded by emergencies, feel the terrible pressure of time, or often run behind schedule, pacing skills can help you manage your stress and save your energy.

Stress Management   **Coping with Stress**

Schedule your time and make allowances for emergencies. Schedule your tasks to fill but not overflow the time you have available. If you have an hour, don't plan 2 hours worth of work. Keep up and don't allow yourself to get behind schedule. Just as important, don't allow yourself to get ahead. Practice plodding. Be consistent. Try to eat healthy meals, sleep, and exercise at about the same time each day on your shift. It will bring order into your chaotic life and give your body a chance to prepare for the demands you're going to make on it. Set aside several short periods each day for quiet time.

6. SLEEP MANAGEMENT

An insufficient quantity and quality of sleep is a major stress factor. Your actions before going to sleep directly affect your ability to achieve restorative sleep. The following helpful sleeping tips were gathered by Dr. Launi Treece of the FOCUS Psychological Services, San Diego Police Department.

- Maintain regular hours of sleep from retiring to rising.

- Ingest no caffeine (coffee, tea, soda, pain killers, and chocolate) after 1:00 p.m.

- Exercise any time during the day except within the last two hours before going to sleep.

- Keep a cool breeze in the room.

- Drink a glass of warm milk. It contains a chemical which aids sleepiness.

- Melatonin tablets, a nutritional supplement, may be helpful. Check with your physician before adding to your diet.

- Do not use alcohol or other drugs to relax or make you drowsy. After the sugar in alcohol is metabolized by your body, a rebound occurs which will wake you after a few hour's sleep.

- If you get very little sleep at night, nap around 3:00 p.m. the next day.

If you have trouble falling asleep, try this activity.

PREPARING FOR SLEEP

1. If you have troubling thoughts, write them out or talk them out at least 2 hours before bedtime. Then, put the thoughts aside. Tell yourself that you can focus on them again tomorrow, and that you can do no more about them now.

2. Engage in non-stimulating tasks the final hour before bedtime.

Coping with Stress **Stress Management**

3. Practice physical relaxation techniques such as deep, diaphragmatic breathing and progressive muscle relaxation. Have a relaxing massage or a hot bath.

4. Do not go to bed unless you are drowsy, and get out of bed if you do not feel close to sleep.

5. In bed, count backwards from 50, mentally imagining the numbers being formed in different ways.

6. In bed, do a relaxing visualization. If thoughts intrude, do not fixate on them; simply allow them to "pass through" your mind, as you return to the visualization.

7. If you cannot sleep, get out of bed, write out your thoughts, and/or engage in non-stimulating or "boring" activities until you are drowsy again.

---

7. COMMUNICATION SKILLS

There are many pitfalls in communication. Check out the do's and don'ts below. Are you a good communicator or a bad one?

Bad Communicators:

Don't listen.

Mind read.

Say "Yes, but...."

Cross complain.

Drift off-beam (drag in kitchen sink).

Interrupt.

Do a standoff.

Engage in heavy silence or escalate quarrels.

Don't ever take a "Time Out."

Insult each other.

Don't validate, and say "That's nuts...."

Good Communicators:

Check out clearly what the other person says and make sure they understand.

Ask for feedback and use active listening.

Give good feedback—sticking to the facts rather than interpreting.

Listen to both the content of the message and the feeling or tone of the message.

Summarize what has been said and validate the agreements and the understandings received.

Communicate that when they see things from the other's perspective, it makes sense and is reasonable to feel that way. They are not agreeing, just admitting that another view can make sense.

Managing Conflicts

Being able to resolve verbal conflicts shows good communication skills and reduces the stress experienced by both persons. The following tips on resolving conflicts show the importance of focusing on the conflict, not the person.

- Each person needs to respect the opinions of the others.

- The relationship is more important than "one-up-man-ship."

- There is a willingness to compromise when necessary.

- Unresolved conflicts will fall into the wrong hands.

- Anger has no place in conflict, except when the energy is used as motivation to find out the truth.

- There is a kernel of truth in every point made in conflict.

- Honesty and moving on are indispensable in the resolution of conflicts.

- When conflicts are handled properly, everyone grows.

- Good opening statements include:

    "I feel we've gone 'round and 'round about things in the past. Maybe if we focus first on steps we can take now, we won't get trapped."

    "I know I sometimes let myself get caught up in getting my own point across and I don't listen. Can we agree to really listen to each other and check things out before we move on?"

- Acknowledge successful conflict resolution with the person since this reinforces resolving conflicts in healthier ways.

8. EFFECTIVE STRESS MANAGEMENT

The following tips will help you assume responsibility for your own mental and physical health. Good mental and physical health leads to more effective stress management. Remember: Stressed out equals angry time bomb!

Coping with Stress   **Stress Management**

1. Eat three meals a day, including breakfast.
2. Reduce intake of sugar, salt, animal fat, and treats in the diet.
3. Pursue physical and leisure activities four times a week.
4. Form new friendships and maintain old ones. Friendships outside of work are encouraged.
5. Get 6 to 8 hours of sleep each night.
6. Practice abdominal breathing and relaxation techniques daily.
7. Schedule time alone for yourself, and time to spend with others socially. You are worth taking care of.
8. Stop smoking.
9. Limit alcohol and caffeine intake to twice a day.
10. Pace yourself and allow for an even flow of demands, when possible, in your work and lifestyle.
11. Identify and accept your emotional needs. Try not to save up conflicts/problems. Deal with them in the here and now.
12. Recognize early warning signs of stress such as apathy, withdrawal, defensiveness, irritability, headaches, changes in eating and/or habits, overworking, worrying, and alcohol misuse.
13. Allocate time and energy to express yourself in outside interests and hobbies. Try some community involvement.
14. Take vitamin supplements such as Vitamins C, E, and B complex.
15. Avoid "self-medicating" with alcohol/pain pills, etc.
16. Take one thing and one day at a time.
17. Give in once in a while!
18. Talk out your worries to people you trust. This helps to keep you in better control. Make yourself available to family and friends.
19. Learn to accept the things you cannot change.
20. Be aware of the pressures of "group think" in the squad room that, by influencing you to either clam up or "go with the flow," may build stress or resentment.

21. Use your sense of humor! Recognize that most of your personal problems do not stem from the job itself, but from the failure to deal effectively with the stress created by your unique profession of law enforcement.

9. ANGER MANAGEMENT

Unresolved stressful situations, especially those focused on you, can lead to outbursts of anger. On the job, anger expressed can lead to unintended conflicts with co-workers and supervisors. At home, anger will lead to conflicts with your spouse and family. The following anger management activity features steps in managing anger taken from Launi White, Ph.D., Focus Psychological Associates, San Diego Police Department.

Follow the steps in this activity the next time you get angry with someone. Continue using these steps as needed until they become internalized.

MANAGING YOUR ANGER

RECOGNIZE that you are angry. Write out a scale of 1 to 10, 1 being mildly annoyed and 10 being full of rage. Give words or color descriptions to each number. Check yourself on your anger scale.

ACCEPT that you are angry; do not deny it.

SEPARATE from the person or situation when your anger is at level 7 or above, and you cannot think or communicate rationally or in a non-destructive manner. Give the other person a *TIME FRAME* for when you will return. Be realistic for the amount of time you need to calm down, but try to make it as soon as possible, preferably not longer than one hour.

VENT your anger in a non-hurtful way. Some options are to exercise, punch a punching bag or pillow, use a wiffle ball and bat, yell into a pillow or out a window, or throwing rocks into a lake.

RELAX. The fastest way to relax physically is with deep breathing (4 seconds in and 4 seconds out for 4 minutes). Try deep muscle relaxation (tense and release muscle groups), repeating a soothing phrase to yourself, or closing your eyes and focusing on soothing thoughts.

CONSIDER YOUR OPTIONS for how to express your anger only after you are calmed back down to level 5 or lower on the anger scale and can think rationally.

EVALUATE AND CHOOSE the best way to express your anger in a non-destructive way. Remember to use "I feel" statements instead of "you make me feel" or other blaming statements.

Later, *REVIEW* the way that you managed your anger and decide on the aspects you liked about how you handled it, knowing you can do that again.

Coping with Stress — Stress Management

Also be aware of the areas you could improve on, and tell yourself you will attempt to improve on those areas next time.

Anger management is not easy and will take practice! Anger in one person tends to beget anger in the other person. So, the rewards of anger management can be considerable for all involved.

10. THIRTEEN STYLES OF DISTORTED THINKING

A traumatic event can produce physical stress or injury in your body that dissipates or heals fairly soon thereafter. The possibly more damaging psychological reactions to stress and trauma are generated by your mind as you replay the event over and over and by the way you think about the event. Distorted thinking heightens stress, hinders the healing process, and contributes to suicidal feelings. In fact, such feelings are the result of distorted thinking. Study the following styles of distorted thinking to learn how to take control of your mind by not falling into mental traps.

1. *Mental Filtering*: You take the negative details and magnify them while filtering out all positive aspects of a situation.

2. *All or Nothing / Polarized Thinking*: Things are black and white, good or bad. You have to be perfect or you're a failure. There is no middle ground.

3. *Overgeneralization*: You come to a general conclusion based on a single incident or piece of evidence. If something bad happens once, you expect it to happen over and over again.

4. *Mind Reading*: Without their saying so, you know what people are feeling and why they act the way they do. In particular, you are able to divine how people are feeling toward you.

5. *Catastrophizing*: You expect disaster. You notice or hear about a problem and start multiplying "what ifs:" "What if tragedy strikes? What if it happens to me?"

6. *Personalization*: You think that everything people do or say is some kind of reaction to you. You also compare yourself to others, trying to determine who's better, smarter, better looking, more successful, etc.

7. *Control Fantasies*: If you feel externally controlled, you see yourself as helpless, a victim of fate. The fallacy of internal control has you responsible for the pain and happiness of everyone around you.

8. *Fallacy of Fairness*: You feel resentful because you think you know what is fair, but other people won't agree with you.

9. *Blaming*: You hold other people responsible for your pain or you blame yourself for every problem or reversal.

10. *Shoulds*: You have a list of ironclad rules about how you and other people should act. People who break the rules anger you and you feel guilty if you violate the rules.

11. *Emotional Reasoning*: You believe that what you feel must be true automatically. If you feel stupid and boring, then you must be stupid and boring.

12. *Labeling/Mislabeling*: You generalize one or two qualities into a negative global judgment.

13. *Disqualifying the Positive*: You reject experiences by insisting they don't count for some reason or other. In this way you can maintain a negative belief that is contradicted by your everyday experience.

11. GOLDEN RULES FOR COPING WITH PANIC

Panic attacks are a common result of the fear and anxiety associated with the exaggeration of your normal reactions to stress experienced following a traumatic incident. These rules can help you quell a panic attack.

- Remember that although your feelings and symptoms are frightening, they are neither dangerous nor harmful.

- Understand that what you are experiencing is merely an exaggeration of your normal reactions to stress.

- Do not fight your feelings or try to wish them away. The more willing you are to face them, the less intense they will become.

- Don't add to your panic by thinking about what "might happen." If you find yourself asking, "What if?", tell yourself, "so what!"

- Stay in the present. Be aware of what is happening to you rather than concern yourself with how much worse it might get.

- Label your fear level from zero to 10 and watch it rise and fall. Notice that it doesn't stay at a very high level for more than a few seconds.

- When you find yourself thinking about fear, change your "what if" thinking. Focus on and perform some simple, manageable task.

- Notice that when you stop thinking frightening thoughts, your anxiety fades.

- When fear comes, accept it, don't fight it. Wait and give it time to pass. Don't try to escape from it.
- Be proud of the progress you've made. Think about how good you will feel when the anxiety has passed and you are in total control and at peace.

12. ALCOHOLIC THINKING

Alcoholic thinking is a type of thinking that is created during alcoholic drinking and withdrawal. It is also called negative thinking, drunk thinking, "stinking thinking" or alcohologia.

Alcoholic thinking is a learned behavior that is picked up during drinking, from families (from parents), in marriages (from spouse), and from friends. Alcoholic thinking is related to the thinking of people with temporary or permanent brain damage. Such people commonly suffer from poor memory, disorientation, poor judgment, confusion, and have the tendency to repeat stories. Often they have difficulty in knowing (feeling, sensing) their environment and being able to respond with appropriate behavior.

Alcoholic thinking is characterized by:

1. *NEGATIVE THINKING.* The person:
   Believes nothing is good, everything and everybody is bad. Has poor self concept, *e.g.*, "I'm a failure"; "Everything I do is wrong." Engages in self criticism and doubting.

2. *PARANOID THINKING.* The person:
   Thinks "they're out to get me." Is suspicious, self-conscious, and unable to check out feelings, even more so during withdrawal.

3. *RESENTMENT.* The person:
   Holds resentments and grudges, while not checking with others for the truth of the matter. Avoids communicating.

4. *REPETITIOUS.* The person:
   Repeats the same stories; says the same thing over and over; and remains stuck on the same thoughts (usually negative ones).

5. *DENIAL.* The person:
   Does not admit what is going on; *e.g.*, "I'm not an alcoholic"; "I can quit"; "Everything will be O.K. when I leave"; "I can control my drinking"; "My only problem is booze"; "Everything is fine."

6. *CONFABULATION.* The person:
   Makes up stories, lies to him or herself and to others for cover-up/entertainment.

7. *GUILT.* The person:
   Constantly feels guilty as a way of punishing the self.

8. *NOT TAKING RESPONSIBILITY.* The person:
   Believes "it's not my fault; it's someone else's fault."

9. *WANTING TO STAY HIGH.*

10. *WANTING TO FORGET OR ESCAPE.*

11. *SUPREMACY OF THE EGO.* The person:
    Is self-centered; *e.g.*, "I can control myself"; "I need more will power"; "I am not good enough." Does not understand other's views.

12. *DIFFICULTY CONTROLLING FEELINGS.* The person:
    Expresses anger, rage attacks, crying, laughing too much, and chronic sadness. Has chronic anger management problems.

13. *FEARS.* The person:
    Experiences unknown fear, a feeling of dread, fear of sudden catastrophe, and panic attacks.

14. *LIFE IN A RUT.* The person:
    Does the same thing everyday; acts locked in.

13. ASSERTIVENESS TRAINING

How you interact with others can be a source of stress in your life. The goal of assertiveness is to stand up for your rights in such a way that the rights of others are not violated. Beyond just demanding your rights, you can express your personal likes and interests spontaneously, talk about yourself without being self-conscious, accept compliments comfortably, disagree with someone openly, ask for clarification, and say no. In short, when you use an assertive approach, you can be more relaxed in interpersonal situations. Each of the following mistaken assumptions violates one of your legitimate rights as an adult.

Mistaken Traditional Assumptions

1. It is selfish to put your needs before others' needs.

   Replace with: You have a right to put yourself first sometimes.

2. It is shameful to make mistakes. You should have an appropriate response for every occasion.

   Replace with: You have a right to make mistakes.

3. If you can't convince others that your feelings are reasonable, then they must be wrong, or you are crazy.

   Replace with: You have a right to be the final judge of your feelings and accept them as legitimate.

4. You should respect the views of others, especially authorities, and keep your differing opinions to yourself and listen and learn.

   Replace with: You have a right to your own opinions and convictions.

5. You should be logical, consistent, flexible and not question others for their actions.

   Replace with: You have a right to protest unfair treatment or criticism and to change your course of action.

6. Asking questions reveals your stupidity.

   Replace with: You have a right to interrupt in order to ask for clarification.

7. Things could get worse, don't rock the boat or take up other's valuable time with your problems.

   Replace with: You have a right to negotiate change and ask for emotional support and help.

8. People don't want to hear that you feel bad, so keep it to yourself. If they give you advice, they are right and you should take it seriously.

   Replace with: You have a right to feel and express pain, and to ignore the advice of others.

9. Knowing you did something well is its own reward, so don't show off since successful people are secretly disliked and envied.

   Replace with: You have a right to receive formal recognition for your work and achievements.

10. You should try to accommodate others because they may not be there when you need them. People will think you don't like them if you say you want to be alone.

    Replace with: You have a right to say "no" and to be alone even if others would prefer your company.

11. You should always have a good reason for what you feel and do, and if someone is in trouble, you should help them.

    Replace with: You have a right not to have to justify yourself to others and not to take responsibility for someone else's problem.

12. You should be sensitive to others' needs and wishes, and stay on their good side, always giving them an answer when they question you.

Replace with: You have a right not to have to anticipate others' needs or wishes, and not to have to always worry about the good will of others, as well as having a choice about not responding to a situation.

Assertiveness has been found to be effective in dealing with depression, anger, resentment, and interpersonal anxiety. As you become more assertive, you lay claim to your right to relax and are able to take time out for yourself.

The three basic interpersonal styles are a/an:

- *Aggressive style* using fighting, accusing, threatening, and stepping on people without regard for their feelings. The advantage is that people don't push you around. The disadvantage is that people don't want to be around you.

- *Passive style* in which you let others push you around, do not stand up for yourself, and do what you're told regardless of how you feel about it. The advantage is that you rarely experience direct rejection. The disadvantage is that you are taken advantage of and store up a heavy burden of resentful anger.

- *Assertive style* in which you stand up for yourself, express true feelings, and do not let others take advantage of you while at the same time show consideration of others' feelings. The advantage is that you get what you want without making others mad. The disadvantage is that you will be heard and understood, but not necessarily get what you want.

In both the aggressive and passive styles, anger can build up in others or in yourself. The assertive style offers an approach that creates the least anger. The following technique illustrates how you can use an assertive style to resolve problematic interpersonal situations.

Short Form Assertiveness Technique

Your thoughts about the problematic situation is a non-blaming description of the problem as you see it. Stick closely to facts, making no inferences about the motives or feelings of others.

Your feelings are "I" statements about your emotional reaction to the problem. Avoid the implication that you're holding the other person responsible for your feelings. Your main message should be that you are trying to solve a problem, not blame or prove the other person wrong.

Your wants make your request specific and behavioral. Don't ask your spouse to be "more considerate," ask that he or she call if more than 15 minutes late.

In listening assertively, you focus your attention on the other person so that you can accurately hear the speaker's opinions, feelings and wishes. Try the three-step listening activity below.

ASSERTIVE LISTENING

Step 1—*Prepare.*
Become aware of your feelings and needs. Are you ready to listen and is the other person ready to speak?

Step 2—*Listen and Clarify.*
Give your full attention; listen to their perspective, feelings, and wants. If you're uncertain about any of these three elements, ask them to clarify with more information.

Step 3—*Acknowledge.*
Communicate that you heard the other person's position. Paraphrase their position for them as you heard it. Assertive listening and assertive expressing go together to arrive at workable compromises or new ways of looking and working out problems to mutual benefit.

Avoiding Manipulation
The final step to becoming assertive is learning how to avoid manipulation and blocking gambits from those who seek to ignore your assertive requests. Helpful techniques include the following:

Broken Record. When you find that you are dealing with someone who won't take no for an answer or refuses to grant a reasonable request, you can choose a concise sentence to use and say it over and over.

Content-to-Process Shift. Shift the focus from the topic to an analysis of what is going on between the two of you.

Defusing. Ignore the content of someone's anger and request to discuss the problem later after everyone calms down.

Assertive Agreement. Acknowledge criticism with which you agree.

Clouding. When someone is putting you down as a person, acknowledge something in the criticism with which you can agree. Rephrase the critic's words so that you can honestly concur. By giving the appearance of agreeing without promising to change, you soon deplete the critic of any reason to criticize you.

Assertive Inquiry. Prompt criticism in order to find out what is really bothering the other person.

Responding to Gambits

For each blocking gambit given below, one or more of the manipulation avoidance techniques to break the gambit described above are given.

A. Your assertion is responded to with a joke (laughing it off).

    Respond with *Content-to-Process Shift* and *Broken Record*.

B. You are blamed for the problem.

    Respond with *Clouding* or simply disagree.

C. Your assertion is responded to with a personal attack (verbal "beat up").

    Respond with *Assertive Agreement* ("thank you!"), *Broken Record*, or *Defusing*.

D. Your assertion is met with delays.

    Respond with *Broken Record*, or insist on setting a specific time for discussion.

E. Every assertive statement is blocked with "why" questions.

    Respond with *Content-to-Process Shift* or *Broken Record*.

F. Your assertion is met with tears and the covert message you are sadistic.

    Respond with *Assertive Agreement*.

G. The other person wants to debate with you about the legitimacy of what you feel, etc.

    Respond with *Content-to-Process Shift*.

H. Denial such that you are told "I didn't,...you misinterpreted me."

    Respond by asserting what you have observed and experienced, and use *Clouding*.

14. MARRIAGE AND THE AFFAIR

Affairs are not an easy subject to discuss. The stories change but the theme is the same—discouragement in marriage leads to affiliation with someone else. It does no good to take sides with a couple in this situation. Both of them need to work through this if they want to reconcile their marriage. The key question for the couple will be "Will this affair control our future or will we move on in the marriage and resolve our problems?" It is possible that out of the depths of despair such marriages can be resurrected so that they are stronger than if the affair had not occurred.

Understand that an affair is a redefining of the marriage structure by shifting the primary loyalty away from the spouse. This concept has the advantage of recognizing that what occurred is not just an illicit sexual relationship. It also allows for the possibility of reconciliation.

Affairs are a fact of life whether we like it or not. Freedom of movement, unhappy marriages, and sexual mores in society are the chemistry of affairs. Affairs take place because a spouse is dissatisfied with the marriage vacuum and is desperate for closeness and affirmation. Many people get "hooked" into an affair by just having a good listener available to them.

Critical First Steps

Prior to reconstructing a broken marriage involving an affair, the following facts and insights need to be recognized and understood.

1. If an unfaithful partner chooses to do what is right, and is willing to be patient, he or she can gain new feelings for the other spouse.

2. The reason the spouse is involved in an affair is due to tension in the marital relationship.

3. An affair is not on solid ground. 70% of men and women who have affairs return to their spouses. The numbers are on the side of the spouse. Marriages founded on affairs don't do well since their cornerstone was a dysfunctional marriage.

4. The "affairing" spouse should not be fooled by the ecstasy of feelings and enthusiasm for this relationship. These feelings are temporary and in most cases do not stand the test of time.

5. Most of the time an affair is an unconscious expression of desperation. The person just cannot live with the marriage the way it is. An affair seems the only way to motivate the person and the spouse to get help and change behaviors.

6. Another critical point is the necessity for the "affairing" person to let go of the affair. A marriage can't be resurrected out of split loyalties. The choice is difficult, but the choice must be made.

7. Affairs don't break marriages; affairs come from broken marriages.

8. The person having an affair may also have a spouse having an "affair" with activities, family members, or hobbies (again a shift in primary loyalties).

9. When the wronged spouse gets beyond his or her hurt, there is hope. The affair will test their commitment to marriage. Are they truly committed for better or worse, in sickness and in health, till death do they part? Or are they committed only as long as it does not infringe on their comfort?

Tips on Reconstruction

1. It is usually productive to consult a third party, one who understands relationships.

2. This couple needs to be "quarantined" so that the tremendous emotional strain is restricted within a circle of protection. The fewer people who know about an affair, the better.

3. There is an initial shock wave, and time is needed for settling. Both parties are hurting, but in different ways. Both need time to work through their hurt, and to express their feelings individually and/or together in therapy.

4. The offended party must not be allowed to threaten or issue ultimatums to the "affairing" partner. Ultimatums are an attempt to re-establish security, but they rarely work.

5. Remember, the issue is not the "other person;" the issue is the couple's relationship. Constantly discussing the "whys", does not improve it. It is best for the offended partner to discuss these feelings with a therapist.

6. The "affairing" spouse needs to regain confidence that the marriage relationship can work. Once he or she gains some of that confidence, there is more motivation to put energy into the marriage and to make it work.

7. The "management stage" lasts anywhere from 2 weeks to 3 months. The next stage is the work and commitment stage.

8. The work needs to be extended not in promising each other that there will never be another affair, but in working to strengthen the relationship so it can be a source of fulfillment.

9. The marital problems should be addressed in therapy and can take anywhere from 2 months to 1 year. Counseling need not be every week, but at least once a month.

10. Each partner needs time for healing. At least 6 months to 1 year is normal, but it can take as long as 2 years. Each experiences guilt, loss, despair, tension, and frustration. Neither has a corner on the emotional doldrums.

11. Trust is a major issue, and rebuilding it is a tricky task. The offended spouse has been deceived and now expects the "affairing" party to prove trustworthy. Both must give themselves into the relationship so it can work and not return to the ho-hum relationship of the past.

12. This difficult and heart wrenching experience can be turned around. Affairs are never to be encouraged, but they do happen and must be dealt with when they occur by understanding and gutsy commitment monitored and supported by a wise third party.

15. BURNOUT

Job burnout, an impairment of motivation to work, is increasingly common in today's complex world and especially for law enforcement. It begins with small warning signs such as feelings of frustration (feelings of "why bother," and "so what" increase), emotional outbursts, and enthusiasm replaced by cynicism. On the job, the burned out person acts withdrawn, looks bored, and the quality of his or her work declines.

A burned out person will increasingly suffer from minor health problems such as minor colds, headaches, backaches, insomnia, and complaints of feeling "tired" and "rundown." He or she is likely to increase use of alcohol and/or drugs, eat more or less than normal, smoke more, drink more coffee, and seem jittery and tense.

Burnout is neither a physical ailment nor a neurosis even though it has physical and psychological components. It is an inability to mobilize enough interest to act. To prevent job burnout, a person needs to maintain motivation. Motivation is determined largely by what happens after the person acts. For example, a good idea leads to feeling satisfied which leads to recognition; or, a person feels blue, talks to peer who listens, and feels better.

Causes and Recommendations

The following points are demotivators faced by law enforcement personnel that can lead to job burnout.

The officer experiences:

- A critical boss who always finds a nit to pick.

- High recidivism of crime and community violence.

- A lack of recognition or praise for good work.

- A lack of clear directions or goals for assignments and a lack of support when things don't turn out as planned.

- A lack of information to complete the job.

- Tasks without end and the use of inadequate equipment.

- "No-Win" situations. One boss wants speed, one boss wants quality.

- Conflicting roles in the workplace, as well as conflicting expectations at home.

- Value conflicts in the job. The officer believes in the necessity for police work, but is everywhere criticized for the work done.

- Work overload for too long without using strategies to cope with stress and fatigue.

The following recommendations will help alleviate the problems that lead to job burnout.

1. Recognize what is going on with your peers, supervisors, and yourself.

2. Refer to your agency's Employee Assistance Program.

3. Use stress management techniques.

4. Build a support system.

5. Use skill building, goal setting, and self rewards.

6. Modify the job.

7. Manage your mood with thought control. If you are the victim of "runaway thinking" you'll respond to every red flag waved before you. Personal power comes in knowing how to empty your mind of negative chatter so that you can focus productively on the moment and the tasks at hand.

8. Practice detached concern. Let go of "how things ought to be" that can imprison you and make you feel helpless. Focus on what you can do in the situation; stay in the "here and now;" shift your viewpoint to add to your perspective; and use some humor.

Stress Management

Stress is the fever of burnout. Bringing down the level of stress preserves health, but reducing stress will not eliminate burnout. As implied by the demotivators above, a job situation likely to lead to burnout is characterized by powerlessness. When a person faces a loss of control, the body perceives this as a threat. This triggers the body's

Coping with Stress — Stress Management

"fight or flight" response. Muscles tense, blood rushes, and breathing quickens. In normal situations, this response is temporary and subsides when the threat disappears. But, when you remain in the powerless situation the result is chronic stress. Chronic stress causes the symptoms of burnout such as exhaustion, health problems, irritability, intellectual impairment, and emotional outbursts. Some of the recommendations given above deal with changing the powerlessness of the job situation. Other possible action includes treating the stress.

The objective is to keep the stress or tension level within the optimal range (not too high, or not too low). Too little stress leads to boredom, apathy, dullness, and depression. Too much stress leads to hyperactivity, forgetfulness, frequent mistakes, lack of concentration, and irritability.

The following actions and techniques will help you control stress associated with the job.

1. Identify the situations that stress you and gather information on how you can respond to them differently.

2. Keep a stress log and identify your stress patterns (What responses do you use over and over that do not help? Do you eat to manage stress? Do you avoid situations?).

3. Use these stress reduction techniques:

    a. Breathe slowly and deeply (use abdominal muscles).

    b. Systematically tighten muscle groups for 10 seconds then relax them. Start with feet and slowly work up legs, abdomen, chest, neck and shoulders, arms, head and face.

    c. Empty your mind, or focus on one word ("relax", "calm", etc.) as you breathe slowly.

    d. Find a quiet spot to relax in daily—yard, bed, or sofa.

    e. Walk for 45 minutes five times a week.

    f. Find quiet spots for meditation—garden, ocean, etc.

    g. Instead of a coffee break, take five minutes at work and close the door and darken the room. Then, tense and relax muscles and do abdominal breathing with eyes closed.

    h. Imagine a pleasant scene and focus on this to relax.

4. Build a support network and begin to talk with "safe" people regularly about what bothers you. Friends and family buffer us against burnout and stress.

5. Keep a healthy diet, decrease cigarette smoking, drink 6-8 glasses of water daily, use Vitamin E (400 mg), Vitamin C (500 mg), Vitamin B6 (50-100 mg), decrease coffee (use Ginseng instead), and avoid excesses of alcohol.

Vasoactive Substances and Stress-Inducing Chemicals

Many vascular headaches, including the classical migraine can be induced by vasoactive stimuli. Vasoactive stimuli are factors that have the ability to stimulate the Sympathetic Nervous System and consequently the blood vessels in the brain.

The primary vasoactive stimuli include:
- Tyramine (found in processed foods and in meat)
- Monosodium glutamate
- Sodium nitrate
- Histamine (found in decongestants)
- Bright lights that create glare
- Changes in barometric pressure (rapid declines)
- Strenuous physical exercise
- Prolonged loud noise
- Some Sympathomimetics (substances high in caffeine)
- Some foods such as: liver, cheeses, caviar, sausages, coffee, tea, chocolate, hot dogs, Chianti & red wine, foods containing Brewer's Yeast, fava beans, fermented or over- ripened foods.

Sympathomimetics are chemical substances that initiate a stress response by stimulating the sympathetic branch of the Autonomic Nervous System.

Some common sources for these substances are:
- Coffee—one 5 ounce cup contains 150 mg of caffeine.
- Tea—one cup brewed 1 minute contains 25 mg caffeine.
- Cocoa—one cup contains 15 mg caffeine.
- Colas—one can ranges from 30 to 65 mg caffeine.
- Chocolate—one bar ranges from 30 to 65 mg caffeine.
- Medications containing caffeine:
    Fioricet 40 mg
    Anacin 32 mg
    Excedrin 65 mg
    Midol 32 mg
    Fiorinal 40 mg
    No Doz 100 mg
    Stay Alert 250 mg
    Triaminicin 30 mg

This information is from the *Physician's Desk Reference*. Use it to increase your well-being.

16. RELATIONSHIPS

In a relationship, fighting is a legitimate and inevitable part of intimacy. No two people always agree on all things. But, fighting can be done fairly. The following is a step by step guide to fair fighting that, if followed, will increase mutual understanding and respect, and decrease tension and stress.

Fair Fighting

Step 1

"What am I angry about...?" State your anger in terms of behavior. What is your mate doing or not doing in terms of specific behavior in the here and now?

Step 2

Set the time for fighting. "I have a bone to pick with you and I'd like to hash it out now or as soon as the kids go to bed." Frequent small fights are better than periodic explosions of anger and rage.

Step 3

State the problem while your mate listens without interrupting.

Rule 1: State the problem simply, directly, and clearly.

Rule 2: State the problem using the facts of the issue without any emotional overtones.

Rule 3: Deal with only one issue at a time.

Rule 4: Deal with the present here and now aspects of the issue. No complaints and examples from the past!

Rule 5: State the problem in terms of behavior, not attitudes. Describe what your partner does nor doesn't do that you don't like.

EXAMPLES

Unsuccessful Statements:
"I'm sick of sitting around while you work in the garage four nights a week. I'm deserted, you love your table saw more than me."

Successful Statements:
"I'd like you to hear some gripes I have about the way we spend our evenings. Three to four nights a week you are in the garage while I sit around reading or watching TV."

Step 4

Use "I" statements. This makes it easier to avoid blaming. Instead of saying "You are distant and standoffish", a better way of getting the message across is "I feel out of touch with you."

We cause our own feelings by the way we interpret other's words and actions. Others are responsible for their words and actions but they are not responsible for your feelings. Blaming others for your feelings is not only inaccurate, but can be dangerous. When you blame others for your feelings, you give them power over you—you hand over the controls. If others make you feel bad, they must also be in charge of feeling good. "I" statements put the power in your own hands.

Describe your feelings in a normal tone of voice and make sure body language is non-threatening. You do not act out by yelling, clenching your fists, or pounding on the table. Avoid all scornful sarcastic tones in your voice.

Discuss your anger, as well as other secondary feelings such as hurt, anxiety, agitation, apprehension, suspicion, or alienation you may also be experiencing.

EXAMPLES

Unsuccessful Statements:
"Where have you been? You're late. Not much of a mother. The kids and I are a mess, and we're supposed to take cupcakes to the school tomorrow."

Successful Statements:
"I'm glad you're back. I feel overwhelmed when the kids cry and get demanding. I feel resentful too, because I expected to go off the kidsitting an hour ago, and I also feel I got cheated out of 45 minutes of peace and quiet."

Step 5

Propose change. State your proposed changes as specifically as possible and in terms of behavioral changes that are easily measurable.

EXAMPLES

Vague: "I want you to trust me more."

Clearer: "I request you do not phone me five times a day and peek at my paperwork on my desk."

Vague: "I want you to be more responsible around the house."

Clearer: "Son, I want you to mow the lawn by noon every Saturday."

Sarcasm has no place in a fair fight. Sarcasm is a hostile way of combining blaming and suggesting that the other partner is stupid.

Step 6

State the consequences. The key here is to remember that honey is sweeter than vinegar, a carrot is tastier than a stick, and seeking pleasure is better than avoiding pain. Accentuate the positive by pointing out the advantages of the changes you want. After that, you can casually mention the negative consequences your partner will incur if the proposed changes, compromises, etc., are not put into effect. Avoid empty threats! They are impossible to carry out, and destroy the fair fighting process.

EXAMPLES

Unsuccessful Statements:
"Pizza and movies. That's all we do. I'm bored, and if you don't want to do anything else, I'll find someone else who will!" (Complain and Threaten style)

Successful Statements:
"I'm tired of eating pizza and going to the movies so often. How about next Friday we eat Japanese and go listen to jazz at the new club? I'd enjoy the change, and I think you would, too."

The Receiving Partner
As the receiving partner, your role is simple—just listen. Do not argue, refute, disagree, or interrupt. The only time you open up is to ask for more information or further clarification. You listen carefully, understand the problem, appreciate your partner's emotions, grasp the changes your partner wishes to make, and understand the consequences of making or not making the suggested changes.

A response is always made to the proposal for change. You do not respond to the validity of the problem, the emotion, or to the fairness of the consequences. Your partner has made a serious proposal and it is to the proposal alone you are expected to respond.

The response can take several forms: you agree; you agree, but have some conditions that are related to the issue at hand; you may agree to the necessity for change but have a better idea for change and make a counter-proposal; you ask for time to think about the proposed change (time out for 1 hour to 1 day); you suggest a trial period for the proposed change; or you may just say "no." When a "no" occurs to your partner's carefully made proposal, it usually means you have suppressed hostile feelings of your own that need to be worked out via the fair fighting routine. It's time to get clear what you really want and how you feel, so that you and your partner can

Managing Anger Within a Fair Fight

Here are some points to consider that will keep outbursts of anger from ruining a fair fight.

- Keep an anger log and look for patterns to your anger.

- Cool those "hot thoughts"; *e.g.*, "this battle isn't worth it."

- Think problem solving; *e.g.*, "OK, what's the first thing to do?"

- Use an escape route; *e.g.*, "I can always walk away rather than lose it."

- Reward yourself; *e.g.*, "Good, I'm hanging in there and not yelling."

- Reduce anger images. Use humor not sarcasm to get distance.

- Decide your battles:
  For the large indignities, use direct action.
  For the small indignities, use distraction.

- Difficult people? See your part in the situation and avoid focusing only on flaws; look for their strengths.

- Disarm difficult people by listening (calm assertiveness).

- Disarm the other person by telling what is done right, then mention your problem and explain what you want.

- Don't take "bait." Stay focused on problem solving.

- Agreeing with difficult persons shuts them up and takes the wind out of their sails. Then immediately clarify your point of view again, calmly and firmly.

- Paraphrasing defuses anger and helps everyone feel understood.

- Rewrite the rules. Although it would be nice, we are not "entitled" to love, honesty, etc. Reduce your "should" statements.

- Examine how you feed your rage. Anger often masks fears.

- There is a time to move from righteous anger to closure.

- Develop empathy—it's your thoughts that create your anger, not the other person's behavior. Our behavior reflects our point of view.

- Develop a daily stress reduction plan. Stress fuels anger.

CHAPTER 6

POST TRAUMA

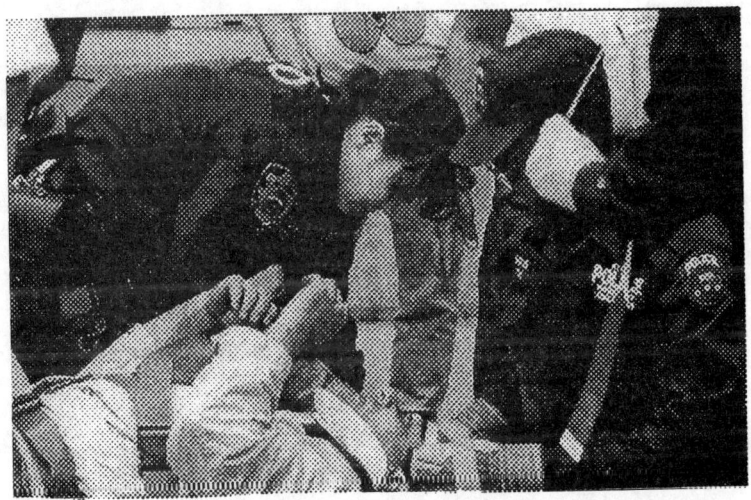

A. "THE MORNING AFTER"

A police officer shoots and kills a criminal for the first time, his or her partner has just been killed in the line of duty, or he or she is involved in a serious incident involving multiple deaths. What happens to these officers who are involved in such traumatic psychological and physiological experiences? Do we send them back to the front lines the next morning? Years ago, in many instances, this was the case.

Today there is an awareness of serious psychological impairments that result from involvement in these types of traumatic incidents. For example, at approximately 9:02 a.m. on April 19, 1995, a bomb ripped through the Alfred P. Murrah federal Building in Oklahoma City, killing 168 men, women, and children, and seriously injuring hundreds more. The result was a tragedy to the victims and families of the blast, and to the security and safety we as Americans hold dear.

However, there is another very sad statistic connected to the bombing that is rarely spoken about. There are only whispers amongst the people, families, and agencies directly involved. Six more lives are gone. These six people took their own lives. Three of the six were family members of the bombing victims. The other three were bombing rescue workers; police officers and fire and rescue personnel who were assigned the arduous task of not only rescuing the blast survivors, but also locating, bagging, and labeling the bodies and parts of the dead.

Suicide by members of the victims' families is a double tragedy for those involved. But, for those professionals who had witnessed firsthand the horrific carnage from the blast, leaving behind torn lives, suicide was an unexpected release from the incurred trauma. This, despite the hundreds of hours of debriefing and counseling by on site debriefing and trauma teams, peer counselors, and psychiatrists. What follows is an examination of the nature of trauma reactions and the events that produce them.

B. TRAUMA AND NEUROSIS

Psychological trauma includes anything that overwhelms the person's available resources. In other words, any event that poses a seemingly unsolvable problem for an individual or which creates a conflict of such significant proportion as to bring the person to an impasse is a trauma.

In severe cases following an incident that has left an impact upon a police officer, either psychologically or physiologically, a condition called neurosis may exist. Neuroses following trauma include reactions that have their onset following severe physical or acute psychological-emotional trauma incidents. The resulting physical and emotional consequences are highly variable in degree and in duration, as well as in time of origin. In general, in neuroses, there are significant attitudinal and behavioral manifestations whose presence indicates the existence of emotional tension and conflict, termed "conflict indicators." They may include stuttering, nightmares, certain mannerisms, or persistent insomnia.

Clinical indications that a trauma occurred resulting in a neurosis include the following:

1. Symptoms or changes in personality noted by observers less biased than the subject date from the external threat or from the first attempt to return to the activity during which the threat occurred.

2. The subject has repetitive dreams of being in the traumatic situation.

3. Increased irritability and startle reaction and a tendency toward explosive-aggressive reaction patterns are observed.

4. A phobia for the situation or activity in which the threat occurred exists. This phobia may be masked by physical symptoms or behaviors that preclude return to the feared situation or activity.

5. A diminished interest in the outside world, or constriction of the ego, may be an extreme form of avoidance against a phobia.

The early recognition of the presence of trauma and the encouragement to return to the activity in which the trauma occurred is analogous to the common-sense method of preventing a neurosis after a rider has been thrown from the back of a horse. It is well-known that immediately remounting the horse to master the beast is the best method of treating the anxiety produced and of preventing a phobia for horseback riding. Such intervention and treatment by police department counselors can shorten the duration of a traumatic neurosis and facilitate an early return of the officer to active duty.

C. TRAUMATIC INCIDENTS

The psychological violence connected with a gunfight or similar serious confrontation can be a dangerous enemy. Sometimes the effect upon the police officer is felt immediately; sometimes it may be days, weeks, or months before trauma symptoms may appear. The human mind has a tendency to dwell on unpleasant, emotionally charged events in the wake of their actual occurrence. In post trauma, an officer might relive and react to the memory of an experience, churning over and over in his or her mind what he or she did and what might or should have been done differently. Under the best of circumstances, the psychological strain of being in law enforcement is immense. There is no time when stress is greater than after a serious confrontation or incident such as a shooting. During the incident, an officer might not be aware of all the happenings caught in the moment. But, afterward, he or she is most certain to feel a psychological input in some form. Men and women who have been involved in shootings know they can never predict how someone will react afterwards. The ones who least expect to be damaged psychologically may be hit the hardest. To understand post trauma and its effects is the key to survival, both mentally and physically.

A shooting incident evokes many emotions and feelings. Besides physical stimulation, the officer may be confused as to what is actually happening, and why it is happening to him or her. Seconds feel like minutes, and minutes feel like hours, as time seems to stand still. The officer reconnects his or her awareness to reality by taking responsible action. A call on the radio for help, a talk with a supervisor, or a simple report will refocus the officer's attention from bewilderment to the actual task at hand. This refocusing of attention allows the officer to function efficiently and may offer a break psychologically, but it also holds off the emotional impact of the shooting, leaving it to haunt him or her at a later time.

Depending on what type of person the officer is, emotional trauma may set in quickly or linger below conscious awareness for some time. A sensitive, compassionate officer will feel the impact almost immediately. The officer may become very somber, feeling quite disturbed, mulling over the incident again and again. He or she may remain silent on the subject, but may feel it necessary to, in some way, make amends for what was done.

An officer who is emotionally stable and more rational may treat the shooting as if it were an everyday occurrence. He or she may say, "it was nothing!" This reaction only delays the emotional impact of what actually occurred. By behaving in this manner, the officer places little importance on the incident; thus, no one really approaches him or her to talk about it. The memory of the incident stays hidden, behind the scene; the officer hoping it will somehow disappear. The officer feels if the subject is avoided or treated lightly, it will go away. This is definitely not so! As time goes by, signs of psychological turmoil may show up in unexplained headaches, backaches, stomach problems, nervousness, forgetfulness, and a short temper that becomes explosive for no reason at all. Nightmares and panic wakening in the night may also be experienced.

The officer who was so good at avoiding the emotional impact of the shooting incident can no longer avoid the symptoms that avoidance has brought on. The officer needs help. Repressing his or her feelings is no longer possible. The time has come to be honest with his or her emotions and recognize the traumatic nature of the experience. The officer must understand the need for guidance through this tunnel of darkness; someone to relieve the inner anxieties; someone to help him or her to deal with the feelings before it is too late—before the feelings turn into psychiatric problems with which he or she can no longer cope.

As in any other incident where there is gunfire, a complete investigation will take place; only this time the officer will be under scrutiny. Commanding officers will be involved, as well as the news media. The officer may be treated as a "suspect." The news that is printed and statements that are made may sound ambiguous—and they are not retractable. Some officers will feel their privacy is being invaded. They may feel like they are a standing target, helpless in trying to share their side of the story. These events also add to the emotional turmoil of the officer. The officer may begin to complain of feeling ill, with many symptoms, but no real disease. As the officer's homelife fills with tension, the marriage may suffer. Sexual problems are not unusual. The officer may mask these symptoms by telling everyone how sexually active he or she really is and how the marriage has never been better; once again, hiding the truth, leaving reality out of the picture.

The psychological wounds experienced after a traumatic incident are handled differently by each officer. Some choose to resign from the law enforcement field. Other officers, unable to handle their first shooting experience, vow never to pull the trigger again. This is not an attitude an officer would want a partner to have. When an incident evolves in which shooting would be the only means of survival, an officer does not want a partner who would put him or her in danger by trying to be persuasive with words instead of a gun. While believing him or herself to be a hero, the partner would not be a hero for long.

Some positive results can develop from a shooting experience. The officer who can acknowledge the emotions felt and express them honestly to him or herself, and to others, will come away from the experience a better person. He or she will truly understand the scope of police work. What was once thought of as impossible, is now a reality. The officer's views on police work will now include the extreme danger that is really involved—the danger of possibly having to shoot a suspect; the danger of being hit by a suspect's bullet; and the danger of death. Police work is no longer routine, going from one assignment to another. The officer will be more aware of his or her responsibilities and more cautious of surroundings. He or she will be able to give firsthand information to fellow officers on how to deal with a shooting incident before it occurs. The most rewarding result that could emerge from an officer's traumatic experience is being able to help other officers who are going through similar feelings of guilt, sorrow, and uncertainty by comforting them and enabling them to handle the situation which seems to be suffocating their lives. These other officers will know that their experiences are not unique.

Traumatic Incidents

An officer who survives a shoot-out may receive departmental awards or favorable press coverage, with even fame and glory attached. This may seem like enough restitution to such law enforcement officers, but in many instances these surface or cosmetic factors are not able to repair all of the internal damage that takes professional expertise to correct.

CHAPTER 7

POST TRAUMA— TREATMENT AND REHABILITATION PROGRAMS

Today, police departments and all law enforcement agencies realize the impact and serious consequences of post-traumatic stress on their people. This has led to a concerted effort to properly "treat and cure" those who are affected and succumb to after effects that can seriously damage both individuals and the morale of an entire agency.

A. THE McMAINS STUDY—FINDINGS AND RECOMMENDATIONS

Back in 1983 and 1984, a study was conducted by Dr. Michael J. McMains, Ph.D., Police Psychologist of the city of San Antonio, Texas, in relation to post-trauma/shooting incidents. This study acknowledged and proved the success of professional counseling, as well as peer counseling by police officers, some of whom had already been involved in shooting incidents.

In November 1983, a questionnaire was sent to police departments of the 20 largest cities in the United States. The questionnaire focused on professional and peer support systems for managing "post-shooting trauma" in these major departments. Demographic data included population of the city, size of the department, number of patrol officers on the force, and average number of shootings by police officers over the previous five years. The findings and recommendations of this study were as follows.

The emotional impact of a shooting on a police officer has been a growing concern of both officers and behavioral scientists involved with police officers over the last decade. Professional publications in law enforcement have touched on the emotional trauma frequently experienced by officers. The cost of losses to departments as the result of "post-shooting trauma" has sensitized departments to the need for effective and efficient support systems to deal with the emotional impact of shootings. Studies of the impact of post-shooting trauma have defined the sequence and nature of the emotional impact of shootings on officers, as well as the stages through which officers pass in reaction to the use of deadly force.

Suggestions about the management of "post-shooting trauma" have included the idea that a peer support system could be an effective method of managing officers' reactions. Major concerns were to explore the programs currently used by police departments across the country in light of the suggestion that a peer support system might provide effective intervention, to present preliminary data on the effectiveness of such support programs, and to address these issues based on the knowledge gained by military psychologists and psychiatrists in the management of the trauma of combat.

Most large departments have recognized a wide range of events as traumatic. Consequently, they provided formal professional and peer support services for more than shooting incidents, and they have had a greater opportunity to experience the effectiveness of such programs. In addition, the cost effectiveness of support services has probably been more obvious to larger departments. Not only have larger departments tended to have more resources invested in their personnel, but when the cost of maintaining a support system was compared with the benefit derived, it seemed reasonable that larger departments had greater use for the same services, thus decreasing the per person cost for services.

The fact that larger departments have had support programs longer than smaller departments has given them more experience with the benefits of the services than that had by smaller departments. Not only have long established programs developed proven track records, but the very fact that larger departments have been parts of systems for a number of years has provided for trust to build throughout the systems. Services have attained credibility just because they have been in place for a period of time.

The use of peers as counselors in police departments seemed to have gained greater acceptance. In setting up a peer support system, it did not seem to matter whether the system allowed the officer to decide to use the service or whether the department required the officer to use the service. Both voluntary and mandatory programs appeared equally effective. The use of a voluntary system had the advantage of a greater commitment on the part of the officer choosing to participate. Under a mandatory system, required participation by every officer involved in a traumatic event provided a "face saving" way for officers who would not otherwise have used this service.

The responsiveness of both peer and professional support systems seemed fairly sensitive to the needs of officers involved in traumatic incidents. Most departments that provided services, provided them within 24 hours of the time of the event. Most departments recognized the need to provide support and counseling services to other officers on the scene of a shooting and to officers who have experienced other incidents that are considered traumatic. An impressive percentage of departments that provided services to officers were sensitive to the fact that many events could bring an officer to the realization of his or her own vulnerability.

Research on the usefulness of counseling demonstrated that effective counseling required an ability to understand people's emotional experiences and to communicate that understanding, the ability to be honest with people, and the ability to value people and to communicate that valuing. Also, research on the effects of trauma intervention in combat stress by non-combat personnel supported the importance of understanding feelings to facilitate recovery. Thus, a key factor in successful treatment was selecting, as officers' counselors, people who were empathetic individuals who could understand fear, guilt, remorse, anxiety, etc., regardless of its origin. These peer counselors would then be trained in effective communication skills and in the ability to provide a non-threatening and accepting atmosphere for officers involved in traumatic incidents.

Likewise, training on the psychology of trauma was considered as important. The thinking was that if a basic understanding of the stages of trauma was provided to counselors, they would feel more secure in their management of others in trauma. Counselors could also help provide security for others because they would show that trauma was not an unpredictable or uncontrollable phenomena.

Training of peer counselors in two other areas of social problems seemed to be called for due to the large number of police officers involved nationwide. Training peer counselors in alcoholism and alcohol abuse and in family counseling would be helpful because the use of peer counselors could provide even the smaller departments with an early warning system. Such trained counselors could identify and intervene in problems before administrative action became necessary.

B. POST-SHOOTING/COMBAT STRESS REACTIONS

1. POST-SHOOTING STRESS REACTIONS

Authors of articles on post-shooting trauma and on combat stress reactions have described similar physical and psychological reactions and similar factors that influence the individual's susceptibility to the stress of traumatic situations. For example, Stratton (1983) has described the reaction of officers involved in shootings as including:

1. Time distortions;
2. Emotional numbing (emotional hardening);
3. Feelings of isolation;
4. Denial;
5. Flashbacks;
6. Sleep disturbances;
7. Worry about legal proceedings; and
8. Guilt.

Stratton (1983) has suggested that an officer's reaction to a shooting incident will depend on his or her personality, the stability of his or her life situation, the nature of the event, and the available support systems.

2. COMBAT STRESS REACTIONS

Belensky (1981) has reported similar symptoms in combat stress reactions, including:

1. Fugue states (time distortions, emotional numbing, denial, and isolation);
2. Anxiety (worry);
3. Restlessness (sleep disturbances); and
4. Distortions of the senses (flashbacks).

Belensky (1981) reported the results of Israeli studies that concluded that a combat soldier's reaction to combat stress was dependent upon the stability of other life situations (family, finances, and so on), and group cohesion in the combat unit (support system).

3. CONCLUSION

Though there are recognized differences between the police officer who has to decide and act alone and whose decisions and actions are subject to departmental and judicial review and the combat soldier who acts as a member of a group and who is relatively immune to review and accountability, there are enough similarities in their reactions to trauma and stress to justify the application of knowledge gained in one area to the other.

C. PRINCIPLES OF MANAGING TRAUMA

In managing the impact of combat stress and trauma, several principles have been developed that facilitate a constructive return to duty and that minimize the long-term disabling impact of combat (Schultheis, 1982). They include:

1. Brevity;
2. Immediacy;
3. Centrality;
4. Expectancy; and
5. Proximity.

In reviewing the crisis intervention research relevant to combat stress and trauma, Manglesdorf (1984) has pointed out that these principles have applicability to traumas other than combat, including mass casualty management and terrorist operations. Consequently, the application of these principles to post-shooting trauma seems reasonable.

The design of an effective and efficient post-shooting trauma program needs to consider each of the following principles and its explication.

1. *Brevity.* Intervention should be short-term, focused on supporting officers during the time of crisis and returning them to the field at the earliest possible time.

2. *Immediacy.* Intervention should begin as soon after the trauma as possible, so as to provide officers a way of understanding the experience in the most constructive way, and before they solidify their thinking about the event in maladaptive and self-critical ways.

3. *Centrality.* Intervention should be centralized to provide for the most efficient and effective use of time and resources. A centralized

response team will provide a more timely response (immediacy) closer to the actual location (proximity).

4. *Expectancy.* Intervention should convey to officers from the first interaction an expectation that the officer acted properly, can manage the situation, and will be returning to duty soon.

5. *Proximity.* Intervention should occur as close to the shooting as possible to maximize the desensitization of officers to any possible trauma.

D. PROFESSIONAL AND PEER SUPPORT SYSTEM

The following section outlines a sequential program for supporting officers who experience the impact of post-shooting trauma based on three phases through which officers pass in their adjustment to trauma: shock, impact, and resolution (Solomon, 1984). A professional and peer support system would be put into effect which would make an efficient use of manpower and which would integrate the crisis intervention principles discussed previously with an understanding of this sequential reaction to trauma.

1. DEBRIEFING AND COUNSELING PROGRAM APPLIED

Stage I: Incident

The main principle after an incident requires that the counselor, whether professional or peer, establish contact with the officer involved in a trauma at the time of the incident. Being available as soon after the incident as possible, provides the counselor an opportunity to view the scene and to review the events on the location. Information is gained which will allow for the building of desensitization at a later time. In addition, the counselor can make initial contact with the officer, giving the officer an opportunity to talk about the incident on location, so as to begin the desensitization process. The counselor can begin the process of evaluating the emotional impact of the trauma, thereby shortening the intervention process.

Stage II: Investigation

A frequent stress for officers involved in traumatic events is the internal investigation required by most departments. The availability of the counselor during the investigation integrates several principles of trauma intervention into the counseling program. Support, evaluation, and recommendation can be provided for during the stress of the investigation. The briefing of an officer during this period about the emotional impact of trauma on persons involved, about the procedures of the investigation, about the emotional impact of delays in the investigation on officers, and about the services available from the peer counselor can set the expectations of the officer. These expectations are commonly about the interest of the support service in him or her, about the normal nature of emotional reactions to traumatic situations, about his or her own capacity to deal with the up-coming stress, and about the belief that the officer will be returning to full day in the shortest possible time.

Stage III: Forty-Eight Hour Follow-Up

In the sequential analysis of the impact of post-shooting trauma, Solomon (1984) has suggested that the shock phase lasts from 24 to 48 hours after the incident. Follow-up by a peer counselor two days after the incident provides the officer another opportunity to discuss his or her feelings in a non-critical and non-threatening environment. It allows the counselor to evaluate the officer's progress in resolving the trauma and to make decisions about the need for formalized relaxation training, the development of a desensitization program, and professional intervention at a time when the shock phase is remitting. The teaching of systematic relaxation techniques during the time of the most intense emotional response to shooting can reassure the officer by providing a renewed confidence in the officer's ability to control his or her own physical processes.

Stage IV: One Week Follow-Up

Solomon (1984) has pointed out that the impact stage of post-shooting trauma begins after approximately 48 hours and can last from six to eight weeks. A one week follow-up, initiated by the peer counselor, can allow the officer the opportunity to express his or her feelings about departmental management and concerns about the rightness of the shooting. It provides an opportunity for the peer counselor to explore the beliefs the officer holds about the shooting, to help guide him or her to a more rational interpretation of events, to evaluate the presence or absence of frequent emotional reactions, and to reassure the officer that the symptoms he or she is experiencing are normal reactions. It demonstrates interest and support, but it reinforces the expectation that the officer can manage the incident by pointing out that the peer counselor will be available to him or her when the officer needs to talk.

Stage V: Six Week Follow-Up

A six week follow-up allows the peer counselor to evaluate the officer's progress in accepting the incident, his or her emotional reaction to the incident, and his or her vulnerability. It provides the counselor an opportunity to evaluate the officer's comfort with the incident by giving the counselor the chance to return with the officer to the scene of the incident, to monitor non-verbal signs of anxiety, and to coach the officer in systematic relaxation techniques at the scene.

Stage VI: Six Month Follow-Up

An evaluation by a professional at six months provides the opportunity for the professional to evaluate the integration of the officer's experience into his or her life. It provides protection against liability and it provides a quality control check of the peer counselor's work.

The total amount of time involved in the resolution of a traumatic situation will vary from case to case depending on the personality of the officer involved, the seriousness of the incident, and the other support systems in the officer's life (Stratton, 1983). However, the model outlined above, utilizing the principles of crisis management developed in combat, promises to reduce the amount of professional and peer time necessary to support an officer after a traumatic incident.

As outlined, time allotments would vary, depending on how the programs were implemented. For instance, it might be that the peer counselor would provide the initial contact, evaluation, and support at the time of the incident and during the investigation, leading to more time invested by the peer counselor and less by the professional. The advantages and disadvantages of such reallotment is a local decision and it hinges on available budget, available professional resources, the liability incurred with and without professional services, the acceptance of the professional by officers, and a host of other administrative and political issues. The point is that in developing a professional or peer support system to meet the needs of officers involved in traumatic events, the principles of brevity, immediacy, centrality, expectancy, and proximity, coupled with compassion and understanding, need to be applied. It is through the use of these hard won and time tested principles that a constructive return to full functioning is maximized for officers dealing with the sometimes overwhelming trauma of police work.

2. DR. MARTIN SYMONDS—COUNSELING WITH COMPASSION

Years ago, I had occasion to personally interview Dr. Martin Symonds, who is, in 1999, Deputy Chief Surgeon of the New York City Police Department. Dr. Symonds' involvement with police work lasted from 1940 to 1947, when he was a police officer himself. He left the Department to go to medical school. From 1961 to 1968, he served as Honorary Police Surgeon. Among his other credentials are Director of Victims' Treatment Center, helping the victims of serious crimes, and consultant on hostage situations for the State Department.

Dr. Symonds became personally involved in the New York City Police Department's Psychological Services Unit from 1978 to 1985, and became Director in 1981. During that period, Dr. Symonds, through his influence and persistence, led this Department to its current high standing in the area of post-trauma treatment and rehabilitation. As a psychiatrist, Dr. Symonds now devotes his time administratively and personally to seeing police officers who have been seriously injured or involved in traumatic incidents, and helping them return to a sense of well-being, as well as back to full duty, if possible.

In terms of lending assistance to police officers who have been psychologically and/or physically damaged, Dr. Symonds states that compassion and understanding are important factors to their well-being. Early contact and debriefing are his primary concerns, letting the officer know, "I'm here to help; I'm sorry about what happened to you." He tries to be responsive to the individual, and not to what happened. This personal interaction on a one-to-one basis is his key to a successful debriefing.

Professional and peer support systems that provide intervention programs for the traumatized police officer help to keep officers from slipping through the crack and succumbing to illness, or worse. Tribute should be paid to the New York City Police Department's Post Trauma Unit and to similar units nationwide. Special thanks should go to Dr. Martin Symonds and others for their devoted interest and accomplishments.

This page intentionally left blank.

CHAPTER 8

*POST TRAUMA—
RESPONSES AND HEALING*

A. THE TRAUMA RESPONSE

An incident occurs; it is sudden, random, violent, and senseless. It affects not only the victim, but co-workers as well. The incident can shatter an officer's sense of safety and well-being and temporarily destroy his or her ability to function normally.

This reaction is called the "trauma response." Although individuals will react with different intensities and recover at varying rates, most people will go through some form of the trauma response, which may appear as an alternation between the following two states.

Numbness is characterized by withdrawal from others, depression or emotional flatness (not feeling much of anything), or the feeling of being "lost in a fog." These signs may be accompanied by problems with concentration on and off the job.

Hyperarousal is characterized by irritability, flashbacks to the incident, nervousness, extreme emotions, nightmares, and being easily startled.

It's not uncommon to go back and forth between these two states. A person may feel numb for a while, then move into hyperarousal, and back again. Some people may ultimately stay in one of the two states. It's also quite common for the traumatic event to evoke memories of past events and associated feelings of helplessness, shock, or loss.

1. BUILDING A WALL AROUND PAIN

When crisis strikes, the normal human tendency is to try to stop the pain. It's normal for a person to build a "wall" around the incident in an attempt to keep it separate from the rest of his or her life.

The problem with building a wall around the pain is that it usually doesn't work. A critical incident causes a traumatic reaction, and refusing to think about or discuss it does not undo the incident. Even if the pain can be denied for a while, it will push through later—often in the form of increased illness or turnover, decreased productivity or morale, and a breakdown in the normal communication between the person and those they care about.

2. COMMON RESPONSES TO TRAUMATIC EVENTS

Although trauma affects people differently, there are some common reactions. Signs and symptoms may begin almost immediately, or one may feel fine for a couple of days or even weeks, then suddenly be hit with a reaction. The important thing to remember is that these reactions are quite normal. Although one may feel some distress, that is a normal reaction to an abnormal situation.

Post Trauma Healing — The Trauma Response

Some common responses to traumatic events are listed below.

Physical Reactions

- Insomnia/nightmares
- Fatigue
- Hyperactivity or "nervous energy"
- Appetite changes
- Pain in the neck and back
- Headaches
- Heart palpitations or pains in the chest*
- Dizzy spells*

*These symptoms require a physician's attention.

Emotional Reactions

- Flashbacks or "reliving" the event
- Excessive jumpiness or tendency to be startled
- Irritability
- Anger
- Feelings of anxiety or helplessness

Effect on Productivity

- Inability to concentrate
- Increased incidence of errors
- Lapses of memory
- Increase in absenteeism
- Tendency to overwork

Usually, the signs and symptoms of trauma will lessen over time. If a reaction causes concern, the officer should note the specific symptoms. Then for each symptom, note its duration and intensity. If the symptoms do not lessen in intensity and disappear within a few weeks, or if the reaction interferes with the ability to carry on life normally, he or she should seek help. An Employee Assistance Program, community mental health center, physician, or religious leader may be able to offer referral to a qualified counselor.

Whether seeking counseling or not, the following tips can help the officer keep his or her life in order while experiencing the trauma response.

The officer should:

- Maintain as normal a schedule as possible, but not overdo it. Cut out unnecessary "busyness" and not take on new projects.

- Acknowledge that he or she will be operating below normal level for a while.

- Structure his or her time even more carefully than usual, keeping lists and double checking any important work. It's normal to forget things when under stress.

- Maintain control where possible by making small decisions, even if they are seemingly unimportant.

- Spend time with others, even though it may be difficult at first.

- Allow plenty of time to adjust to the new realities. He or she may feel better for a while, then have a relapse. This is normal.

3. GETTING OVER THE TRAUMA RESPONSE

The trauma response is a temporary reaction to a serious incident. Creating a barrier to the pain caused by the incident should be avoided. If the employer provides debriefing and/or counseling, the officer should take advantage of this opportunity to talk about how the incident has affected him or her. If the officer chooses not to seek counseling, he or she should talk about the event with friends. Understanding the trauma response, and then making a conscious effort to work through it, will ultimately help the traumatized officer to overcome the pain and resume a productive career.

B. THE HEALING PROCESS

Although the healing process is so individual and personal, there are some common steps that most people go through. Although this process is natural and normal, it is also painful and difficult. Moving through the healing process means acknowledging a painful reality and integrating it into your life in a meaningful way. That may require a lot of time and patience.

1. CARING FOR PHYSICAL HEALTH

In a crisis, a person may forget to eat and sleep, revert to old habits, like smoking, or find that nagging physical ailments flare up. This is precisely when it is most important to take care of one's physical health. Emotional upheaval can make a person especially vulnerable to physical illness. In general, major changes in lifestyle should not be attempted, while at the same time, good habits should be reinforced and bad habits minimized.

Pay special attention to the areas outlined below.

Stress is completely normal when dealing with a crisis. A person will feel many unpleasant emotions—sadness, anger, loss of control, impatience, etc. Learning and practicing relaxation techniques and cutting back on responsibilities can lessen the amount of stress a person will experience during the healing process.

Sleep is always important, but especially so when undertaking the healing process. Nightmares that can disrupt sleep are a common reaction after a crisis. A person should allow sufficient time each night for a full sleep cycle. Any serious sleeping difficulties that last longer than a week or so, should be brought to the attention of a physician.

Exercise such as that gained from brisk walking is not only good for the body, but also has a calming effect on the mind. A regular exerciser should resist the temptation to use exercise as a way to literally "run away" from his or her feelings. A relaxed exercise session can help combat stress, but an intense, all-out workout every day can increase stress and may become a way to avoid facing a painful reality. Also, over- exercising can easily lead to injury.

Smoking is always a health risk. Unfortunately, many ex-smokers become current smokers during a crisis. The act of smoking is oftentimes a way to repress feelings and put psychological distance between the person and his or her problem. A stressful time is probably not the best time for a person to try to quit smoking; yet, at the same time, he or she should try to avoid using cigarettes as a crutch.

Alcohol and other drugs may be tempting, but they cause far more problems than they solve. People under extreme stress may tend to "self-medicate" with alcohol, tranquilizers, coffee, and other drugs, both legal and illegal. For a person in pain, it's hard to tell how much is too much, so perhaps the best idea is for him or her to try to avoid mood-altering substances as much as possible.

2. MOVING THROUGH THE HEALING PROCESS

The following points summarize what we know about the healing process. Move through the process by:

Connecting event and response. The response to trauma may be immediate or delayed, mild or intense. It may include numbness, or a strong connection with another event that caused feelings of loss or helplessness. The traumatized person needs to have the support of others, and at the right time, make the connection between his or her pain and the event itself.

Finding a safe environment. A very natural human response to trauma is to deny or "wall off" the painful reaction to the event. While a person may need privacy to deal with events and feelings in his or her own way and time, a person also needs to talk about these feelings, either with friends, family and colleagues, or with a counselor or trauma specialist.

Thinking the event through. In order to heal, a person must be able to acknowledge his or her feelings of sadness, anger, confusion, or guilt. Talking about the event with others who went through it too, can help each person make sense out of what may have been a senseless event.

Allowing painful memories. Trauma brings back memories of trauma. An incident can make a person remember and sometimes rework experiences that don't usually intrude into his or her life. This is normal. Consciously remembering and re-experiencing previous painful events causes the memories to eventually recede into the background. The mistake many people make is to push them down again too fast, too soon.

Discovering meaning, both individual and group. A healing group might conclude: "As a result of this, we recognize how important we are to one another and how little time we spend communicating. We need to examine our values more closely." This helps encourage acceptance of a new, more difficult reality and the beginning of being able to move on with life.

The healing process doesn't always proceed in a straight line. A person may seem to be recovering, but then something—the anniversary of the incident—can cause a setback. Keeping in mind the above points about the healing process will better equip a person to eventually work through the pain.

C. FINDING MEANING IN TRAUMA

Finding meaning in a traumatic event can be a long and difficult process, but it is very important. Without putting the event into some sort of perspective, it can be difficult or impossible for a person to let the wounds heal and move on with life. While a person may never forget the trauma, he or she can recover and get on with life.

The points below may offer some "food for thought" to a person trying to find meaning in a traumatic incident.

A person should:

Remember that he or she is not a "target." When tragedy strikes, it's easy for people to feel as if they're being punished or singled out by some evil force. But the fact is that bad things can happen randomly to good people, to bad people, and to everybody in between. A person should not try to lay blame or establish his or her own "guilt."

Ask the "big" questions; seek answers. "Spirituality" doesn't have to mean religion, although religious belief can provide comfort and a framework for dealing with traumatic events. A tragedy can cause a person to re-examine the values and the basic beliefs that have given meaning to the his or her life by asking the questions that have no answers. Some examples are: "Why does it always happen to the good guy?" "What's the point of living if we can be struck down so suddenly?" "If there is a God, then why does He/She/It allow things like this to happen?"

Give it time. It may take some time before a person can find any meaning in a traumatic event. First the shock, then the pain may prevent him or her from being able to think clearly about the event and put it into some sort of perspective. Normally, however, as the pain begins to subside, the person will find it easier to think about the incident.

Seek professional counseling, if necessary. That person for whom the trauma response is not subsiding, but growing worse, affecting the perceived quality of life, might want to seek professional help. Referrals are often available from a person's company's Employee Assistance Program, the crisis consultant (if any) who has been called in to work with the company, the community mental health center, the person's physician, local hospital, or friends and family who have seen a counselor themselves.

Not expect to be the same as before. "Healing" after a tragedy doesn't necessarily mean going back to exactly the way things were. A person undergoing the healing process necessarily changes from the change in circumstances. While the emotional pain eventually recedes, memories of the event remain for life. That's why it's especially important for a person to find a way to understand the event and make it part of him or her.

D. FAMILY SUPPORT

A person's spouse or other loved one has been through a major trauma. What can that person do to ease the pain? The following are some suggestions for offering support and comfort during a trying time.

The person should:

Listen, listen, listen. One of the most important needs after a trauma is to talk about the event—often, to talk about it over and over. This talking is a crucial part of the loved one's recovery. The person should be supportive and sympathetic, but try to avoid over-reacting and upsetting the loved one. The loved one who tries to shield the person from the event by refusing to talk about it, obviously can't be forced to talk. But, the person can encourage openness and listen to whatever else the loved one wants to say.

Not encourage the loved one to quit work. After a crisis, emotions run high. It's easy to rush into an unconsidered action, such as quitting a job. While it may be difficult for the loved one to face going back to work, returning to work may actually be the best way to recover from the crisis. Work can provide the company of others who have been through the same thing, but by quitting the job, the loved one may fail to face the event and work through the emotions. Also, by quitting, the loved one will not be able to take advantage of any counseling on the job.

Include the whole family in the healing process. As parents the spouses may feel that they should protect their children from an upsetting event. But, the children will undoubtedly know something is wrong. By trying to hide the truth from them, the kids may think that they are somehow to blame. This can be a stressful time for them too, and they may need some help to get through it.

Watch for signs of strain in the marital relationship. Marital problems are common after a traumatic event. A person should not assume that he or she just needs to be "more understanding." If a couple decides to seek counseling, they should check to see if their employee assistance professional, local hospital, or mental health clinic can help.

Take care of him or herself. A person having a spouse or loved one who has undergone a traumatic event has his or her own responsibilities, and now he or she may also feel responsible for keeping the loved one and the children from too much strain. While it's important to be supportive, the person needs some support too. He or she may ask friends or family members for help, and should not be afraid to seek counseling.

Enjoy the little things. Even after a personal tragedy, there are things to be grateful for. A person might take time out for the family and for his or her spouse by having a special meal together, or taking a small outing. Appreciating the little things doesn't make the pain go away, but it does help the healing process and strengthen the bonds with the people he or she loves.

E. CO-WORKER SUPPORT

What can a co-worker do when a person at the same job is either the victim of or a witness to a traumatic event? A co-worker may feel awkward or embarrassed, have feelings about the event that are difficult to resolve, and simply not know what to say. The tips below may help the co-worker formulate a response that shows to the traumatized person his or her care and support.

A co-worker should:

Acknowledge the event. Pretending that nothing happened may seem to a co-worker like the easiest thing to do, but it doesn't help affected individuals recover. The co-worker may want to acknowledge the event with a ritual such as sending flowers or making a donation.

Not ask questions, just listen. A co-worker who asks detailed questions about what happened usually comes across as ghoulish and intrusive. If the person wants to talk about the event, just listen; he or she may repeat the details many times. This is often an important part of healing. But, if the person is not yet ready to talk about it, a co-worker should not push.

Offer long-term emotional support. It takes a person longer to recover from a trauma than most people realize. For instance, a year might seem like enough time to "get over it;" yet, the first anniversary is often very difficult for people.

Become involved in a re-entry process. When the person returns to work, a co-worker will have natural concerns about the person's ability to work, appearance, willingness to talk about the event, etc. If appropriate, a co-worker might get involved in planning for the person's return.

Offer practical support. Instead of the catch-all, "If there's anything I can do ...", a co-worker should offer to do specific things such as give rides to and from work, run errands, pick up part of the person's workload (check with the boss first), or other favors.

Watch for signs of abnormal reactions. Behavior that would usually be considered strange (irrational anger, crying spells, a period of seeming to be okay followed by a relapse, etc.) is quite normal after the person has suffered a trauma. But, if the person seems to be seriously disturbed, if the symptoms go on for weeks, and if he or she is not in counseling, then the manager or Employee Assistance Program counselor may need to get involved.

Here is some advice for what a co-worker should and should not say to a fellow employee who has been involved in a traumatic event.

WHAT TO SAY
- "Would you like to talk about it?"
- "This must be very painful for you?"
- "Don't worry about work while you're gone; we'll take care of things for you."
- "We're glad to have you back."

WHAT NOT TO SAY

- "I understand how you feel." (A co-worker may think he or she does, but to a victim, his or her pain is unique.)

- "What happened? You'll feel better if you talk about it."

- "When this happened to me ..." (Even if a co-worker has had an identical experience, the victim's need to talk about his or her own trauma is probably greater than the need to listen to other people's experiences.)

CHAPTER 9

SPECIALIZED FIELD AND TESTING UNITS

A. CRITICAL INCIDENT DEBRIEFING TEAMS

A critical incident is a situation which is not in the normal range of a person's routine, and overtakes one's control over a situation. It is any situation which causes strong emotional reactions which may interfere with one's ability to function either at a scene or later on. Law enforcement personnel are at high risk of being exposed to such events and their devastating consequences. And, to make matters worse, the stress of the critical incident itself is compounded with subsequent investigations where the officer may be second-guessed by his or her supervisors, the news media, and the public.

The most common critical incident associated with law enforcement is a shooting or the use of other deadly force. An officer may be shot or killed, or may injure or kill an innocent bystander, or may be simply a witness to a shooting. Other critical incidents include the death of a family member or colleague, community disasters such as riots, and observation or participation in the investigation of horrific crimes. Major natural disasters such as hurricanes, tornadoes, floods, and earthquakes also have devastating results and create high stress levels for officers who must take control of a chaotic situation while coping with their own possible losses from the disaster. Unique stresses faced by law enforcement personnel include separation from family members, dual duty to family and community, and being a victim of a disaster.

The devastating effects of critical incidents upon officers affect their families and their department as well. It is found that structured treatment and immediate support can help prevent or diminish these effects. As a result, critical incident debriefing has become a common service offered by law enforcement stress programs. In some departments, participation is mandatory because some officers feel they can handle any fear, guilt, anger, or emotions stemming from the incident on their own. In fact, this is not true. Such officers need support, and mandating they attend debriefings makes them face this reality.

Critical incident debriefing involves a brief, structured intervention of counseling and support immediately or shortly after an incident occurs. Debriefing offers individuals a chance to express their feelings and to understand that their reactions are normal. A critical incident debriefing is led by a licensed mental health professional, and is not meant to take the place of regular counseling which may be needed at a later date.

Officers in need of critical incident debriefing are those who were directly involved in the incident and others who are part of a follow-up investigation. If the incident is of high notoriety, then debriefing of others, including those not even involved but who know of the incident, is necessary. This may require debriefing fellow officers, dispatchers, and even officers' families and friends. These debriefings of large magnitude help reinforce the fact that all law enforcement personnel and their families are on the same side and support each other. Command officers benefit by attending these sessions to show their sensitivity and support. It may benefit them psychologically as well, as they are also affected by the crisis that surrounds them.

Critical incident debriefings are held as soon as possible after an incident for those directly involved, but no later than 48 to 72 hours afterward. In many departments, counselors do not reach out to an officer until the officer has had an opportunity to speak with his or her union representative or lawyer who can discuss the facts of the incident. A debriefing for any others involved indirectly can be held within one week of the incident. Stress program staff must be sensitive to the needs of officers and family members during this time limit. Time and time again, it has proven beneficial to have critical incident debriefing as a necessary factor in the handling of stress and trauma in law enforcement.

B. PEER SUPPORT UNITS

Peer support is given by those individuals, present in every department, who are always there for other officers in times of crisis. There are stress programs that take advantage of this fact by providing training to these officers and letting it be known that the officers' services are always available. Peer support or counseling units are rapidly becoming a primary resource in combating stress and trauma in law enforcement.

Admitting to the department of having certain psychological problems might very well destroy that officer's career. For this reason, many officers have a fear or mistrust of their department or agency. This is where a good solid, well-advertised peer program may overshadow all other programs for at least the initial personal contact with another person. Like professional counselors, peer support sworn officers have the ability to empathize, because many have experienced similar incidents. Besides being able to know how the officers feel, peers are in daily contact with fellow officers and are able to detect problems before they become more serious. This makes the peer program a preventive measure as well.

Peer support must not be a substitute for the services of other health professionals. Many departments feel they can keep their budget in order by not allocating money for professional services and rely strictly on peer support programs. They must be reminded that peer support programs must compliment employee assistance programs and professional counseling, not replace them. Keeping a peer support program in good order takes time, planning, and supervision. Without these factors, it is hard to keep a peer support unit effective. Staff members must be cognizant of any trained peers who become "counselors" on their own.

The peer members must be screened carefully and trained properly so they do not overstep their boundaries.

Listening is a major role of peer supporters. They must provide an ear for officers' expressions of frustrations, fears, and other emotions. The listening process enables the peer to note signs that indicate an officer may have more serious problems which possibly need immediate attention. They can tell if the officer is depressed, suicidal, or even homicidal and needs professional help.

Many peer supporters are recovering alcoholics who can help an officer with a drinking problem. They are aware of the programs which are accessible for this problem such as Alcoholics Anonymous, detoxification programs, and inpatient treatment. These peers can help an officer get through his or her problem with support from one who understands.

Critical incidents are a major factor in law enforcement, and most officers have, unfortunately, experienced one or more. Officers who have had to use their weapons feel no one else can understand what they've been through, except for another officer who has had to do the same. Officers in this situation are even more stressed by what they believe to be their department's lack of support in these situations. Most of the time the officer is stripped of his weapon, subjected to internal investigation, and even, at times, lawsuits from the person shot. Peer supporters in shooting instances can offer the support and comfort to the officer that all the pent-up emotions being felt are normal, especially after such a traumatic critical incident.

In starting a peer support unit, it is necessary to have the support of department administrators. If they don't take it seriously, no one else will. Supervisors need to give on-duty peers the time to assist those officers in need as long as it does not take them away from another emergency situation. In this way, management support is of vital importance. Without it, the program will not succeed.

Also, for an effective program, there must be properly chosen officers available for training. Some programs choose peer supporters on the basis of their desire to help others, while others say this is not enough. Some program staffers select candidates on the basis of their reputation of already being a person sought out by troubled officers seeking help, referral by other officers or supervisors, quality of social skills, previous education and training, experience on the streets, previous use of the program, and the ability to complete the training program successfully.

Most peer supporters are chosen because they have experienced critical incidents and recovered from them. It is important to remember, however, the peer group must have a variety of experience represented among peer supporters so that the peer support program is not labeled as being useful for only one type of critical incident. For example, all peer supporters are recovered alcoholics and that is all they know how to deal with. This would not be a good representation of peer supporters for they would not be able to help those officers who have experienced shootings, family traumas, or the death of a police partner.

Peer support means just that. Obtaining help from someone at your own level. Most officers are unwilling to accept support from anyone of a higher or lower rank. Therefore, it is important to have peer support members from every rank within the peer support program.

Peer training is a crucial factor for a peer support program to be effective. Candidates receive on an average of three to five days training which focuses on developing listening skills, assessing problems, determining the need for referral to professionals, and selecting the proper resource as a recommendation for professional assistance. It also covers topics such as dealing with death and responding to relationship problems.

When training peer support candidates, it is emphasized that they try not to be therapists and to know their limits with regard to what they are capable of handling. They are instructed to contact program professionals whenever needed, especially if they have questions on how to continue with the troubled officer. Confidentiality is of major importance, but peer supporters are trained to inform the officer when confidentiality may be broken, for instance, if the officer begins talking about hurting someone else.

Most departments' training includes lectures, demonstrations and role-play exercises, emphasizing rapport, active listening, and taking action. Some departments have the program director, assisted by other staff members, train the peers, while others send them outside the department to attend special courses designed specifically for this purpose. Others have staff from local Employee Assistance Programs attend the training so they and the peers can work together. Many programs provide some kind of follow-up to the initial training to reinforce or expand the peers' skills, enable them to share and learn from their experiences, and monitor their activity.

There are also stress programs to monitor burnout among peer supporters. Providing ongoing support and helping others through intense critical incidents generates stress. Yet, peer supporters must remain strong to help the needs of others. Stressed-out peer supporters will be of no use to others, and a possible danger to themselves. Keeping abreast of peer supporters' feelings, and taking necessary action when problems arise, are of paramount concern so that everyone will benefit from the program.

In order for any program to be successful, everyone must know it exists. That is why it is so very important to advertise the peer support program in any department through memos, bulletin board messages, police paper articles, and word of mouth. The program will only be successful if it is used. No one program covers all circumstances. In order to provide all the services police officers and their families need, outside organizations and services of professionals may be required. Peer support is only a very good beginning.

C. PSYCHOLOGICAL TESTING UNITS

1. PSYCHOLOGICAL TESTING OF POLICE RECRUITS

A police officer shoots and kills an unarmed person without just cause or provocation. Another officer brutally assaults an innocent bystander, again without cause or provocation. Still another is involved in the selling of narcotics, and, in fact, was himself a user. Unfortunately, there are a few law enforcement officers who fall into the category of those who should have never been hired in the first place. Could these people have been more carefully investigated and weeded out before they entered their respective jobs as law enforcement officers? Let's explore some related issues in recruit screening.

In the last decade or so, psychological testing for police has become as important, if not more so, than the testing for physical requirements. The key question in psychological testing of police, as in all other areas of recruit selection, is validation—whether it can be proved that selection procedures are related to doing the job of a police officer. Elaborate validation studies have been undertaken on most standard psychological tests to demonstrate their reliability. But, few such studies have been conducted specifically on police performance, largely because it is so difficult to define and measure the quality of any officer's work.

More testing today looks to predict a recruit's success or non-success in police work and looks to weed out the clearly unsuitable people. Although psychologists say there is no test in existence that will weed out those officers with a propensity toward brutality, they will show instability and red-flag that tendency.

No one doubts that police psychologists, or even standardized tests, can do a good job of screening out applicants suffering from acute mental illness. But, many psychologists are more ambitious. They want to develop testing procedures that identify recruits who might be brutal, corrupt, cowardly, or lazy once they are in the field. The goal of many psychologists is to pinpoint the very best recruits, not merely to eliminate a few misfits.

The issue is complicated by the frequent court challenges to recruit testing procedures. Most direct court challenges to police hiring practices have focused on written aptitude tests and height requirements, and they have been successful when departments could not demonstrate that these tests and requirements related to on-the-job performance. Many police psychologists seem to be looking over their shoulders, fearful that someone will haul them into court to challenge the validity of their tests. Is the test job-related? Does it have to do with picking successful police officers?

2. FUNCTIONS OF SCREENING

The first and most important function of psychological screening is to identify those who are totally unfit for police work. This would include those who are truly dangerous, as well as "people who see spots on the wall and invisible turkeys," in the words of one psychologist. A second group targeted by psychologists are those who might not be considered acutely mentally ill in the general population, but who could not function as police officers. These would include those beset by internal conflicts, hypochondriacs, impulsive people, those suffering from high anxiety or low self-esteem.

Most psychologists agree that a thorough background check, including talks with an applicant's neighbors, teachers and acquaintances, or even a tough interview, will identify most of these people. But, the most common method is to use a standard multiple question test, such as the Minnesota Multiphasic Personality Inventory (MMPI).

3. HOW TESTS WORK

The multiple question psychological test consists of statements that the respondent labels true or false. Some of the statements, such as, "I feel suicidal," will automatically disqualify a candidate if answered the wrong way. But, most of the statements are parts of groups that, in the aggregate, will tell the tester whether the test-taker has tendencies toward mental illness. For instance, there are about 30 statements scattered throughout the test that are designed to measure depression. "I sometimes feel down in the dumps," and, "I sometimes have trouble getting out of bed," are two such statements. A normal person might mark seven or eight of them true. Someone who answers almost all of them that way is depressed and will probably be disqualified.

4. THE ASSESSMENT CENTER

Departments in a few cities, wanting to learn more about their police recruits than they can learn from pencil-and-paper tests or face-to-face interviews, have turned to an expensive option, the assessment center. An assessment center approach was developed during World War II by the military to select undercover agents. It was later adapted by private industry as a means for evaluating executives. Many police departments use assessment centers to evaluate candidates for higher ranks. A few, however, have used them to select raw recruits. The consensus is that they can yield some powerful insights into the future behavior of potential officers, but at a high cost.

Some of the more elaborate tests can show the following:

- Logical reasoning skills—the ability to process disparate bits of information and to act with forethought.

- Decision-making skills—the ability to make decisions and to know when more information is needed in order to make a decision.

- Organizational compatibility—the ability to work with others in a paramilitary organization.

- Self-confidence—the ability to control a situation and to know when not to try to control it.

- Sensitivity to other people—includes the ability to listen.

- Stress tolerance.

- Non-verbal communication.

- Positive motivation—having more than a passing interest in law enforcement.

- Behavioral flexibility—the ability to adapt behavior to the demands of the situation.

Psychological testing and screening procedures are as variable and complicated as are the recruits being evaluated. The tests are a necessity and do play a major role in recruit selection.

Police officers vary mentally, as well as physically. While recruits possess basic qualifications and have natural talents, the bottom line is training. Police work is a learned skill, and if the recruit is not properly taught, he or she will not only fail to take a productive place in the department, but could, in fact, fall victim to another police killing, or worse yet, succumb to the pressure of the job and commit suicide. The potential for such disasters is boundless. All preventive measures, including psychological testing, must be taken.

CLOSING

Yes, there is enormous stress and frequent traumatic situations encountered in the profession of law enforcement. Prevention and teaching are the keys. The cure is caring and attention.

Explicitly teaching police officers the stressful pitfalls of police work will act as a parachute to be opened when they feel like they are free falling toward destruction. The information presented in this book may save a career, a contribution to a community and department, and even a life—the life of the police officer.

Life is a gift. We must believe wholeheartedly that all human beings are entitled to keep and protect it. Sometimes we forget that our law enforcement officers are also these very same human beings and have these same rights. In memory of those officers whose lives were cut short, let us please never forget.

This page intentionally left blank.

GLOSSARY

Abuse/addiction - a condition which exists when job performance, personal health, or interpersonal relationships are impaired by an employee's use of alcohol or other addictive substances.(p. 140)

Alcoholic thinking - a type of thinking that is created during alcoholic drinking and withdrawal.(p. 57)

Compassion stress - occurs when we are exposed to the trauma experienced by others whom we come into close contact.(p. 35)

Countertransference - feelings that occur when the wounds of the helper are triggered by the victims they are trying to help, by similarities between the victim and the helper, or by recent traumas in the life of the helper.(p. 35)

Critical incident - a situation which is not in the normal range of a person's routine and overtakes one's control over a situation.(p. 100)

Critical incident debriefing - a brief, structured intervention of counseling and support immediately or shortly after a critical incident occurs.(p. 100, 163)

Denial - A psychological defense mechanism that a person builds around alcohol abuse.(p. 126)

Emotional hardening - a reduction in the capacity to experience emotions.(p. 25)

Hyperarousal - a trauma response characterized by irritability, flashbacks, extreme emotions, nightmares, etc.(p. 90)

Job burnout - an impairment of motivation to work.(p. 65)

Minnesota Multiphasic Personality Inventory (MMPI) - a written multiple question psychological test.(p. 105)

Negative discipline - that style of discipline which takes the form of punishment or chastisement.(p. 14)

Neurosis - significant attitudinal and behavioral manifestations whose presence indicates the existence of emotional tension and conflict.(p. 74)

Numbness - a trauma response characterized by withdrawal from others, depression or emotional flatness, lack of concentration, etc.(p. 90)

Pacing - the skill of taking on no more and no less than you can handle and work on steadily.(p. 49)

Positive discipline - that form of training and attitudinal conditioning which is used to correct deficiencies without invoking punishment.(p. 13)

Post traumatic stress - defined as a normal reaction to an abnormal event.(p. 120)

Post-Traumatic Stress Disorder (PTSD) - the mind and body's re-occurring psychological and physical responses to a highly stressful event from the recent or distant past.(p. 34)

Psychological autopsy - profile of a suicide death.(p. 45)

Quota system - a promotional system of selection, whereby one candidate is placed over the next, based upon his ethnic background.(p. 17)

Stress - Physiological and psychological effects produced by emotional states of sufficient intensity and duration.(p. 10)

Sympathomimetics - chemical substances that initiate a stress response by stimulating the sympathetic branch of the Autonomic Nervous System.(p. 68)

Trauma - any event that poses a seemingly unsolvable problem for an individual or which creates a conflict of such significant proportion as to bring the person to an impasse.(p. 74)

Trauma response - a reaction to a traumatic event characterized by an alternation between the states of numbness and hyperarousal.(p. 92)

Validation - whether it can be proved that selection procedures are related to doing the job of a police officer.(p. 104)

Vasoactive stimuli - factors that have the ability to stimulate the sympathetic nervous system and consequently the blood vessels in the brain.(p. 68)

APPENDIX

LAW ENFORCEMENT STRESS AND TRAUMA MANAGEMENT PROGRAMS, SOLUTIONS, AND PERSONNEL

Law enforcement assistance programs can vary, but most have a few factors and objectives in common: to offer and lend help when needed, to be there when despair and depression strike, to be available 24 hours per day, 365 days per year, and to administer preventive measures. The programs can assume many forms, such as critical incident debriefing teams, psychological services units, or peer support teams. These services can be run by the private sector, the departments, or by the law enforcement unions themselves.

The following is a sampling of the various police departments' stress management programs from across the U.S. We have highlighted them and profiled some of the people who have implemented or assisted in the operation of successful programs.

A. NEW YORK CITY POLICE DEPARTMENT / NYPD

Over the past few years, the NYPD has implemented some new and very effective stress, trauma, and suicide prevention programs. By way of training officers, department counseling units, chaplains, confidential hotlines, open campaigning, and videos for officers and their families, positive results have been achieved.

One of the more successful programs, the Membership Assistance Program (MAP), was assembled in March of 1996. Using Federal money, MAP was set up in the Police Benevolent Association Headquarters, and has been supported by the NYPD Superior Officers' Unions as well. The program has officers of all ranks who receive professional training and provide peer support. Handbooks have been created for peer support officers, and almost all commands citywide, will have such officers available 24 hours a day.

The program falls into three categories: those who have recently been exposed to a grisly scene on the job, and have nightmares or are not eating well; newly married cops whose spouses are having a tough time adjusting to the job's demands; and others who recognize they are turning to alcohol for solace. On average, each peer support officer volunteers about 12 hours per month, which is spent either answering beeps on the program's hotline, or meeting face-to-face with officers to offer guidance. About half of all the peer support officers have had troubles themselves, making it easier for those they counsel to relate to them. The experience of a troubled officer turning him or herself around is a strong incentive.

New York City Police Dept. Programs

The impetus for the program was the record number of suicides the NYPD experienced over the past years. The alarming rate of suicide prompted city law makers to study the occupational hazards associated with the police profession, and a rough profile emerged of the type of officer who was likely to commit suicide. With the study came a realization that early intervention was important, but also that the counseling services being provided by the NYPD itself were not working. When troubled officers went to the department for assistance, they feared their careers would be jeopardized, and therefore, many avoided voicing their problems.

In the past, research has shown that the family has always been a vital unit that has been left out of consideration. Under the new program, the family has been brought into the picture. Family members can help their loved ones recognize the signs of stress, and get help for themselves. It is common for the spouse of a cop whose partner has been injured or killed to have an adverse and emotional reaction when the officer returns to work.

MAP seminars have been conducted by licensed mental health professionals and peer support officers. They discuss such topics as an overview of stress and its effects on officers and their families, the specific stresses in officers lives, and teach stress management techniques. They also have focused on some common problems, including marital and relationship difficulties, alcohol and substance abuse, eating disorders, and gambling and indebtedness problems.

1. TRAUMA COUNSELING AND RESPONSE PROGRAM

The main focus of the Trauma Counseling and Response Program services are to provide support and trauma counseling when any member of the service has been involved in shooting incidents, disasters, or other violent occurrences resulting in death or injury. Counseling is available for incidents that include, but are not limited to, the following:

- Member is shot or otherwise seriously injured.

- Member discharges a weapon causing injury or death to another.

- Member causes, accidentally or otherwise, serious physical injury or death to another.

- Member is directly involved in an incident where his or her partner was killed or seriously injured, etc.

- Member is directly involved in incidents or serious disasters where multiple serious injuries and deaths have occurred.

Programs Los Angeles Police Dept.

2. TRAUMA COUNSELING TEAM

The Trauma Counseling Team responds to all incidents involving members of the service who are shot, killed, or seriously injured in the performance of duty, and any incident pursuant to a request from a captain or above. The Team:

1. Responds to target locations and reports to the designated contact person at the scene.

2. Responds, if required, to the station house of the precinct of the occurrence or some other location, to make contact and converse with member(s) of the service involved in the incident.

3. Visits the place of occurrence if necessary.

4. Schedules and arranges for a follow-up meeting 48 hours after the event or initial contact, as appropriate. Any additional counseling/interview sessions after this meeting are scheduled within one to six weeks after the incident.

The Trauma Counseling Team is staffed by the Chief Surgeon Director, Psychological Services and licensed certified Professionals of the Health Services Division. This program does not prevent, in any way, the voluntary use of or referral to any of the Employee Assistance Programs or units in the department for any reason at any time. The services of the Trauma Counseling Team are also available to members who are involved in personal or family tragedies, *e.g.*, violent criminal incidents involving themselves or their families, death in the family, etc. All conversations with the Trauma Counseling Team by members of the service are strictly confidential.

B. LOS ANGELES POLICE DEPARTMENT / LAPD

The Los Angeles Police Department has a wide variety of programs to combat the effects of job stress and trauma. The LAPD's chief police psychologist, Debra F. Glaser, Ph.D., heads the Behavioral Sciences Services, and has devoted a major part of her life and career to the assistance of police officers and their families.

1. LAPD BEHAVIORAL SCIENCES SERVICES / SCOPE OF SERVICES

Counseling/Therapy

Behavioral Sciences Services (BSS) provides individual and couples counseling to all Department personnel and their spouses/significant others. When self-referred, these sessions are voluntary and confidential. The focus of care can include issues related to relationship challenges, job stress, family or personal health. Employees may also be directed to BSS for evaluation or counseling on a limited confidential basis by supervisors or administrators in certain job-related situations.

Los Angeles Police Dept.

Consultation

Consultation is regularly provided to supervisors and managers within the Department. The consultations involve a variety of management and organization issues. BSS staff is available to assist detectives in developing psychological "profiles" of suspects, evaluation of danger in threat cases, and to consult in other crime-specific situations.

Balanced Health—The LAPD Wellness Program

BSS has undertaken the systemic review and design of a Departmentwide holistic wellness program ("Balanced Health"). This Program is designed to promote both physiological and psychological health and well-being. Participation will be voluntary and open to both sworn and civilian employees. The program will introduce positive incentives to encourage both participation and the achievement of positive health results. The program will consist of various confidential health screenings with appropriate recommendations, referrals, and treatment. Psychological classes and workshops designed to alter negative health behaviors will also be introduced.

Research

Basic and applied research is conducted by BSS psychologists on a number of issues important to LAPD and law enforcement. BSS has sought and obtained federal funding to conduct research into ways in which early intervention can mitigate stress reactions. Members of the staff design research projects, facilitate their implementation, and are trained in advanced statistical analysis. BSS has also consulted on research design and grant applications for other Divisions within the Department.

Emergency Response

Crisis Response Team (CRT)

The Crisis Response Team is comprised of a BSS psychologist, Department chaplains, and specially trained Department personnel. One team is assigned to each of the four geographic bureaus. These teams provide emergency response and immediate on-scene support for unusual or potentially traumatizing situations. The CRT also provides management consultation, roll-call defusing, training, and debriefings as appropriate.

Crisis Negotiation Team (CNT)

Staff psychologists are members of the Crisis Negotiation Team and respond to hostage situations and certain suicide and barricaded suspect incidents.

Training/Education

A large number of seminars, classes, and workshops are presented by BSS staff to assist Department personnel with a variety of issues, including stress management, communications skills, conflict resolution, suicide prevention, and anger management. BSS staff also teach at various Department schools, Division training days, and during roll-call.

2. LAPD MENTAL EVALUATION UNIT AND SYSTEM WIDE MENTAL ASSESSMENT RESPONSE TEAM

One of LAPD's most dedicated officers, Detective Walter J. DeCuir, Jr., has been working in the field of law enforcement/developmental disability—mental interface for over 15 years. He is a recognized national expert who is responsible for the development, training, and on-going evaluation of the Los Angeles Police Department's Mental Evaluation Unit (MEU). The MEU is the LAPD's mental health/developmental disability command post. This complement is operational 24 hours a day and provides meaningful expertise to officers in the field. Before the start of the MEU, LAPD officers were spending more than 28,000 officer hours a month on calls involving developmental disabilities and/or mental illness. Due to the rare skills of the MEU, the LAPD now expends less than 14,000 officer hours per month addressing the various issues involving these populations.

In spite of the effectiveness of the MEU, there was still a necessity to provide a more effective and reliable way to handle acute cases in the field. Detective DeCuir, in concert with the Los Angeles County Department of Mental Health (DMH), conceptualized, selected, and trained the System-wide Mental Assessment Response Team (SMART) as it is currently formed. The SMART consists of specially trained LAPD officers and DMH clinicians who respond to calls for service from law enforcement units. This resource allows officers to handle other high priority calls. The SMART members identify and attempt to access the needed resources the criminal justice, mental health, and regional centers should provide. These assets enable the SMART to provide a meaningful delivery of service that reduces the inappropriate hospitalization or incarceration of these citizens.

C. CLEVELAND POLICE DEPARTMENT

1. OFFICER PROFILE

Carolyn M. Tenerowicz, Ph.D., LPCC has a history within her profession that is rich in the experience of law enforcement personnel and all the stress-related disorders that accompany this field. For the past 22 years, she has dedicated herself to the recognition and treatment of these problems among hundreds of officers in both urban and suburban departments. For the past 15 years, she has maintained an office inside the Cleveland Police Headquarters and is currently the Stress Consultant for the City of Cleveland, Department of Public Safety, Division of Police. Dr. Tenerowicz's responsibilities are vast and crucial to the mental health of the city's police officers that need her. She has planned, developed, and administered a program that offers stress services to officers who display stress-related behavior. She has also implemented in-service training as well as a training program for the recruits of the Cleveland Police Academy. Other key accomplishments include the implementation of a program that deals with officers involved in critical incidents, the forming of a support group for female officers, and a series of lectures titled "Stresses of a Police Marriage."

Dr. Tenerowicz's knowledge of what goes on inside the mind of a police officer is remarkable and has been proven extremely accurate. Through her many years of service, Dr. Tenerowicz has helped hundreds of officers succeed in their careers and relationships where they very well may have failed without her help. She offers training seminars for all recruits and sworn, in-service personnel. Chiefs, administrators, and officers in charge of training along with members of their respective agencies attend these seminars.

Dr. Tenerowicz is a highly sought after lecturer. Her credits include articles in the *Cleveland Plain Dealer*, as well as numerous appearances on radio talk shows and local television. She has also been interviewed for segments on the national television show *20/20*.

2. DR. TENEROWICZ'S PROGRAM

Dr. Tenerowicz considers her program high profile as it is located in Police Headquarters in an office attached to the Police Academy. She chose this location because it has an academic purpose, as she believes therapy is education. When people come into her office for their appointments, they ultimately learn.

Also her location allows her to "be there" as a consultant to any and all specialized units in police headquarters. She can be in the hall, the elevator, or on the phone receiving a call from homicide, narcotics, SWAT, SIU, etc., with a question about a case or a personality. She is there to help. Her location allows her to do much informal counseling. People see her, stop her, and say, "Hey, Doc, can I ask you a question?" It gives cops who are assigned to in-service training the opportunity to interact with her. Because she has taught all these officers before, just seeing her reminds them to watch their stress levels, and if they feel overwhelmed, they can call her. She says this is informal, but powerful.

Dr. Tenerowicz's program is entirely voluntary and confidential. This, she says, is the ultimate key. Officers who come to see her for therapy do so on their own. They are not referred or forced to come. Someone may have suggested they talk to the "Doc," but again, there is no coercion. Also, she keeps absolutely no records of any kind. She does not write in "anyone's jacket." In her 15 years, no one, not anyone from Safety Director to the newest police hire, has ever asked her who she has talked to or what she does with her time. She has developed this trust from others over many years.

The only exception to her voluntary counseling is the debriefing sessions she does with Cleveland police officers involved in a shooting or other critical incident. These officers are required to go through debriefing with her, but are returned to duty by an outside psychiatrist (M.D.). Her debriefing for shooting incidents is as follows:

1. Officers involved are put on 3 days administrative leave. During this time they complete their paper work and interviews and see her for the first debriefing.

2. The officers are assigned to the gym for 45 days or until the prosecutor rules on their case. This time is designed to give them a break from all the routine stress of police work, keep them out of the limelight, give them an environment to work-out, exercise in, and give them time to spend with their families. Debriefings continue weekly until the examination by the M.D.

3. Full return to duty follows.

Along with Employee Assistance, Dr. Tenerowicz works to prevent suicides. She has stepped in and worked with many domestic problems. Officers and their wives come jointly to see her, but she sees too many divorces. Employee Assistance composed of three Cleveland Police Department officers makes arrangements for and follows up with alcoholism cases. The officers come to Dr. Tenerowicz after treatment and enrollment in Alcoholics Anonymous. Employee Assistance is located away from police headquarters, and operates on a confidential basis. Dr. Tenerowicz is their consultant.

The cornerstones of Dr. Tenerowicz's success are high visibility, people who believe in her work, and long-term commitment. Her dedication and loyalty to the Cleveland Police Department is special, and she feels the department does its best to give each police officer the opportunity for a healthy career in law enforcement.

D. SAN FRANCISCO POLICE DEPARTMENT / SFPD

The San Francisco Police Department has had the support, commitment, and hard work of many of its members who have developed and contributed to the well-being of its officers. Some of these dedicated people are: Sergeant Forrest Fulton, Ph.D., Captain Allen Benner, Ph.D., Chief of Police Fred Lau, Sergeant Vicki Quinn, Deputy Chief William Welch, Police Officer David W. Tussey, Sergeant Lynnette Hogue, and Police Officer Mick Shea.

1. BEHAVIORAL SCIENCE UNIT

This Department, developed by the San Francisco Police Department, is a relatively new unit that provides support for all members of the department. The Behavioral Science Unit is commanded by Captain Allen Benner, Ph.D., the first San Francisco Police Department

San Francisco Police Dept. — Programs

Psychologist. Dr. Benner has been studying many of the institutional stresses of law enforcement officers and emotional demands on department members.

Chief of Police Fred Lau has mandated that Dr. Benner examine the many issues that place stress on officers and support staff. In Dr. Benner's review of the multi-dimensional issues that negatively impact the law enforcement community, the concept of "police stress" continues to reappear at the core.

Dr. Al Benner has developed the Behavioral Science Unit to help coordinate the many support services that are available to San Francisco Police Department members. Dr. Benner's philosophy is to help department members obtain early access to services and entitlements during times of need. Making helping systems available and empowering members to take control over their problems is the best way to reduce negative stress and alleviate personal crisis.

Dr. Benner and Sergeant Vicki Quinn have been developing one of the most valuable resources for department members. They have been the driving force behind the SFPD Peer Support Program for the past 14 years. The Peer Support Program operates on the basic principle that, "no one takes care of cops better than other cops." Taking this premise, the SFPD Peer Support Program is one of the most revolutionary and sometimes controversial programs in modern law enforcement. Peer Support takes volunteers from both sworn and civilian department members and instructs them in the latest helping skills and theories.

Every SFPD Peer Support member attends a three day approved class, certified by the California Commission on Peace Officers Standards and Training (POST). Members are instructed and evaluated using practical and interactive scenarios that expose students to real life helping techniques. Students are trained in the proper responses to life's many serious stressors and tragedies. Peer Support members learn to challenge themselves and still remain aware of their limitations and resources.

The Peer Support Program operates 24 hours a day, 365 days a year at no additional cost to the police department. The Program functions because members are caring and willing to help other members in need. Members of the Peer Support Program operate during their normal duty hours and support the Program as a non-financed additional duty.

The Program functions by the combined efforts of all its members. The certified Peer Support members are in all sworn ranks of the department. Chief Lau and Deputy Chief William Welch are both long time Peer Support members. The San Francisco Police Department is now totally committed to the theory of officers supporting officers.

2. BEHAVIORAL SCIENCE UNIT PROGRAMS PROFILED

The Behavioral Science Unit of the San Francisco Police Department is responsible for managing several department programs. These programs are the Employee Assistance Program, the Catastrophic Illness Program, Critical Incident Response Team (CIRT), the Stress Unit, Police Chaplains, and the Peer Support Program. The unit is currently involved in establishing and managing the department's association with the United Behavioral Health Program.

These programs have one purpose in common that is unique to units within the police department. They exist solely for the well-being of police officers and their loved ones. This is the only unit within the department that does not provide service to the public. It has been established to provide help and support to police officers and their loved ones in a confidential and supportive atmosphere. The following is a profile of each program.

Employee Assistance Program (EAP)

This program provides resources for officers facing difficulties in their work or personal lives that require help or support of one form or another. This help could be anything from a friendly ear to referrals for services or counseling. Years ago, EAP was pretty much the only program available. Now, many of the services formerly provided by either this program or the Stress Unit have been expanded and are being provided by additional programs.

Headed by Sgt. Lynnette Hogue, EAP also coordinates the Psych Pros program and its steering committee. This program is unique in that it selects and trains dedicated psychologists to deal specifically with police officers and their loved ones. Police work-related problems are as varied as police work and difficult for many people to understand, including psychologists. These "cop docs", as they are sometimes called, go through extensive training by San Francisco Police officers to familiarize them with police work and its ramifications. This includes, but is not limited to, ride-alongs with police and paramedics and training at the academy. Hopes are that this training and familiarization will help allay the reservations that some cops have toward consulting counselors, as well as create a better link of communication between the doctor and the client.

Catastrophic Illness Program

This is a relatively new program and is an extremely valuable resource which provides officers with additional sick time should they be faced with a life threatening illness or injury. This is a voluntary program wherein an officer, who finds him or herself in such a situation, can apply for and receive additional sick time through donations from other officers. This program is open to all city employees of the City and County of San Francisco, as well as the police department. These hours can be cross donated from one city agency to another.

San Francisco Police Dept. **Programs**

Since its inception in 1990, more than 33 police department members have been helped through the program. All that is needed to join, either as a recipient or a donor, is to fill out a short form following simple guidelines. This is done at the Behavioral Science Unit and takes only a few minutes.

The Critical Incident Response Team (CIRT)

Under the umbrella of the Behavioral Science Unit, this team is comprised of a number of officers from various ranks and assignments who are assigned the task of debriefing personnel involved in on-the-job occurrences in which a death results from an officer's actions. Participation in the debriefing process is mandatory for involved personnel and the debriefing is to take place within 72 hours of the incident.

In such an incident, a police supervisor will contact the on-call CIRT team member and a determination will be made whether or not to respond to the scene to begin the debriefing process. Presently, efforts are being made to amend the general order and broaden the definition of a critical incident and define it as any event that is likely to cause "post-traumatic stress." Post-traumatic stress is defined as a normal reaction to an abnormal event.

The Behavioral Science Unit urges any officer, who wishes to do so, to notify CIRT if they think an event qualifies as one that might negatively impact an officer. CIRT team members are available to respond to the scene if they can be of help to officers in the event of a traumatic situation. This incident could be anything from witnessing a death or serious injury, gun take-aways, line-of-duty injury or death, traffic accidents, or even close calls.

CIRT members operate under the same confidentiality guidelines as those in the Peer Support program. Remember, CIRT officers are not investigators. They respond solely to support and assist in a stressful situation.

Peer Support

Very often misunderstood, this Peer Support program is quite simple. It might be thought of as a training program that teaches a more effective way of listening to another person. Originally called "Peer Counseling", the name was later changed to "Peer Support." The word "counseling" seems to evoke a wary response in most people, especially cops, and makes a person feel a little apprehensive of whatever follows.

In the past, most would be dragged kicking and screaming to a counselor to discuss the simplest concern, yet we'd readily talk to another officer, usually a partner, about our most intimate problems. Recognizing this, Captain Allen Benner and Sergeant Vicki Quinn developed a training program to teach cops how to be better listeners. They realized that cops are not likely to seek out a stranger with whom to discuss a serious issue, but most would talk to their trusted friends all the time. Capt. Benner and Sergeant Quinn decided to start a system of training "the friends" at how to be better at "being there" and how to become more skilled at listening.

This is done at the Basic Peer Support training class and is reinforced on an ongoing basis at Peer Support Update training which is held at regular intervals. At these classes, volunteers are trained in active listening skills in order to become more adept at guiding another person through a problem. These classes are extremely beneficial.

Peer Support members are not therapists. They are just cops who have taken it upon themselves to be better prepared to be of support to others. They don't solve problems for others nor are they expected to take on that person's responsibilities. They simply try to be supportive as the individual helps him or herself to a successful solution.

Stress Unit
This is probably the oldest assistance program in the department and deals primarily with alcohol/substance abuse problems of its members. The unit is an office separate from the rest of the Behavioral Science Unit. Officer Mick Shea is in charge of the program. He has information, as well as referrals, and is of valuable assistance and support to members or loved ones who need this type of assistance.

The Behavioral Science Unit, through the leadership of Capt. Benner, has negotiated a contract with United Behavioral Health in order to provide additional mental health benefits and substance abuse counseling to department members and their families or domestic partners. These benefits are in addition to any and all benefits provided by the officer's health insurance provider and are underwritten by the City and County of San Francisco at no cost to the member. The counselors include those in the Psych Pros program and are all highly qualified, hand picked individuals who have been specifically trained to deal with police officers and their loved ones.

The Behavioral Science Unit is not Psych Liaison, EEO, Management Control, or Medical Liaison. It does not investigate anyone nor does it represent anyone for disciplinary purposes. It supports and assists police officers in need whether those needs be large or small, and it does so in a positive and confidential atmosphere.

E. LAS VEGAS METROPOLITAN POLICE DEPARTMENT / LVMPD

1. OFFICER PROFILES
The Las Vegas Metropolitan Police Department has instituted and maintained a variety of stress, trauma, and suicide prevention programs, none of which would have reached such levels of success

without the dedication and hard work of some of its members. These people work in the field as counselors, intermediators, debriefers, and department program directors. Three of these officers who deserve honorable mention are Sergeant Thomas. G. Harmon, Lieutenant Edward H. Jensen, and Detective Michael Bryant.

Sergeant Thomas G. Harmon

Sergeant Thomas G. Harmon has been employed as a police officer with the Las Vegas Metropolitan Police Department (LVMPD) since 1985. He has held assignments in the Patrol Division and in the training of new officers in the Field Training Program. In March of 1992, he was promoted to the rank of Sergeant where he continued in the training and instructing of new officers.

Because of Sergeant Harmon's personal life experiences, along with his experiences as an officer and supervisor, he was drawn to the LVMPD Police Employees Assistance Program (PEAP) where he has worked as a peer counselor since February of 1994. As a peer counselor, Sgt. Harmon provides assistance, emotional support, and professional referral to all LVMPD employees and their immediate families who are affected by relationship problems, parenting problems, death and loss issues, post-traumatic stress, alcohol/chemical dependency, job performance problems, and many other personal or job-related issues. Sergeant Harmon has also facilitated more than 70 critical incident debriefings to date for events such as police officer-involved shootings, suicides, fatal vehicle accidents, and deaths or serious injury to police officers.

He is also a certified instructor for the Police Officer Standards Training (POST) for the State of Nevada, and is currently instructing in the LVMPD academy, as well as the In-Service Training Section. Sergeant Harmon has instructed courses on the Critical Incident Stress Debriefing Process (CISD), Understanding Grief Issues, Post-Traumatic Stress, Communication Skills, Stress Management, Family Orientation to Police Life, and the Psychology of Retirement. He has attended 150 hours of Death & Grief Studies, as well as several classes and seminars on the topics of stress management, critical incident stress debriefing, substance abuse/intervention, and communication skills/conflict management.

Lieutenant Edward H. Jensen

Lieutenant Edward H. Jensen is presently the Director of the Police Employees Assistance Program. He co-implemented the program in 1984, and is presently assigned with two other officers. His major responsibilities are to provide peer counseling and referral service to all employees and their families; critical incident debriefings; and through the Ministry of Presence, companion all employees experiencing the trauma of loss. He also provides training both at the academy and in-service level to enhance the overall well-being of employees.

Lieutenant Jensen has received a number of awards including one for Outstanding Service for work in the Police Employees Assistance Program presented by the Nevada Conference of Police and Sheriffs. He also received the August Vollmer Award for Outstanding Criminal Justice Student/Worker-UNLV in 1989.

Lieutenant Jensen holds a Master of Arts Degree in Pastoral Ministry from Saint Mary's University in Minnesota, where his thesis was "The Ministry of Contemplative Presence to Traumatized Police Officers." He also received a Death & Grief Studies Certificate of Award from the Center for Loss & Life Transition in Colorado, a Bachelor of Arts Degree in Criminal Justice from the University of Nevada Las Vegas, and an Associates of Science Degree from Alexandria Technical College in Minnesota.

As a police officer in the Las Vegas Police Department, Lt. Jensen has worked a variety of assignments including Patrol, Narcotics, Vice, Gang Unit, Intelligence Unit, and the Police Employees Assistance Program. He has provided training for Family Orientation to Police Life, Stress Awareness, Post-Shooting Trauma, Communication Skills, Stress Management, The Psychology of Retirement Seminar, Understanding Grief Issues, and Critical Incident Debriefing.

Besides presenting multiple seminars around the country, Lt. Jensen has participated in over 130 debriefings within the Las Vegas Metropolitan Police Department related to police officer shootings where over 250 police officers were involved. In 1988, as a result of the Pepcon explosion, he helped debrief fire departments in Clark County, Las Vegas, Henderson, and Boulder City.

Detective Michael Bryant

Michael J. Bryant has been employed as a police officer with the Las Vegas Metropolitan Police Department since 1976. He has held assignments in the Detention Division and Patrol Divisions. While in the Patrol Division, he was assigned to the Field Training Program where he trained new officers after graduating the police academy. He also worked as a Resident Police Officer in Laughlin, Nevada for 5 years and was responsible for normal patrol functions along with criminal and traffic investigations. In November of 1988, Mike Bryant was promoted to Detective where he was assigned to Larceny, Auto Theft, Robbery, Criminal Intelligence (Undercover) and Homicide details.

Detective Bryant has had many personal and work-related experiences that resulted in his having a strong desire to help Metro employees and their families. While a Homicide Detective, he assisted in peer counseling as the need would arise. In November of 1996, he transferred from Homicide Section to the Police Employees Assistance Program (PEAP) and assumed the duties as a peer counselor on a full-time basis. As a peer counselor, Detective Bryant provides assistance, emotional support, and professional referral to all LVMPD

Las Vegas Metro. Police Dept. **Programs**

employees and their families. Just some of the issues he provides assistance for are death and loss issues, post-traumatic stress, alcohol/chemical dependency, and relationship problems.

Detective Bryant also facilitated more than 35 critical incident debriefings to date (9/98) for events such as police officer involved shootings, suicides, fatal vehicle accidents, and deaths or serious injuries to police officers. He is a certified instructor by Police Officer Standards Training (POST) for the State of Nevada, and is currently instructing in the LVMPD academy, as well as the In-Service Training Section. He has received 150 hours of Death & Grief Studies, as well as training in the areas of stress management, critical incident stress debriefing, substance abuse and intervention, and communication skills/conflict management. Detective Bryant has also instructed courses on the Critical Incident Stress Debriefing Process (CISD), Understanding Grief Issues, Post-Traumatic Stress, Communication Skills, Stress Management, Family Orientation to Police Life, and the Psychology of Retirement.

2. LVMPD POLICE EMPLOYEE ASSISTANCE PROGRAM (PEAP)

The LVMPD Police Employee Assistance Program (PEAP) is a counseling and referral service run by the LVMPD for employees and their families. It is set up to prevent, and when necessary, to treat the personal and family casualties which are caused directly or indirectly by the stress of the police job. PEAP provides an avenue for voluntary short-term, confidential counseling for those experiencing these problems. The Program helps with such problems as marriage, divorce or relationship difficulties, job performance problems, parent/child conflicts, post-shooting trauma, death of a loved one, problems with alcohol, and chemical dependency.

The Police Employee Assistance Program helps with brief individual assistance, group counseling, stress awareness training, performance assistance, and referral to community resources when the problem requires professional assistance. The Program helps all LVMPD employees and members of their immediate families. PEAP portrays the image that seeking assistance is a sign of courage.

PEAP is staffed by three police officers who have a variety of training skills and life experiences. Additionally, there are several professional resource people within the community who have made themselves available on short-term notice to provide assistance when needed. Participation in the program is voluntary, and all services or assistance provided is kept confidential. Only those records necessary for the orderly administration of the Program are maintained. Phone numbers are available for appointments, and a beeper number for urgent needs.

3. LVMPD SUPERVISOR'S GUIDE TO EMPLOYEE JOB PERFORMANCE AND ASSISTANCE UNDER THE POLICE EMPLOYEE ASSISTANCE PROGRAM

At every level of management, the key to success of this or any other program, is the supervisor, whose effectiveness is twofold. First, the immediate supervisor is usually the first individual to become aware of the employee's decreasing job performance. This may be the earliest significant evidence of a developing problem. Second, the supervisor can motivate the employee to seek appropriate professional help. The resources available to the troubled employee are of little value unless he or she is made aware of those resources and realizes that seeking help is the employee's responsibility. The supervisor is the one who can most effectively provide the motivation for the employee to seek help before his or her job performance has deteriorated to the point where employment must be terminated or he or she self-destructs.

The supervisory guide contains much useful information on supervisory skills and employee performance criteria. Some of that information directed at supervisors is summarized below.

Supervisor's Five-Step Plan

Step 1
Recognize that a problem exists. Recognize signs, symptoms, and behaviors characterizing troubled employees. If work performance is deteriorating, don't ignore it; the problem will only get worse. Describe problems factually, not judgmentally. First, use a one-on-one confrontation.

Step 2
Document the problem. Keep accurate up-to-date records of the employee's work performance. This is the basis of an effective intervention. Additionally, the employee may actually be aware that his or her work performance is affected. Documentation presents the problem as it is.

Step 3
Take action. Whatever is done in terms of discipline, it is important to follow through. No one is helped by avoidance. Problems should not exclude employees from disciplinary job action or intervention.

Step 4
Refer. Refer the employee to the employee assistance program once it is determined that normal supervisory corrective measures are not working. PEAP will serve as a liaison between the employee and appropriate sources of help.

Step 5
Return and follow-up. In the case of some employees, *e.g.*, chemically dependent persons, the supervisor will need to be involved in the process of reintegration. PEAP is helpful as well in this situation.

The following three points must be emphasized.

1. The supervisor's responsibility is to observe and document job performance deficiencies.

2. The supervisor must not attempt to diagnose alcoholism or substance abuse or any other problem, nor does he or she mention them in his or her confrontation with the employee. It would be useless and inappropriate to label the employee's problem as alcoholism or substance abuse. On the one hand, the problem may actually not be alcoholism (*e.g.*, marital, family, financial, and a variety of other personal problems may also cause deteriorating job performance); on the other hand, if the problem is indeed alcoholism or substance abuse, the supervisor will be unable to penetrate the denial syndrome characteristic of the illness. However, the employee cannot deny documented job performance deficiencies. This is the only ground on which the supervisor has sure footing.

3. Once the employee has been referred to PEAP, the supervisor should discontinue attempts at counseling and work with PEAP to establish outside assistance.

Alcoholism: Dealing With Denial

Although the police supervisor cannot be concerned with the causes of an employee's performance problems, a concern must exist for the effects. Performance problems, regardless of their cause, result in increased use of sick leave, disciplinary problems, errors in judgment, accidents, poor public relations, and a host of other problems.

Alcoholism is a disease, a physiological addiction and a mental illness. The mental and physical components of this disease are so interwoven that even in the field of alcoholism study it is difficult to separate the issues. However, the main point for the supervisor to remember is that the active alcoholic employee is not going to want to listen to anything that threatens his or her self-image or points to his or her drinking as a cause of problems. This protection that the employee builds around alcohol use is called "denial" and it is expressed in a multitude of ways.

Denial is a psychological defense mechanism with many facets. It is used to protect one's self-worth and keep out painful or damaging information. When supervisors counsel an active alcoholic employee on his or her work performance, they will most certainly encounter this barrier of denial. In fact, it is this very mechanism that creates problems in counseling such employees.

The denial system expresses itself in many ways, and on the job it can be seen in the problem employee's false self-image of being a good performer. In this way, the denial system can filter out an input that would attack the self-image and force the employee to see that his or her alcohol use is having a negative impact on his or her employment. Without this denial system, the employee would be pressured to view many painful behaviors and past decisions that he or she both consciously and unconsciously desires to avoid. Unless confronted, however, this denial system will "protect" the alcoholic to his death.

Supervisors must realize that the department holds a strong hand in its ability to break down the officer's denial system. The beginning of that break occurs when the supervisor counsels the employee on his or her poor job performance. The supervisor must also realize how the denial mechanism works within him or her as a supervisor.

Supervisor's Denial

When a supervisor is in denial, he or she is aware of irregularities in the job performance, but joins the troubled employee in the delusion that there is really not a problem. The supervisor will accept even the flimsiest excuses for problem behavior (such as grandmothers who die every week, near terminal cases of the sniffles, and alarm clocks that fail only on Mondays and Fridays) in order to give the employee the benefit of the doubt.

Why would someone intelligent enough to become a supervisor accept these or any recurrent excuses? The reason is that the supervisor wants to believe them. For reasons of ego preservation, a supervisor may need to believe such excuses. To supervisors who see themselves as nice persons and who supervise employees by inspiration and a winning personality, a troubled employee can represent rejection. To those supervisors who see themselves as tough and who lead by intimidation and fear of consequences, a troubled employee can represent defiance. To a supervisor who is indifferent, a troubled employee can indicate that action needs to be taken and that involvement is necessary. Empathetic supervisors feel a troubled employee represents personal defeat, while an insecure supervisor admitting to an employee problem feels he or she is admitting personal incompetence.

Therefore, denial is the easiest solution. The idea seems to be, "What I don't know, can't hurt me." The easiest way to break through denial is to provide supervisors with instructions on how to document employee problems. Usually, if a supervisor gets a chance to objectively review the symptoms of a problem and can see a pattern of progressive deterioration, the supervisor will be better able to address the problem and less able to deny it.

Understanding his or her own denial system will allow the supervisor to realize that he or she is the main thrust in the police department's ability to break down the employee's denial system. Like the resistant patient who has difficulty accepting a recommended course of treatment, the supervisor may have to confront an employee's resistance to resolving the problem. To help address the problem of resolving

Las Vegas Metro. Police Dept. **Programs**

this resistance, the following are fifteen expressions of the employee's denial system a supervisor may encounter when counseling an active alcoholic/substance abuser on his or her work performance.

1. Expect to be faced with an employee who believes his work performance is acceptable.

2. Expect the employee to try to deflect the focus from the issue of job performance.

3. Expect the employee to "push your button" so that you get sidetracked on trivial issues or become angry and argumentative.

4. Expect the employee to blame others for all the events that are happening to him or her: the wife, the kids, the car, the partner, the supervisors, the department, etc.

5. Expect the employee to become defensive and angry about being counseled and to argue with your data observations.

6. Expect the employee to minimize the extent of his or her poor job performance. "There are a hundred guys worse than me!"

7. Expect the employee to be very convincing about how others are to blame for his or her present problems. Remember, an alcoholic cannot drink without having people cover for him or her.

8. Expect the employee to test your position and the rules set forth within the counseling session.

9. Expect the employee to get personal and direct some ambiguous comments at your qualities as a person or supervisor.

10. Expect the employee to accuse you of favoritism and offering others special privileges.

11. Expect the employee to constantly interrupt your focus on his or her job performance.

12. Expect the employee to demonstrate some strong emotions throughout the entire session.

13. Expect to see a bold front put up by the employee as evidenced by staring and periods of silence.

14. Don't expect to see any lasting results after just one counseling session.

15. Expect to keep pressure on by continuous job performance monitoring.

Programs   Las Vegas Metro. Police Dept.

What must be remembered is that no matter how "good", how intelligent, or how experienced a supervisor may be, interaction with an employee reflects the supervisor's own personality and ego. It also is an interaction of both the employee's denial system and the denial system of the supervisor. Adherence to these guidelines will provide supervisors with a specific mechanism that will short-circuit the supervisor's and the employee's denial system.

The following information can help a supervisor identify behavior patterns that constitute poor job performance in an employee who has an alcohol/substance abuse problem.

Patterns Identifying the Impaired Employee
The patterns and component behaviors are as follows.

1. *Increased Absenteeism*
   a. Unauthorized leave
   b. Excessive sick leave
   c. Repeated tardiness or absenteeism to briefings
   d. Improbable or peculiar excuses for absenteeism
   e. Higher than normal absences for minor illnesses such as cold, flu, etc.
   f. Requests time off more frequently than others
   g. More illness coinciding with RDO's

2. *"On-The-Job" Absenteeism*
   a. Continued absences from detail or work station
   b. Increased number or length of coffee breaks
   c. Increasingly long lunches
   d. Increased number of trips to the restroom
   e. Physical illness on the job (headaches, stomachaches, etc.)
   f. Leaving work early

3. *High Accident Rate*
   a. Lost time due to accidents on the job
   b. Lost time due to accidents off the job
   c. Minor accidents on the job
   d. More disability claims filed (SIIS)

4. *Repeated Complaints of*:
   a. Civil rights violations
   b. Use of excessive force
   c. Being discourteous
   d. Excessive use of "resisting arrest" or "obstructing an officer" type of charges
   e. Poor grooming, dress, or personal hygiene

5. *Repeated Reports and/or Complaints of Inappropriate Brandishing of His or Her Weapon*

6. *Repeated Failure to Respond to Radio Dispatches*

7. *Sporadic Work Patterns*
   a. Extremes of high or low productivity
   b. Extremes in the quality of work produced
   c. Having to put in extra hours to complete work
   d. Needless risks taken to raise productivity after admonishments from supervisor

8. *Lowered Job Efficiency*
   a. Missed deadlines
   b. Increased number of errors
   c. Wasted time and materials
   d. Careless handling and maintenance of equipment and supplies
   e. Poor decision making
   f. Work requires greater effort
   g. Jobs, projects, or handling calls takes longer
   h. Easily distracted

9. *Coming To/Returning to Work in an Obviously Abnormal Condition*
   a. Hangovers on the job
   b. Showing up intoxicated
   c. Hand tremors
   d. Deteriorating personal appearance and hygiene
   e. Red or bleary eyes

10. *Police Officer/Employee Relations On The Job*
    Friction in employee relationships including supervisor/employee relationships, usually results in decreased job performance efficiency. The following is indicative of behavior that affects job performance and may be indicative of some sort of problem.
    a. Over-reacts to real or imagined criticism
    b. Wide swings in mood and or morale
    c. Avoidance of supervisor or associates
    d. Unreasonable resentments
    e. Change in mood after lunch or coffee breaks
    f. Borrowing money from co-workers
    g. More aggressive towards co-workers
    h. More of a tendency to blame other workers for performance problems
    i. More suspicious of fellow workers
    j. Sensitive to opinions about his or her drinking
    k. Complaints from co-workers

11. *Unusual Behaviors*
    a. Temper tantrums
    b. Physical violence
    c. Regard for co-worker's safety

12. *Miscellaneous Symptoms*
    a. Increasing complaints about problems at home, or with family and friends

Confrontation

One of the most crucial aspects of this program is the supervisor's confrontation with an employee whose job performance is deficient. It is extremely important that the supervisor not make any attempt to diagnose the cause of the employee's job performance problem and that the supervisor not attempt to counsel the employee.

Meeting with an employee face-to-face to discuss a problem situation is never an easy task. A supervisor is often tempted to put off confronting an employee who is troubled. Sometimes a supervisor will meet with an employee but hesitate to recommend counseling. Despite his or her initial reaction, an employee who is in trouble knows it and is often relieved to have it out in the open so it can be handled with the supervisor's support.

A supervisor who has identified a definite pattern of unsatisfactory on-the-job behavior should handle it as soon as possible. An appropriate time is right after an incident which is indicative of the problem. The following guidelines may be helpful to a supervisor when meeting with a troubled employee.

The supervisor should:

1. Come prepared to the interview with a clear sense of the job criteria and the facts to be addressed. For example, in the case of excessive absenteeism, the dates should be readily available.

2. Focus on specific job performance issues or behavior, not on vague personality or attitudinal problems which can be easily denied. The supervisor should indicate the effect that the worker's problem is having on him or herself, the workload, and the other workers in the unit.

3. Remain calm and firm while always returning the conversation to the specific on-the-job problems, despite an employee's excuses, defensiveness, or hostility.

4. Avoid any diagnosis or labeling of the employee's personal problem. The supervisor should stress that whatever is troubling the employee, it is the employee's responsibility to do whatever is necessary to make it possible to perform adequately, *e.g.*, contacting the Police Employee's Assistance Program.

5. Emphasize and reiterate exactly what is expected in order to resolve the problem. Once the supervisor is sure the employee understands, then a commitment should be secured and monitored.

6. Set a definite date, *e.g.*, in a month's time, for the next meeting at which time a marked improvement in the employee's performance is expected.

7. End the interview on a positive note with his or her expectation that given the resources available, the problem will be resolved in the near future.

Giving Criticism

Before criticizing, a supervisor should examine his or her motive. A supervisor should ask him or herself, "Why am I preparing to say these things?" and "How will my criticism help the other person and/or improve our relationship?"

Responsible criticism has five characteristics illustrated by the acronym **C - L - E - A - R**, and is described as follows:

Current
Limited
Expresses
Acknowledges
Re-evaluates

Current: "What is the individual presently doing wrong?"

Limited: "What specific behavior(s) do I find offensive or unacceptable?" "What specific change or changes do I wish to see implemented?"

Expresses: "How can I phrase this criticism so that it expresses my belief, opinion, feeling or perception?"

Acknowledges: "How will I acknowledge this person as a unique human being?" "How would I feel if these things were being said to me?"

Re-evaluates: "Have I set aside a date and a specific time to evaluate progress toward the desired objective?"

Documentation

Proper and careful documentation is an essential part of management on all levels and is necessary at all times for efficient department operations. Proper documentation provides an authentic record of what has gone on in the past and helps to avoid the lack of clarity that usually occurs when one attempts to evaluate an employee's performance on the basis of memory.

It is important that the supervisor understand that documentation should cover problems that occur on the job only. Mention of incidents that take place outside the work setting (such as public drunkenness) could be construed as an invasion of privacy. The supervisor can only legitimately become involved when an off-the-job problem interferes with job performance. The employee's actions while not on the job are of concern only to the employee, they are his or her own private business. When such off-the-job problems create job performance difficulties, however, the difficulties should be carefully and thoroughly documented.

If the supervisor follows the established procedures for documenting performance deficiencies, the initial discussion with the employee will be based on objective performance data rather than vague references to the employee's unsatisfactory work. Remember that everyone has an occasional "bad day." It is a pattern of deficient job performance which may indicate a continuing problem, and warrant constructive confrontation.

When documenting a disciplinary action, care should be taken to include the following:

1. *Facts*: This means names, dates, times, places, witnesses, etc. If possible, a reaction to the incident should be included.

2. *Statement of Violation*: State how the above mentioned facts constitute a violation of department rules, regulations, and/or policies, and cite the violation specifically.

3. *Previous Warnings and Incidents*: State whether the employee has committed this offense before; and, if so, whether he or she was disciplined for it. Describe the employee's disciplinary history as to this type of action.

4. *Expected Improvement*: Be explicit; state what improvements are expected of the employee and what is expected to be achieved by way of disciplinary action.

5. *Review Period*: Indicate that follow-up will occur on this matter within a specified period of time. This is a check to see if the employee has attempted to correct the situation.

6. *Warning of Further Action*: Inform the employee that should his or her behavior not improve, a more severe disciplinary action will follow.

7. *Signature*: Make sure the employee signs the notice. An oversight here might be alleged by the employee as a disciplinary action administered without his or her knowledge. If an employee refuses to sign, affix your own signature and one of a witness, and indicate that the employee has been given the opportunity to sign but has refused.

Documentation Example

When counseling someone for repeated job performance deficiencies, the supervisor may want to consider using the critical incident report form as described in the LVMPD Performance Appraisal Guide. This

Las Vegas Metro. Police Dept. **Programs**

procedure is to be used when performance has not been corrected through normal supervisory measures.

PHASE I
- Observe and document patterns of job performance deficiencies such as:
  > Repeated absences of tardiness;
  > Frequent accidents (on the job);
  > Repeated complaints of "use of excessive force;"
  > Repeated failure to respond to radio dispatches; and
  > Frequent absences from assignments (details).
- Conduct the first interview in a private setting.
  > Have documentation in hand.
  > Tell the employee your observations. Cite specific incidents and situations.
  > Ask the employee for an explanation.
  > Offer the services of PEAP.
  > Jointly set up a plan for improvement.
  > Explain what the department's standard disciplinary procedures are.
  > Make it plain that standard departmental disciplinary action will follow unless improvement is noted.
- Document interview.
  > Record the date, time, main points of discussion, response to PEAP offer, and employee's declared and signed commitment.

PHASE II
- Continue to observe and document employee's job performance. If there is no job performance improvement:
  > Conduct a second interview;
  > Have documentation in hand;
  > Review the plan for improvement;
  > Inform the employee that the pattern of work performance remains unsatisfactory;
  > Ask for an explanation;
  > Discipline appropriately;
  > Again offer employee services of PEAP; and
  > Document the interview.

PHASE III
- Continue observations.
  > If deterioration continues, conduct a third interview.
  > Have documentation in hand.
  > Again refer the employee to PEAP. At this point, the supervisor should emphasize that an employee whose work performance continues to be deficient (according to department standards) is subject to continued disciplinary actions, including employment termination.

Programs **Chicago Police Dept.**

- Apply appropriate progressive discipline.
- Document the interview.
     Record the date, time, names of those present, employee's response to PEAP offer, and employee's signature.

F. CHICAGO POLICE DEPARTMENT

One of Chicago's finest, Lieutenant William Powers, from the Personnel Division, has dedicated a major portion of his career to the members of the department, as well as to the objectives and goals of the Chicago Police Department itself. As such, he was kind enough to supply information regarding some of Chicago Police Department's programs related to the intervention of personnel concerns.

The Chicago Police Department values its employees. It also recognizes that Department members are subject to the frailties of humankind and that, sometimes, the problems of the human experience may negatively impact on work performance and expected conduct. Each member is responsible for his or her performance and behavior. Any issues which affect a member's ability to perform at an acceptable level, or impact the Department's ability to serve and protect, must be recognized and confronted by management. Once recognized and confronted, it then becomes the individual member's responsibility to change the subject behavior and the Department's responsibility to assist in that change.

1. PERSONNEL CONCERNS PROGRAM
The Personnel Concerns Program is a structured program of supervision designed to provide an Individualized Performance Plan (IPP) for an employee who has been identified as having difficulties affecting his or her competency as an employee of the Department. The thrust of the Personnel Concerns Program is non-disciplinary. Through the Program, the Department attempts to intervene in an employee's problems, behavior, or performance issues which, without assistance, may lead to severe disciplinary measures or separation from the Department.

Placement into the Program is made through written recommendations by the appropriate exempt command staff. This listing includes, but is not limited to, the subject member's exempt commanding officer; the Assistant Deputy Superintendent, Internal Affairs Division; the Administrator of the Office of Professional Standards; the Medical Services Section Administrator; Department-contracted psychologists; the Police Board; or the Executive Director of the Police Board. Program records are maintained separate and apart from Department disciplinary records.

Chicago Police Dept.   Programs

Each recommendation for the Program is forwarded to the Director of Personnel and specifies the reasons for the recommendation. The request for placement into the Program must be approved by the Director of the Personnel Division prior to any Unit Staffing.

The types of behaviors/allegations necessary to be recommended for Personnel Concerns Program consideration are as follows:

1. Certain sustained Complaint Register investigations in which unnecessary physical force was found to be used.

2. Multiple verbal abuse Complaint Register investigations.

3. Sustained domestic violence Complaint Register investigations.

4. Sustained on- or off-duty intoxication Complaint Register Number investigations.

5. Sustained cases in which a penalty of 10 or more days has been recommended.

6. Five or more sustained Complaint Register Number investigations within the last five years.

7. Sworn members receiving two performance grades below 76 on performance evaluations within the past two years.

8. Two Summary Punishment actions within one year or one sustained Complaint Register investigation for being Absent Without Permission.

9. Recommendation by a Department contracted or employed psychologist due to behavioral issues, medication, or psychological symptomology.

10. Incidents for which the member has already received counseling as part of the Behavioral Intervention System (BIS), yet the member failed to comply with the IPP and did not change the subject behavior to the satisfaction of his or her exempt commanding officer within 12 months of being identified for the Behavioral Intervention System.

Watch Commanders monitor the performance of all employees under their command and supervision and make written recommendations, through channels, for the inclusion of specific employees in the Personnel Concerns Program when situations merit.

They participate in Unit Staffings that are convened by the exempt commanding officer for the purpose of discussing the problem behavior of a subject employee. Watch Commanders will also gather and review all pertinent, recorded documentation. Documentation may include, but not be limited to, the member's medical use history, performance evaluations for the past five years, previous involvement in the Behavioral Intervention System, complimentary history, available disciplinary history, and unit documentation—especially past counseling records. He or she also discusses options and strategies which may assist the member in correcting the noted problems.

The Watch Commander is mindful that the focus of the Personnel Concerns Program is the correction of problem behaviors relating to performance and conduct and that the final responsibility for behavioral change rests with the employee. Some of the Watch Commander's corrective actions may include, but are not limited to:

1. Recommending placement in the Personnel Concerns Program.

2. Consulting with Employee Development Unit of the Personnel Division.

3. Requesting a mandatory physical.

4. Requesting a Psychological Fitness for Duty Evaluation.

5. Changing of a partner.

6. Requesting the member to voluntarily participate in the Professional Counseling Services/Employee Assistance Program.

7. Requesting the member be retrained in a certain area.

8. Recommending that the member attend a stress reduction seminar.

9. Recommending a change of unit duty assignment.

10. Weekly performance reviews by supervisors.

11. Assigning the employee to various supervisors for individual tours of duty.

12. Requesting assistance from the Medical Services Section.

13. Participating in daily conversations with the employee.

14. Conducting any combination of the above suggestions or any other appropriate strategies within the guidelines of Department directives/collective bargaining agreements.

Watch Commanders prepare Personnel Concerns Progress Reports bi-monthly based upon weekly reports submitted by designated watch supervisors, and submit a Personnel Concerns Report to the Personnel Division twice each month through the chain of command.

Chicago Police Dept.   **Programs**

2. PERSONNEL DIVISION

The Personnel Division manages the Personnel Concerns Program and also determines the level of Department intervention which is appropriate for each member who is categorized as a Personnel Concern. The Personel Division provides unit exempt commanding officers with the necessary information and feedback about Personnel Concerns Program employees, and assigns a member of the Personnel Division to participate in Personnel Concerns Conferences. A member of the Personnel Division prepares the Individualized Performance Plan for all Personnel Concerns Program employees who are categorized as an Intervention Level Two, where the employee's case is staffed at the Personnel Division. The Personnel Division is responsible for the confidentiality, security, and destruction of all records and reports pertaining to the Personnel Concern employee as indicated by retention schedules.

3. BEHAVIORAL INTERVENTION SYSTEM (BIS)

It is the policy of the Chicago Police Department to support members experiencing personal problems which may be affecting their work performance and offer them the counseling resources currently available through the Department. One such resource, the Behavioral Intervention System, is a systematic review of a Department member's behavioral pattern to alert supervisors to the need for possible intervention and Department counseling. This System is designed to identify Department members who may be in need of Department assistance. It is not a disciplinary process, nor is the System designed to interfere with promotion, transfer, bidding, or other employment benefits. However, it must be understood that the behavior or performance issue which placed a member in the BIS may be used by Department managers in making decisions regarding the member. BIS records are maintained separate from the Department's disciplinary records. An essential element of the effective personnel management system is the early identification of members who may exhibit some troublesome behavioral characteristics. Command and supervisory members are responsible for monitoring the performance of their subordinates, relative to both positive and negative aspects.

Placement into the Behavioral Intervention System is initiated when the Director of the Personnel Division approves of placing a member in the System. The Director of the Personnel Division may consider Department members for inclusion in the BIS based on recommendations by any Department exempt member, the Executive Director of the Police Board, or a Department-contracted psychologist. These recommendations are to be made in writing, and must set forth the reasons for the recommendation.

Some behavioral intervention indicators are:

Programs   **Chicago Police Dept.**

1. Recommendation by the Administrator of the Office of Professional Standards, or the Assistant Deputy Superintendent of the Internal Affairs Division.

2. Any pending registered complaint where there is evidence to support the claim and the nature of the allegation suggests that intervention may be appropriate.

3. A performance grade of 75 or below, or a significant reduction in a member's performance evaluation.

4. Any excessive or pattern of tardiness, summary punishment actions, absenteeism, and medical roll misuse.

5. Significant deviations from the member's normal behavior or the conduct expected of a member of the Department.

6. Multiple sustained Complaint Register investigations within a 12-month period.

7. Multiple excessive force complaints, not sustained, within a 12-month period.

The Personnel Division is responsible for overseeing the BIS, maintaining liaison with all Department units involved in dealing with Department members exhibiting unacceptable behavior, and establishing and maintaining a fair and consistent set of practices to ensure the cases of all personnel are treated in an equitable manner.

4. PROFESSIONAL COUNSELING SERVICE / EMPLOYEE ASSISTANCE PROGRAM

The Professional Counseling Service/Employee Assistance Program is responsible for specific counseling programs and/or referrals that address the needs of members seeking assistance and support. These counseling services are offered at no expense to the member(s). A member's participation in a counseling service is voluntary and confidential.

Watch Commanders do not delay intervention and/or the offering of a Professional Counseling Service referral until a particular member qualifies for placement into the Behavioral Intervention System. Should the member be experiencing performance problems, early intervention/counseling is initiated and the Counseling Session Report is completed to document the counseling. Early intervention/counseling is not considered part of the formal Behavioral Intervention System.

5. PROFESSIONAL COUNSELING SERVICE

The Professional Counseling Service provides a variety of services to active Department members, their families, and retired members. A Department member, a member of his family, or a retired sworn member contacts the Professional Counseling Service by letter, telephone, or in person for information regarding a counseling appointment. Also,

Chicago Police Dept. **Programs**

General Counseling and Referral Services may be recommended by Department supervisory and/or command personnel.

General Counseling and Referral Services are available for the following:
- Individual, couples, marital, and family counseling.
- Referral for financial counseling.
- Stress management training.
- Referrals for death/bereavement groups.
- Family violence issues (physical, emotional and verbal abuse).
- Counseling, assessment, and referral for "troubled teens."
- Traumatic incident debriefing.

6. ALCOHOLISM AND OTHER ADDICTIONS SERVICES UNIT

The Alcoholism and Other Addictions Services Unit is administered by a supervisor who reports to the Director, Professional Counseling Service. The Unit is staffed by certified alcoholism and other drug abuse counselors who are specially selected Department members.

Abuse/addiction is defined as a condition which exists when job performance, personal health, or interpersonal relationships are impaired by an employee's use of alcohol or other addictive substances.

The Alcoholism and Other Addictions Services Unit provides services to Department members and/or their families who may be experiencing difficulty with problems related to alcoholism or other addictions. The Unit can be contacted on a 24 hour, 7 day a week basis. The Unit serves as a resource to command and supervisory personnel and other Department units whose function involves them with employees experiencing impairment due to alcoholism or other addictions.

The Unit is responsible for that portion of supervisory training that focuses upon employee impairment due to alcoholism or other addictions. When an employee is identified by Department supervisory personnel as possibly having problems related to alcoholism and/or other addictions, an addictions counselor will be available to evaluate and provide appropriate support services and/or guidance. When a disciplinary action/investigation is initiated against a member impaired by alcoholism or other addictions, involvement in an Alcoholism and Other Addictions Services Unit program does not delay the disciplinary or investigative processes.

7. TRAUMATIC INCIDENT DEBRIEFING PROGRAM

The Traumatic Incident Debriefing Program provides Department members the opportunity to understand and put into perspective the emotional and/or psychological impact of a traumatic incident. The debriefing process is not a critique of any assignment or action taken by the Department member, but rather a technique by which the stresses of the traumatic incident are dissipated.

8. DEPARTMENT REFERRALS TO THE PROFESSIONAL COUNSELING SERVICE

Department command and supervisory personnel have the authority and the responsibility to recommend the Professional Counseling Service to members under their supervision when appropriate. The member should be assured that the consultation is recommended solely for his or her benefit and that the session will be confidential. Recommendation or referral to the Professional Counseling Service is not used as a substitute for the disciplinary process. Unit commanding officers and/or supervisors may contact the Professional Counseling Service for information about the counseling program or the referral process.

G. BOSTON POLICE DEPARTMENT

The Boston Police Department has varied programs targeting stress management, family counseling, and suicide prevention. One such successful program, The Boston Police Stress/Support Unit, is directed by Police Officer Michael O'Sullivan. His dedication and background make him a natural for the position.

1. OFFICER PROFILE

Police Officer O'Sullivan is actually the founder and coordinator of the Critical Incident Support Team. He has been a police officer for five years, coming on the job in his mid forties, and was sort of "drafted" to start the team due to his experience in treating critical incident stress from his other jobs. He worked in various psychiatric and substance abuse programs for the V.A. as a registered nurse in the 1980's. As a U.S. Marine Veteran of Vietnam, he was able to start Vietnam Vet groups in the facilities that had none at the time. He moved on to work in the Boston City Hospital Emergency Department for six years where he was part of a team that managed all psych emergencies and sexual assault cases. The toughest part of his job was making death notifications to families of trauma victims. He did this during the years Boston experienced its highest homicide rate. Boston City treated probably 90% of Boston's victims of gunshot wounds at that time. It was at City Hospital where he got involved with attempting to help Emergency Nurses, Emergency Medical Techs, and Police Officers cope with critical incident stress. His "past" followed him onto the job when, after a couple of years "in the street," he was asked to start a critical incident support team for the Stress/Support Unit.

2. BOSTON POLICE CRITICAL INCIDENT SUPPORT TEAM

The new Boston Police Critical Incident Support Team has been officially active as a subsection of the Stress/Support Unit since July 10th of 1998. The Team consists of 20 active members that represent most of the police districts. It is in the process of developing a 24-hour call system that should be on-line in the fall of 1998. A pre-incident awareness course is available for supervisors and patrol officers alike, to attempt to ensure compliance with the new special order that lays out the procedure for team access.

A major priority will be to build on the substance abuse piece of the puzzle and increase involvement in other problematic areas such as critical incidents, depression and suicide, marriage and relationship problems, as well as a host of other mental health and job-related problems.

At present, The Boston Police Stress/Support Unit has Police Officer Michael O'Sullivan and two other officers, plus one retired police officer assigned on a full-time basis to the Unit. They are on call 24 hours a day, 7 days a week.

In the near future, the Unit is going for a grant to fund their most ambitious project yet. They want to train at least several hundred officers of all ranks in the International Critical Incident Stress Foundations Peer Support course. They believe this type of training on a large scale will help to decrease the stigma of seeking help for officers' personal problems. Also, with large numbers of trained peer support personnel, they hope to be able to respond to incidents that in the past might have been missed.

H. OKLAHOMA CITY POLICE DEPARTMENT

When we speak of law enforcement officers, the word hero is often used. Now, that word must be used again, and this time it is not used to describe a street cop, but to pay tribute to two more people who have worked behind the scenes, dedicating their lives to aiding those men and women in law enforcement who are in need. Chaplain Jack Poe and Diane Leonard, both of Oklahoma City, are the backbone and originators of the Critical Incident Workshops. Through these workshops they have counseled and cared for those involved in the Oklahoma City bombing.

1. OFFICER PROFILES

Jack O'Brian Poe, Director Chaplain, OKC Police Department
Jack O'Brian Poe, D.Min., received his B.A. in Sociology from the University of Central Oklahoma, his B.D. from Southwestern Baptist Theology Seminary, Ft. Worth, Texas, and his Doctor of Ministry from Phillips University, Enid, Oklahoma. Dr. Poe has also spent a year in training at the Family Life Center, Ft. Sill, Oklahoma, in family counseling training. He has additional training in Post-Shooting Trauma, Stress Management in Law Enforcement, Critical Incidents in Policing, and Advance Peer Support. He joined the Oklahoma City Police Department in 1984 where he was involved in setting up their peer support program.

Dr. Poe teaches at Oklahoma City Police Academy. He has been on the staff of Oklahoma Baptist University as an adjunct professor.

Dr. Poe is responsible for facilitating all officer-involved shooting debriefings, and has extensive experience working with officers and their families who have undergone extreme emotional trauma. He worked with the officers and families who were impacted by the bombing of the Alfred P. Murrah Federal Building in Oklahoma City, and has conducted seminars on Stress Management and Critical Incident Stress. He has been sought after as a speaker on the response of the clergy to the bombing in Oklahoma City. This one presentation was given over 50 times last year to organizations which included The Royal Canadian Mounted Police Academy in Regina, Sask, Canada, the annual training conference of the International Conference of Police Chaplains, the Oklahoma Sheriff and Peace Officers Meeting, police chaplains meetings in Maryland, Wisconsin, Texas, Tennessee, Illinois, Kansas, Missouri, and military chaplains in Kansas, Oklahoma, Utah, Texas, and Missouri.

Dr. Poe is listed in *Who's Who in Religion* and the *International Who's Who of Professionals.* He is presently the STARC Chaplain for the Oklahoma Army National Guard. He holds the rank of Colonel.

Diane Leonard, Administrator, Critical Incident Workshop

Diane Leonard was born and raised in Tulsa, Oklahoma. She met and married her husband, Don, while working for the Postal Inspection Service. Don was an Agent with the U.S. Secret Service, and shortly after their marriage, Don was transferred to Washington, D.C. While in Washington, Diane worked at Postal Service Headquarters.

After three years in Washington, Don was transferred to St. Louis, Missouri, where Diane started her own business as an independent sales representative and covered the states of Illinois and Missouri. In 1989, when Don and Diane were transferred to Oklahoma City, Diane continued her sales rep business, covering the states of Oklahoma and Arkansas.

On April 19, 1995, Diane's husband, Don, was killed in the bombing of the Alfred P. Murrah Building in Oklahoma City. Three weeks after the bombing, she began working with a small group of bombing victims on death penalty reform. During this effort, she spoke at several news conferences in Washington, D.C., and also lobbied many members of Congress. In April 1996, the week after the first anniversary of the bombing, Diane was asked by the White House to be on the podium with President Clinton when he signed the Anti-Terrorism bill into law, which included death penalty reform.

Shortly after death penalty reform was signed into law, Diane left her sales rep business and became a victim/witness coordinator for the Oklahoma Attorney General. In February 1997, while in Washington to speak at a symposium, Diane lobbied Congress once again. This time it was due to a ruling by Judge Matsch that impact witnesses in the bombing trials could not view the trials. A month later she was in Washington again to see the legislation which resolved this problem pass the House and Senate, and signed into law by President Clinton. Due to the passage of this legislation, Diane was able to view both the McVeigh and Nichols trials and to testify as an impact witness in both trials.

In August 1997, Diane began work to obtain a grant from the Department of Justice to fund workshops to help the rescue workers who responded to Oklahoma City. The funding was granted in May 1998, and in June 1998, Diane became the Administrator of that grant.

Diane has three stepsons, Brad, Jason, and Tim, and is currently serving as Administrator of the Critical Incident Workshops in Oklahoma City, and teaching Death Notification at two local Police Departments.

2. CRITICAL INCIDENT WORKSHOPS—A PATHWAY TO PEACE

Over 4,000 rescue and recovery personnel were involved in the aftermath of the bombing of the Alfred P. Murrah Federal Building, April 19, 1995, in Oklahoma City, Oklahoma. In all, 168 persons were killed, including 19 children, and 442 persons were treated in area hospitals. Literally thousands of people in the Oklahoma City area have been affected by the worst terrorist attack in U.S. history.

Not only are the families of victims and survivors affected by this traumatic event, but the responding personnel and their families are affected as well. It is very common for people to experience emotional after-shocks or stress reactions after a traumatic event. Sometimes these reactions are immediate or they may occur days, months, or even years later.

It is common for victims to deny their emotional expressions of trauma. However, traumatic events have a way of freezing images in the memory. As a result, many individuals and families have been impacted negatively by the direct involvement of a family member in the event. When the Office of Victims of Crime, Department of Justice became aware of the continuing traumatization and the beneficial results of the Critical Incident Workshops, they made a huge commitment to those suffering as a result of this crime by awarding a grant to continue the workshops.

Purpose and Design

Critical Incident Workshops are designed to bring together responders, emergency personnel, survivors, and families of victims in a small group setting. Upon completion, participants are better equipped to work through trauma and support others experiencing the ravages of trauma. Although the workshops are not therapy, the training model has very therapeutic results for participants. Participants have included personnel from agencies such as police, fire, and Sheriff's departments, Oklahoma Highway Patrol, federal and state law enforcement, chaplains, mental health professionals, survivors, and families of victims.

The workshops are held once a month on specific dates, and are three days long beginning at 1:00 p.m. on Tuesday and ending at noon on Friday. The results have been overwhelmingly successful as people have discovered ways of processing the effects of a traumatic event that minimizes the impact. The workshops are conducted in a motel setting within an hour's drive of Oklahoma City at no cost to the participants.

Workshop Topics
 "The Nature of Trauma"
 "Individual Experiences and Perspective"
 "Thought and Fact Phase"
 "Reactions—Perception of Danger, Symptoms"
 "Suicide—Potential Warning Signs"
 "Unfinished Business"
 "Ultimate Survivors"
 "Peer Support"
 "Surviving and Prevailing Over Adversity"

Primary Facilitators
 James Horn, M.F.S. Retired FBI, Critical Incident Response Specialist.
 Dr. Roger Solomon, Ph.D. Boston, MA, Critical Incident Recovery Resources.
 Dr. Nancy Bohl, Ph.D. Psychotherapist, The Counseling Team, Los Angeles, CA.
 Dr. Kathy Thomas Stillwater, OK, Counseling Psychologist.

Participation in the workshops leave a positive impact on those attending. Some of their comments follow:

"I was reminded I am not alone and others have the same feelings as I do."

"I finally learned that it's O.K. to talk about feelings, sharing experiences with others.... I wish it had been something required long before now."

"This workshop solved and helped with my stress. My wife and I really fell in love again."

"I did not realize the effect the bombing had on me. By talking about it with others, I released a lot of my pain and found some peace."

"Most of all, the workshop helped me find a new freedom—a freedom to seek help and freedom to trust again."

These comments are feelings of newfound hope, generated from the power of the Critical Incident Workshops which have helped so many learn how to cope and start anew.

I. SAN DIEGO POLICE DEPARTMENT / SDPD

1. FOCUS PSYCHOLOGICAL SERVICES PROGRAM

San Diego has become a national leader in changing the direction of police work. Community orientation, problem solving, and partnering with the community has added pro-active dimensions to traditional enforcement approaches. In keeping with the changing face of policing, the psychological services program titled FOCUS, has been instituted. The FOCUS Psychological Services Program has been designed to address the diverse needs of the San Diego Police Department. All program components are re-evaluated, updated, and revised as needed. FOCUS includes new elements of leadership training, dispute resolution, and critical incident response. An outline of program components follows.

Education and Training

Organizational change necessitates that training and education keep pace with current trends. In addition to the types of training FOCUS has successfully provided to Department personnel for the past eight years, new concepts in skill building and leadership training have been added.

Trauma Treatment and Crisis Intervention

SDPD's new Critical Incident Debriefing Policy was implemented in 1998. The policy formalizes and expands past practices of debriefing personnel following critical events. It addresses trauma treatment and critical incident debriefing, including a description of the most current intervention techniques in use for trauma reduction.

Confidential Counseling and Psychotherapy

Counseling remains the cornerstone of FOCUS' program. Offering counseling services to police personnel acknowledges the stressors inherent in public safety, and demonstrates SDPD's commitment to the health and well-being of its employees.

Family Counseling

Family counseling has become a significant part of the requested services provided by FOCUS. Stepping out of the limitations generally placed on service providers by managed health care, FOCUS family counselors work in concert with parents, schools, and other professionals to design interventions that meet family needs.

Management Consultation and Miscellaneous Research

Restructuring and strategic planning have greatly increased the demand for management consultation services. Work-group problem analysis and development of organizational interventions is a subspecialty of FOCUS professionals, as is alternate dispute resolution. This expands the role of organizational psychology for SDPD's psychological services program.

Consultation to Specialized Units and Teams

Specialized units and teams have relied on FOCUS to provide consultations on psychological aspects of law enforcement and program development. FOCUS provides consultation to units and teams that request expert opinion and input.

Coordinating Committee

FOCUS has established a committee to oversee psychological services. The committee insures contract compliance, client satisfaction, utilization, and programming development as a demonstration of FOCUS' desire to be responsive to the changing needs of the San Diego Police Department.

These components provide SDPD with a psychological services program tailored to meet the needs of an organization in the vanguard of policing for the next millennium.

FOCUS Psychological Services was established by Dr. Jolee Brunton in 1986 to provide psychological services to police and public safety personnel. The psychologists working with FOCUS are trained in the highly specialized field of police psychology, and are experienced in working with police personnel and family members. Each professional brings specialized skills and experience. FOCUS is currently providing a full array of psychological services for El Cajon Police and Fire Departments, North County Fire Department, and the San Diego Police Department. FOCUS provides or has provided training, treatment, critical incident debriefing, or management consultation for numerous police and public safety agencies, as well as private industry.

FOCUS has been the provider of psychological services for the San Diego Police Department since July of 1990, and during that period, has provided over 40,000 hours of services to police personnel and their dependents. This clearly demonstrates both the widespread acceptance of the FOCUS program and the willingness to be flexible in order to meet department needs.

2. FOCUS PERSONNEL

FOCUS is comprised of dedicated mental health professionals with expertise and training in all facets of police psychology, as well as defined counseling specialties. All FOCUS staff members have a doctoral degree in psychology and are either licensed or registered by the State of California as Psychological Assistants. FOCUS is proud of a staff that not only demonstrates clear expertise, but also reflects the cultural and ethnic diversity and richness of the San Diego community.

Jolee J. Brunton, Ph.D., Chief Psychologist

Dr. Brunton has been involved in police psychology since 1984 when she began working for the El Cajon Police Department. She received specialized training at the Symposium for Police Psychology held by the Federal Bureau of Investigation at their facilities in Quantico, Virginia in 1984, 1986, and 1996. She has received basic and advanced training in hostage negotiations, and received Regional Academy training in problem-oriented policing. In her capacity as a police psychologist, she has provided confidential counseling services to police personnel; developed, trained, and supervised Peer Support teams; provided wellness information, newsletters, and training; developed and trained numerous critical incident debriefing teams; trained and consulted to the Emergency Negotiation Team; conducted numerous group and individual debriefings; provided supervisory training and consultations; and acted as coordinator and liaison between the SDPD and FOCUS professionals. Dr. Brunton has an extensive background in the treatment of chronic mental patients, which she utilized when a consultant to committees such as the San Diego Police Department Use of Deadly Force Task Force and In-Custody Death Task Force. She is past chair of the San Diego County Mental Health Advisory Board.

Dr. Brunton specializes in organizational psychology, and in this capacity has facilitated command staff retreats, division workshops, and numerous work group interventions. She assisted SDPD's Equal Employment Opportunity office in developing a pilot Alternative Dispute Resolution program. She is also a recognized expert in assessment and management of employee conflict, including threats of violence in the workplace, providing these and other human relations consultation services to numerous Fortune 500 corporations. As a clinician, Dr. Brunton specializes in brief psychotherapeutic approaches to depression, post-traumatic and other stress disorders, anxiety, marital counseling, substance abuse, grief and bereavement, and habit control.

Dr. Brunton is the primary organizational consultant. She is responsible for ensuring contract compliance, acting as liaison to the SDPD, providing supervision of FOCUS professionals, as well as providing direct counseling, training, and administrative functions.

Robert Burgess, Ph.D., Licensed Psychologist

Dr. Robert Burgess is a Vietnam veteran whose experience of the TET offensive generated an interest in post-traumatic stress disorder (PTSD). He has treated Vietnam veterans for PTSD, along with their spouses and families. For the past eight years, he has counseled employees and dependents of the San Diego Police Department and has specialized in parent-child problems and in individual post-trauma interventions.

Dr. Burgess has trained Peer Support team members, as well as law enforcement officers and their families, and is familiar with the inherent stressors associated with their jobs. He was on the Selection Committee of San Diego County which reviewed applications and interviewed providers who would screen personnel for the Sheriff's and Marshall's Departments. Dr. Burgess has conducted workshops on stress management and communications in the workplace for professional groups, and is a member of the Disaster Response Committee of the San Diego Academy of Psychologists which works in conjunction with the American Red Cross in debriefing and counseling the public in disasters.

Through the FOCUS program, Dr. Burgess is responsible for counseling couples, families, and children; trauma intervention; and mobilization of the trained disaster psychologists team in the event of a disaster.

Mark Marvin, Ph.D., Licensed Psychologist

Dr. Mark Marvin has been associated with FOCUS Psychological Services for 10 years. His vast experience working with law enforcement personnel began with the provision of psychological services to the criminal justice system while in Michigan in the early 1980's. With the FOCUS program, Dr. Marvin is responsible for individual, marriage, and family counseling; trauma intervention; stress management training; organizational development; and consultation to, and training of, the Emergency Negotiation Team.

Dr. Marvin provides diverse services to the San Diego Police Department, as well as providing critical incident stress debriefing (CISD), training development and presentation, organizational development, and counseling services to the United States Immigration and Naturalization Service. Due to his vast experience with post-traumatic interventions, Dr. Marvin was selected to be filmed conducting a CISD for purposes of nationwide training for Border Patrol agents. He also provides a full range of psychological services to numerous fire departments and lectures to emergency medical students at Palomar College. He has extensive experience in the assessment and treatment of the severely and persistently mentally ill, as well as the training of psychology interns.

Lourdes Perez-Williams, Ph.D., Licensed Psychologist

Dr. Lourdes Perez-Williams obtained her Ph.D. from the California School of Professional Psychology in 1986. She is licensed both as a psychologist and a marriage, family, and child counselor in the State of California.

Dr. Perez-Williams has specialized in the treatment of children and families. She has an extensive training history with the San Diego Juvenile Probation Department where she has conducted research with repetitive juvenile offenders and on recidivism. Other research evaluated the effectiveness of parenting programs in decreasing multiple behavior problems with adolescents and their parents.

In 1990, Dr. Perez-Williams came to FOCUS Psychological Services from Children's Hospital. She has continued to provide bilingual-bicultural psychotherapy to families of Hispanic descent. Her specialty is working with children experiencing trauma from sexual and physical abuse, anxiety, depression, illness, divorce, and blended family issues. As a police psychologist, Dr. Perez-Williams is sensitive to the special needs of police families while expertly integrating child development issues. She continues to speak in schools throughout San Diego, Orange, and Los Angeles Counties on children's school success, discipline, enhancing child self-esteem, and treatment of childhood sexual abuse.

Dr. Perez-Williams is responsible for the counseling of children, couples, and families; parenting education, discipline, and behavioral modification; normal and abnormal child development; and bilingual/bi-cultural counseling and psychotherapy.

Trudy Slater, Ph.D., Licensed Psychologist

Dr. Trudy Slater has provided an array of psychological services to law enforcement for over seven years. Her specialty areas are trauma, crisis intervention, critical incident debriefing, and liaison with Peer Support. Dr. Slater has an extensive medical background of 22 years as a RN with charge nurse specialties in psychiatry and obstetrics, and also with continued research in post-partum depression. This medical background is an invaluable resource for the SDPD personnel whose emotional distress may be secondary to their own or a loved one's physical disorder.

Dr. Slater provides a unique medical/psychological approach to law enforcement personnel which includes home visitations related to family illness, disability, pregnancy complications, bereavement, field counseling for anxiety, and in-home family critical incident debriefings. She is particularly skilled in counseling couples and in treatment of anxiety and obsessive disorders, and is a certified EMDR (Eye Movement Desensitization and Reprocessing) clinician, a highly effective treatment for post-trauma disorders. Dr. Slater is well-known throughout SDPD for the quality of her written handouts covering many areas of relevance for law enforcement.

Her responsibilities within the FOCUS program include peer support liaison and training; treatment of trauma, depression, anxiety, grief, and stress; adjustments to injury/illness; and individual, couples, and family counseling.

Launi Treece, Ph.D., Psychological Assistant

Dr. Launi Treece has a diverse background in providing psychological services. She has worked with children in the school setting at all age levels, providing assessments and counseling for the children and their families, as well as coordinating care with school personnel. She has worked with individuals in crisis at several crisis houses in San Diego and has worked with college students conducting trainings and individual and group counseling. She also has experience with counseling individuals experiencing medical health concerns.

Dr. Treece received her doctorate in Clinical Psychology with an emphasis in Health Psychology. She has expertise in understanding and educating others on physical/mental health connections. Dr. Treece has taught numerous workshops and seminars on topics such as depression and anxiety management and is experienced with alcohol abuse counseling. She has conducted critical incident debriefings with police and fire service personnel.

Dr. Treece has completed extensive hours of individual, couples, child, and adolescent counseling for the San Diego Police Department for FOCUS. She is also trained and experienced in Christian counseling and works in conjunction with the SDPD chaplains, and provides Christian counseling to Department personnel when requested. Dr. Treece has conducted critical incident debriefings and is trained as a psychological consultant to the Emergency Negotiation Team while being the FOCUS liaison to the Regional Academy conducting workshops on study skills and test anxiety management.

Adjunct Staff
Other professionals working with the FOCUS on special projects include Stephen G. White, Ph.D., licensed Psychologist who is the President of Work Trauma Services, Inc. founded in 1982. Under his direction, the contributions of Work Trauma Services, Inc. have been widely acknowledged among professionals in human resources, employment law, and corporate security. He is responsible for organizational interventions; management consultation; supervisory and leadership trainings; and critical incident debriefing of major incidents.

Another member of the Adjunct Staff is Dennis A. Davis, Ph.D., Organizational Consultant who has over 15 years of law enforcement experience. He has done pre-employment screening, critical incident stress debriefing, academy training, and management consultation across the nation. He developed a use of force training which was utilized by several California law enforcement agencies. His responsibilities with the FOCUS program include training, management consultation, and critical incident debriefing of major incidents.

3. FOCUS PROGRAM DESCRIPTION
The FOCUS Psychological Services Program includes education and training, trauma treatment and crisis intervention, confidential counseling and psychotherapy, family counseling, management consultation, miscellaneous research, consulting to special teams, and a

San Diego Police Dept.   Programs

coordinating committee. The following information gives more detail on various aspects of the Program.

Education and Training

The FOCUS program has provided a wide array of training for sworn and civilian police personnel over the past 12 years. Familiarity with police issues and culture, as well as the individual areas of expertise represented by FOCUS professionals, provide numerous training topics. FOCUS offers education and training that includes the following components: Leadership, Academy Training, Peer Support, Training for Emergency Negotiation Team, Line-up Training, Management Consultation and Miscellaneous Research, Management and Supervisory Skills Training, and Training Development.

FOCUS on Leadership

As an addition to the types of training FOCUS provides, the program also offers a new concept in supervisor and leadership skills training. FOCUS on Leadership is a program that incorporates workshops, reference material, and individual coaching as career development and enhancement tools for supervisors, or those preparing for promotion. FOCUS on Leadership workshops are designed as one- or two-hour modules to be presented each month at area commands. Each topic is presented at each command, and is scheduled to accommodate shift schedules. Any police personnel, sworn or civilian, may attend the workshop, regardless of division assignment. FOCUS on Leadership offers training and coaching designed to address issues that often impede individual performance and career development.

Listed below are some of the specialized career development training workshops presented by FOCUS on Leadership.

Managing Conflict
Applied Situation Leadership
Structured Performance Counseling
Preparing for Promotional Interview
Supervising a Diverse Workforce
Evaluating Performance
Garnering Respect
Applying Vision, Values and Mission to Supervision
Ethics: Theory and Practice
The Job of Supervision

Reference material for use in each workshop is available through FOCUS and is distributed at workshops and by request. FOCUS professionals are available to provide individual coaching to supervisors facing challenging supervision issues.

Employees who have experienced difficulty in their interpersonal interactions with supervisors, co-workers, or the public are offered the following training and individual coaching.

Orientation to Psychological Services
Spousal Orientation
Overcoming Performance Anxiety
Study Skills Enhancement
Critical Incident Stress
Stress Inoculation
Victims, Witnesses, and Survivors in Crisis

Assistance to Academy Staff and Supervisory Personnel

Assistance to Academy Staff and Supervisory Personnel is a training segment directed to advanced officers, as well as to officers becoming supervisors by way of promotion. All workshops offered by FOCUS on Leadership can be expanded to become academy training classes. Listed below are topics included.

Stress Management
Recognition and Avoidance of Substance Abuse
Gender Stereotyping and Sexual Harassment
New Supervisor Stress
Critical Incidents
Antisocial Criminal vs. the Emotionally Disturbed Criminal

Assistance to Peer Support Teams

Assistance to Peer Support Teams by way of FOCUS psychologists, provides supervision and training for Sworn and Communications Peer Support Teams. FOCUS Psychological Services performs the following: Design and present comprehensive initial training for new Peer Support team members; attend Peer Support meetings and evaluate cases; prepare and present a training exercise/handout for these meetings; be available for supervision to Peer Support team members on a 24 hour, 7 day a week basis; and debrief Peer Support teams as needed. These training topics are included.

Communication Skills
Conflict Resolution
Assessment of Suicidality
Substance Abuse
Confidentiality
Community Resources
Critical Incident Trauma
Coping Skills: Preventing Burnout

Hostage Negotiation Team Training

FOCUS trains negotiators in identifying key personality dynamics of suspects, and the communication skills necessary for effective negotiation. The following training topics are included.

Active Listening
Psychoactive Drugs: Identification and Effects
Psychopathology for the Police Negotiator
Domestic Violence

San Diego Police Dept. **Programs**

Roll Call Line-Up Presentations

Roll Call Line-Up Presentations are given to provide pro-active wellness-oriented interventions. FOCUS offers special 15 minute presentations that are given at line-up for sworn personnel, and at work group meetings for civilian and those employees who do not attend the line-up. The following presentation topics are included.

Habit Control
Communication Skills
Conflict Resolution
Effective Parenting
Coping Strategies
Anger Management
Trouble Sleeping
Stress Management

Management and Supervisory Skills Training

Although topic areas are similar, these training sessions differ from FOCUS on Leadership in that they are developed at the request of specific work groups. One example is the Equal Employment Opportunity office requesting FOCUS to design and present training on Alternate Dispute Resolution.

FOCUS considers education and training as essential to a progressive and innovative organization such as SDPD. Training needs change as the organization changes. Working in conjunction with the Coordinating Committee, FOCUS continues to utilize its wide range of expertise to address those needs.

4. FOCUS—TRAUMA TREATMENT AND CRISIS INTERVENTION

Trauma intervention is an essential component of any comprehensive policy psychology program. Experience has shown that a significant number of law enforcement personnel experience some form of stress-related symptoms following a traumatic incident. Most suffer mild to moderate short-term effects; however, a small percentage are severely affected. Those who receive no psychological intervention may experience negative protracted effects. FOCUS, in concert with the Sworn and Communications' Peer Support Teams, identify and treat personnel, be they sworn or civilian, who are affected by a traumatic event. In recognition of the impact of critical incidents on its personnel, San Diego Police Department implemented a new Critical Incident Debriefing policy which requires Psychological Services to respond to and follow up on every identified critical incident. This increases critical incident interventions, ensuring police personnel receive essential debriefing services in a timely and coordinated fashion. FOCUS is a Southern California leader in assessment and treatment of psychological trauma, and in training of critical incident stress debriefing teams.

Proposed Trauma Intervention Program

FOCUS proposes the following trauma intervention program in response to the new requirements of SDPD policy and procedures.

Training

The purpose of training is to orient Department personnel to the new policy and procedures, recognize a critical incident, and to identify coping techniques to mitigate the resulting symptoms. Training will be conducted in the following manner:

A. *Critical Incident Training.* Training is included in Academy, Advanced Officers Training, and Sergeant's Training curriculum.

B. *Line-Up Presentations.* This consists of a series of 15-minute presentations delivered by FOCUS at each division line-up/roll-call, and work group staff meeting on various aspects of critical incidents.

C. *Informant Articles.* FOCUS requests the "Informant" to publish a series of articles on critical incident stress and interventions.

D. *Training of Peer Support in Critical Incident.* Peer Support members will be trained in the areas of crisis intervention, effects of post trauma, communication/listening skills, and group process.

Clinical Services

Procedures state that FOCUS is contacted by the Watch Commander and put on "stand-by" alert whenever there is an incident that may require debriefing. FOCUS works closely with Medical Assistance and Peer Support. Peer Support is automatically sent out and assesses the need for FOCUS to respond to the scene. If indicated, FOCUS responds to the scene, or wherever necessary. If on-scene response is not indicated, FOCUS is responsible for contacting all involved personnel within 24 hours to offer support and assistance. Medical Assistance provides names and phone numbers for all involved personnel. Critical incidents are responded to by prompt squad/personnel debriefings, provision of pertinent literature, and debriefings with family members as necessary.

Services include:

A. *24-Hour Availability.* FOCUS professionals are available 24 hours, 7 days a week, 365 days a year.

B. *On-Site Defusing.* Defusing is an intervention in which immediate contact is made with traumatized personnel. They are encouraged to express feelings and concerns about the incident and receive information on common symptoms of trauma. If a defusing is indicated, FOCUS professionals respond to the site or station. FOCUS responds to the hospital or to an employee's home should an employee be injured or killed.

C. *Debriefing.* Debriefings differ from defusings in that they are generally held 24 to 48 hours following an incident, are more formalized and structured than a defusing, and usually include all personnel involved in the incident. When indicated, FOCUS conducts critical incident debriefings.

D. *Post-Trauma Counseling.* Individual counseling for post-traumatic stress is provided. Family members are invited to participate in counseling, and when indicated, in-home sessions are scheduled.

E. *Eye-Movement Desensitization and Reprocessing (EMDR).* EMDR is a cutting edge neurological-psychological technique used increasingly by police psychologists and clinicians in the field of traumatology. This respected and researched treatment modality requires extensive training and certification. Drs. Slater and Marvin are trained and certified in EMDR. EMDR is used in conjunction with individual counseling for those who experience post-trauma symptoms.

F. *Mass Disasters.* FOCUS has an established network of trauma therapists throughout the state that are available to respond to any event that requires greater resources. FOCUS is involved in critical incident training for the San Diego Academy of Psychologists' Disaster Intervention Team, the National Association of Victim Assistance, and the county's Disaster Preparedness Team.

G. *Critical Incident Follow-Up.* FOCUS contacts each individual involved in a critical incident within 24 hours, and at least on 2 week, one, three, and six month intervals.

H. *"At Risk" Job Assignments.* At the request of command staff, FOCUS will conduct periodic psycho-educational debriefings for personnel in "at risk" job assignments such as Child Abuse, Domestic Violence, and Homicide.

Confidential Counseling and Psychotherapy

CONFIDENTIALITY
FOCUS maintains confidentiality of all employees who seek counseling services.

COUNSELING AND PSYCHOTHERAPY
The Counseling and Psychotherapy component has been designated by the San Diego Police Department as the cornerstone of Psychological Services. FOCUS will provide counseling and psychotherapy to sworn and civilian personnel employed by the SDPD and their immediate

families employing brief therapy interventions at no charge to the client. Emphasis is placed in brief therapy. In some cases, the therapy utilized needs to be longer, as when law enforcement personnel are exposed to very complex and unexpected situations, and the experience serves as a catalyst to bring up other unresolved experiences that the individual has suppressed. Another example would be when an employee has several distressing events occurring over a period of time. Designing a program which is primarily oriented toward brief psychotherapy, but also allows for therapy of longer duration when needed, provides optimal service for the SDPD, as well as the individual.

The counseling and psychotherapy services proposed by FOCUS include the five areas of concern which follow:

Orientation to Psychological Services
To keep employees informed of the availability of counseling services, several methods are utilized:

a. Psychological Services brochures are continually made available at all stations, through the Police Officers' Association, and through the Medical Liaison Office. Brochures are included in all new employee information packets.

b. FOCUS providers conduct an orientation to Psychological Services during new recruit academy training.

c. FOCUS submits articles for publication in each issue of the "Informant", which includes information on Psychological Services and how to access FOCUS.

d. FOCUS providers periodically go on ride-alongs. This format allows employees access to FOCUS professionals, as well as contributing to a greater understanding of the problems encountered in the field.

e. Line-up trainings provide an on-going presence of Psychological Services in the field, and give opportunity to disburse information about FOCUS services to the rank and file.

Eligibility for Services
All employees of the San Diego Police Department and their dependents are eligible for Psychological Services. Dependents have been defined by the Department as anyone living in the employee's home and all minor children. In order to receive services, an employee or his or her dependents contact FOCUS directly. FOCUS determines eligibility by referencing the current employee roster and information provided by the Department as to leaves, terminations, and retirements.

Initial Assessment
Counseling is initiated by the client calling FOCUS. An initial phone consultation is conducted by a psychologist to ascertain the nature of the

present problem, scheduling and location requirements, and eligibility of services. Based on this information, the psychologist conducting the initial triage refers the client to the appropriate FOCUS psychologist. In almost all cases, clients have their initial session scheduled within a week of the assessment call. Without exception, anyone requesting an emergency appointment is accommodated the same day.

Referrals

Although FOCUS psychologists have a wide range of specialized clinical expertise, there are occasions where the treatment of a client falls outside the range of expertise or scope of services. Examples include parents requesting specialized testing for children or court-ordered custody evaluations, psychological disorders such as anorexia nervosa which require medical interventions, and drug or alcohol detoxification or in-patient treatment. In these cases, FOCUS works with the employee to access appropriate treatment. FOCUS staff has developed a working knowledge of the insurance programs offered to SDPD employees. Liaisons have been set up with other health area providers to facilitate referral and insure the least out of pocket expenses to the employee.

FOCUS has a long-standing working relationship with the City of San Diego Employee Assistance Program. Throughout the years, referral of clients between the EAP and FOCUS has been effectively and efficiently managed. FOCUS utilizes the expertise of EAP staff to facilitate substance abuse treatment, and to manage treatment of supervisor referrals for treatment.

Counseling Services

As previously stated, therapy is the cornerstone of Psychological Services. In addition to years of experience with police personnel, FOCUS staff has expertise in diverse areas of clinical specialties. Counseling is available for, but not limited to, the following issues: stress management, divorce, anger management, health (injury, illness, medical retirement), depression, anxiety, time management, difficulty in interpersonal relationships, grief/bereavement, substance abuse, habit control, and post trauma.

Family Counseling

The family life of police personnel is tremendously affected by the occupational demands inherent in law enforcement; long hours, shift work, and constant exposure to danger are but a few of the unique stressors on law enforcement families. The high rate of marital discord and divorce creates a population of step-families and part-time parents which exacerbate already stressful lives. As such, family and relationship counseling services take on far more importance with police personnel than other employee groups. Family counseling services are available to all San Diego Police Department personnel and their dependents and may be initiated by any family member at no charge to the client. FOCUS is unique in that one of the primary providers, Dr.

Lourdes Perez-Williams is a Child Psychologist. In addition, Drs. Treece and Marvin have extensive experience working with children. Core family counseling includes:

Psychological Services for Children
Relationship Counseling
Marriage Counseling
Divorce Counseling
Parenting and Step-Parenting Skill Development
Communication Skill Enhancement
Counseling for Sexual Problems
Counseling for Childhood Behavior Disorders
Counseling for Adolescents
Consultations with Teachers / School Psychologists

Management Consultation and Miscellaneous Research

Management consultation is divided into the following categories:

ORGANIZATIONAL CONSULTATION

Organizational consultation is requested by the Department to provide assistance to administration and management in the areas of program development, policies, and procedures, and the impact of organizational decisions on the workforce. Examples of organizational consultation by FOCUS psychologists are participation in the Use of Force Task Force, In-Custody Death Task Force, Strategic Planning, Fiscal Restructuring, and the Professional Ethics Committees.

WORK-GROUP PROBLEM ANALYSIS AND INTERVENTION

At the request of a supervisor or manager, FOCUS, through the use of interviews and questionnaires, conducts problem analysis of the work-group to ascertain factors that impede productivity or adversely affect morale. Results of problem analysis are discussed with the supervisor/manager to devise interventions that address relevant issues. FOCUS acts as facilitator and trainer to assist the work-group in resolving issues.

ALTERNATE DISPUTE RESOLUTION PROGRAM (ADR)

As a result of Strategic Planning, SDPD is exploring ADR as an intervention technique to resolve employee disputes before they escalate to the level of grievances or lawsuits. ADR is an effective tool for the resolution of conflict department-wide. FOCUS has experience in designing, training, and conducting ADR programs and interventions. FOCUS works in conjunction with the department's EEO office and provides expanded consultation services for further program development. FOCUS trains mediators and acts as an ADR facilitator.

REFERRAL / CASE MANAGEMENT

FOCUS is always available to consult with supervisors regarding management of a difficult employee, and has developed a Manager's Guide to Employee Difficulties for several other agencies. This guide has been tailored to the San Diego Police Department and is made available to all supervisors experiencing concerns or difficulties with employees.

Consultation to Specialized Units

Specialized units utilize FOCUS professionals as content experts on an as needed basis. For example, the Emergency Negotiation Team (ENT) has designated Drs. Brunton, Marvin, and Treece as psychological consultants to the team. In that capacity, they respond to negotiation scenes as advisers to ENT. The office of Equal Employment Opportunity requested FOCUS to assist in designing a pilot Alternate Dispute Resolution program (ADR), and to train their personnel in the fundamentals of ADR. The Child Abuse Unit has requested FOCUS to conduct periodic psycho-educational sessions with detectives assigned to that unit. FOCUS professionals specializing in child and adolescent psychology consult to the Juvenile Services Teams on the implementation of recommendations from the Juvenile Services Realignment Task Force.

Coordinating Committee

The San Diego Police Department is in the process of developing a strategic plan to guide growth and change over the next decade. To insure that SDPD's Psychological Services program anticipates and plans for dynamic needs of this changing organization, FOCUS has proposed the formation of a Psychological Services Coordinating Committee. The Coordinating Committee will be administered through Personnel, and will periodically review utilization trends, client satisfaction, and recommend program revisions as needed. It will be responsible for establishing measures to assess program effectiveness and efficiency.

FOCUS psychologists are available 24 hours a day, 7 days a week, 365 days a year. Office hours include evening and weekend appointments to accommodate the various shifts and schedules of police personnel, as well as school schedules.

Confidentiality Methods and Procedures

The foundation of every successful Psychological Services Program is its pledge of confidentiality. Without it, there is no credibility. FOCUS points with pride to the utilization of its services over the past eight years as a testament to the trust San Diego Police Department personnel have in its commitment to professional confidential therapy. Records are kept secure in accordance with professional codes of ethics, federal regulations, and state laws and regulations. Information concerning a client is only released at the client's request with a written release of information, or in instances where releasing information to specific persons or agencies is mandated by California law (such as reports of child or elder abuse, etc.). In any instance where a client is requesting that FOCUS give information to the Department, a copy of the client's written release is sent to the Department.

Records are coded with a case number by a therapist and maintained in locked files. Case numbers are then used by the therapists for all record keeping functions. Statistical information reported from FOCUS providers to ProHealth Management (data collection and processing) do not contain names, therefore all reports to the SDPD by ProHealth are completely anonymous. Reporting formats are designed to insure anonymity, and contain only statistical information that cannot be used to identify any individual. Confidentiality and its limits are discussed with each client during their initial session and delineated in the client information letter given to each client.

In addition to protecting confidentiality of records, several other areas must be addressed when dealing with contracted services between an agency and psychological services providers. The areas are as follows:

PRIVACY OF OFFICES
As six psychologists have their offices at FOCUS' primary location, there is a possibility that an employee could see another employee in the parking lot or waiting room. This possibility is discussed with each client during their initial consultation. If this causes concern, arrangements are made to avoid possible encounters, such as scheduling late, early, or weekend appointments, using alternative parking lots, or scheduling at other locations. The main office in Mission Valley is designed to minimize encounters between employees via separate entrance/lobby area and exit.

COUNSELORS / CONSULTANTS
Another situation unique to contracted services is that FOCUS psychologists function both as therapists to individuals and as consultants to the agency. It is not uncommon for a FOCUS psychologist to serve on the same committee as a counseling client, to have clients in a classroom, to be asked by a client to consult on a supervisory issue, or to pass a client in the hallway at a station. To insure the maintenance of confidentiality, each FOCUS psychologist has the policy of "not speaking unless spoken to." It is believed that it is the client's choice whether or not to be acknowledged, and the therapist's responsibility to avoid any awkward or embarrassing contact with the clients.

MEDIA
Interaction with media is another area where clients may feel their confidential communications can be violated. FOCUS has a firm "No comment!" policy to the media. When the media has contacted FOCUS concerning Department activities or personnel, they are referred to Media Relations. Any exceptions to this policy would be at the expressed direction of the San Diego Police Department.

SUBPOENAS
In some cases, psychological records are subject to subpoenas. The Supreme Court held in *Jafee vs. Redmond* that a police officer's

psychological records cannot be subpoenaed in criminal proceedings. In a civil suit where the plaintiff has asserted psychological harm, psychological records can be subpoenaed. This information is explained to all clients. FOCUS does not release records unless the records are formally subpoenaed, the validity of the subpoena is validated by the FOCUS legal counsel, and the client is informed.

5. FOCUS PSYCHOLOGICAL SERVICES SUPERVISOR / MANAGEMENT GUIDE

All supervisors must occasionally deal with a difficult employee or a difficult situation. How the supervisor deals with employees and converts them into top team members is a critical part of a supervisor's job. The *Supervisors Management Guide* is a learning tool for supervisors on how to combat stress and trauma in law enforcement. The information in the *Guide* is designed to provide an alert about particular stressors relevant to law enforcement and to provide information related to when referrals to FOCUS Psychological Services or your EAP are appropriate.

Problem Recognition for Supervisors

It is necessary to recognize and head off problems before a situation becomes a liability or a discipline issue. Problems likely to occur are:

- Substance abuse or chemical dependency issues.

- Indications of marital or family problems.

- Poor peer relations, continual bickering in the team, polarization of team members, and the "scapegoating" of an employee by the team.

- Poor communications skills with peer and public resulting in increased conflict, poor morale, complaints, aggressive outbursts, and sexual harassment complaints.

- Loss of job interest or "burnout."

- Depression with risk for suicide/homicide/workplace violence.

- Anxiety and stress symptoms resulting in accidents, absenteeism, repeated requests for time off/leaves.

- Change in behavior or mood following a "critical incident."

- Physical illness or an acute accident requiring major emotional and physical readjustments.

Signs of Depression

Depression occurs in 10% of women and 5% of men in the general population. Increased stress and the occupational realities of law enforcement may result in mild to severe depressive episodes in personnel. Some signs of depression are:

- Decreased attention and concentration.
- Complaints of fatigue, no energy, and sleep problems.
- Increased irritability with occasional outbursts of anger which are a change from usual functioning.
- Feelings of worthlessness or guilt, or feeling of being punished for something.
- Difficulty sleeping such that it interferes with work where the person seems "not with it."
- Noticeable withdrawal from others, disinterest in the job activities that used to provide pleasure and motivation, and unusual intimidation towards others.
- Sudden weight loss and change for the worse in general appearance and/or grooming.
- Difficulty making decisions and/or unusual requests for assistance in areas of competence.
- Decrease in overall work performance.
- Feeling hopeless about the future and suicidal thinking or statements such as "Now I understand why some people off themselves."

The supervisor should refer promptly and without punishment or censure to FOCUS Psychological Services or EAP for assessment. The notion that depression can be treated and the employee is neither "crazy" nor "weak" for talking about these problems should be supported.

Critical Incident Stress

A "critical incident" for public safety personnel includes line-of-duty deaths, serious injury to emergency personnel, serious multiple-casualty incidents, suicide of an emergency service provider, traumatic deaths of children, serious injuries to children, events with high media interest, victims known to the emergency services worker, or any event that has a powerful impact on personnel. Following such incidents, interventions by FOCUS Psychological Services psychologists or Peer Support counselors (or both) are either conducted immediately or within 24–48 hours and are called Critical Incident Debriefings (CID).

San Diego Police Dept. Programs

A certain amount of psychological distress following a critical incident is normal. Of more concern is when the distress becomes disabling (4% of involved personnel). Peer pressure and concern for "saving face" will influence some personnel to resume work prematurely. The table below lists some early signs of stress, short-term reactions to a critical incident, and long term reactions to a critical incident.

Early Warning Signs

Behavioral

nervous laughter	starring into space	nervous tic
handwringing	foot tapping	worried look
easily startled	high voice	hyperactivity
yelling	clenched fist	

Physical

pounding heart	tight stomach/throat	short of breath
sweating	trembling	rigid posture
sensory distortion	dizziness	weakness
flushed face		

Psychological

excessive:

sadness	guilt	fear
anger	obsessing	euphoria
agitation	impatience	frustration

Short-Term Reactions

Behavioral

aggressiveness	denial	rapid mood
throwing things	isolates	swings
over-hostility	withdrawal	avoidance of
extreme defensive-	blaming others	duties
ness		

Physical

indigestion	fatigue	nausea
gas	diarrhea	headache
blurred vision	constipation	menstrual
backache	chest pain	problems
irregular heartbeat		

Psychological

depression	grief	despair
emptiness	flashbacks	nightmares
preoccupied	survivor guilt	confusion
hopelessness	poor judgment	poor decisions

Programs   **San Diego Police Dept.**

Long Term Reactions: (Non-Effective Coping)

Behavioral

sexual disturbance	sleep disturbance	overworking
reckless behavior	accident proneness	oversmoking
overdrinking	over/under eating	self-medication
extreme behavior changes		

Physical

ulcers	migraines	colitis
arthritis	hypertension	allergies
heart attack	stroke	weight changes

Psychological

alcohol/drug abuse	job loss	divorce
personality changes	depression	suicidality
violence	homicide	disruption of family

Since reactions that last more than 3-4 weeks can interfere with personal or job functioning, supervisors should become "helpers" by actively listening and pointing out what differences are noticeable in the returning police personnel. If referral to FOCUS Psychological Services or EAP is deemed necessary, supervisors should note the nature of the incident, the intensity of the reactions, and the duration of the reactions. Referrals may be mandatory due to work problems or may be voluntary.

Signs of Chemical Dependency in an Employee

Supervisors need to recognize the subtle signs that individually may seem harmless, but when taken together present a startling picture. Whether or not the employee's problem is chemical dependency is not the supervisor's issue. Diagnosing is best left to the experts. The supervisor's role is to monitor job performance. This sets the concern and expectation that the employee will take responsibility for dealing with the problem, and gives the direction for the next step. The signs of chemical dependency in an employee are:

- Swings in the employee's pace of work, productivity, reliability, and/or attendance manifested as peaks and valleys that progressively become more serious and closer together.

- Deadlines for reports or assignments that are missed, or an overall decrease in quality of work.

- Unreasonable excuses for not getting the job done well.

- Tardiness, lengthy lunches, frequent breaks, early departures, and high use of "excuses" for time off.

- Increased accidents causing minor injuries to self, others, and work equipment/cars.

- Increased physical complaints (fatigue and depression) and medical ailments that cause lost time on the job.

- Irritability, rationalizing, complaining of feeling "picked on", stress and tension, borrowing money from colleagues, lack of attention to detail, decrease in concentration, and promises to "shape up" that are evident only for a short time.

- Complaints from colleagues, partners, or the public that suggest conflict, morale problems, and increased tension within the "team" due to the employee's attitude and behavior.

Often, the employee is aware of the performance problems. A supervisor who confronts a performance problem and insists on improvement, but confronts with caring ("You are important and I want you to succeed.") will be more successful than one who uses the time to berate, order, or impose. Above all, a supervisor should not enable the situation by denying or covering up the problem.

Resources: Refer to EAP, FOCUS Psychological Services, Department Services, A.A., Alanon, ACA, CODA.

Absenteeism

Absenteeism forces supervisors to deal with problems of morale, discipline, job dissatisfaction, job stress, team spirit, productivity, turnover, additional administration duties, and overhead costs. How does a supervisor quantify and deal with an absentee problem when it hides among legitimate leaves?

1. Measure and track absenteeism.

2. Discuss absentee issues with employees.

3. Tie compensation to work hours.

4. Help employees maintain and/or improve attendance records.

5. Reward good attendance records.

6. Utilize fair and justifiable discipline so you don't prompt employees to "resist" by using absenteeism.

7. Carefully match employees to jobs and support them.

8. Promote safety and health.

9. Lead by your own example.

10. Give positive feedback.

11. Recognize that a major supervisory role is to facilitate the work of subordinates.

12. Use active listening skills and demonstrate loyalty to staff.

13. Keep the team informed. Encourage and demonstrate healthy conflict resolution and discourage "bickering."

14. Analyze new ideas and suggestions by the team and help make them work when feasible.

15. Make every team member the boss of something.

16. Recognize that absenteeism due to chemical dependency, depression, or work stress needs to be evaluated by experts. Let a referral to EAP or FOCUS Psychological Services be a form of support, not punishment.

Reprimands

When the unpleasant task of reprimanding errant employees comes up, what supervisors don't do is often more important than what they do. Unprepared supervisors may overreact to a situation.

Frequently, team members become defensive when they are receiving criticism, and they fail to hear and understand the suggestions being made to them. To help avoid this, follow these guidelines when having to confront a supervisee:

- Don't ever attack anyone personally. Just address the problem at hand and be specific about what was incorrect. Separate a person's behavior from their personality.

- Don't "save up" critiques. The best time to deal with problems is immediately after the incorrect behavior or action has occurred. Waiting a week and then throwing in other problems observed will lessen the impact and the accumulated griefs will only make for more resentment.

- Don't threaten! This will either immobilize your employee with fear or cause considerable resentment. Just point out the error and then reaffirm their position on the team by telling them they're OK. It's only their actions that need modification.

- Don't rebuke in public. Do it privately. Determine whether he or she knew better. If not, then the person is obviously unfamiliar with the assigned task and needs training or encouragement.

San Diego Police Dept.   **Programs**

- Don't criticize a beginner. It will only cause confusion and discouragement. Help or redirect the person who is having a problem.

- If the problem revolves around self-esteem, don't criticize. In this situation, the proper supervisorial style is to be supportive. The person needs more training, practice, and support from an understanding supervisor.

- Always remember that a manager should only reprimand deliberate, regressive performance or behavior. When needing to deal with these types of employees, be prepared, professional, and prompt in action. At the same time, convey interest in them as people and show the way to success.

Sexual Harassment in the Workplace

In 1980, the Equal Employment Opportunity Commission (EEOC) issued guidelines whereupon the Supreme Court stated these guidelines should be accorded the same weight as laws. According to the guidelines, sexual harassment is described as "unwelcome sexual advances, requests for sexual favors, and other verbal or physical conduct of a sexual nature." These behaviors then have the effect of interfering in an individual's work performance or create an intimidating, hostile, or offensive working environment.

Typical Forms of Harassment

Verbal / Visual

Bawdy jokes, off color remarks	Leers, unwanted propositions
Threats, passes, pin-ups	Unwanted sexual compliments
sexualized cartoons/photos	Repeated requests for dates
Wearing revealing attire	or sexual favors

Physical

Unwanted touching	Unwanted brushing against
Standing too close	another's body
Physical attack	Excessively "lengthy" handshakes

Since more women have joined the workplace, they have moved into jobs traditionally held by males. The "balance" is shifting, and sexual harassment is one result of this shift. Sexual harassment by men may be a response to a real or imagined loss of power. When committed by a woman against a man, it may be an expression of retaliation and/or a flexing of newfound power.

When it comes to sexual harassment, an ounce of prevention is worth a pound of cure. The results of sexual harassment are expensive—lawsuits, terrible publicity, and the destruction of an organization's image that took years to build, causes low morale and results in angry, humiliated people who don't perform well.

Although sexual harassment is illegal, its elimination will come through organizational and individual commitment, not the courts. Most people want a safe and secure workplace, free from intimidation and fear. An organization can take an important step toward creating a safe, secure, positive work environment by implementing a strong sexual harassment policy.

Implementing the Sexual Harassment Policy involves the following:

A. *Communication*: There should be permanent posting on bulletin boards of:

memos;
articles in the organization's internal publications;
meetings; and
training.

B. *Training*: The complexities and subtleties of confronting and preventing harassment require training. The organization will decide whether to use a pre-packaged training or develop one of its own. Classroom training with on-the-job feedback is helpful. The ultimate goal is to give individuals support, training, and reinforcement to develop and consistently use effective interpersonal skills with all people regardless of gender, ethnicity, or other differences.

C. *Counseling*: Rarely will a supervisor possess the expertise to provide in-depth counseling. Even if the person is emotionally sound and carefully lays out the facts, it is advisable to suggest referral sources. Use EAP or FOCUS Psychological Services or the Grievance procedure.

When an individual comes to a supervisor with a complaint of sexual harassment, the supervisor should:

- Be supportive and use empathy.

- Carefully explain the procedures that will be followed.

- Emphasize that the complaint is serious and will be handled as such.

- Explain that separate counseling is available and tell where to find it.

- Explain the procedure and offer to initiate the process when he or she is not the appropriate person to investigate the complaint.

San Diego Police Dept. **Programs**

These complaints must be handled with privacy and dignity. Handling the complaints internally is far more preferable than the person seeking outside help (attorneys, federal/state administrative agencies).

A lot of the subtle behavior that might be tagged harassment continues to occur because the harasser has never been told that his or her behavior is affecting others. As a supervisor, concentrate on the behavior in question, not the harasser's character or personality when you reprimand.

Catastrophic Illnesses

Law enforcement occupations entail the risk of serious injury, illness, or death. In addition, new illnesses have developed that may affect law enforcement agencies. These illnesses are HIV, ARC, and AIDS.

In dealing with employees having these diseases, the first step is to ask the individual how open he or she is to others knowing information about his or her situation. The issue of confidentiality is the main concern and may not be violated unless the individual gives consent.

The American Disabilities Act stipulates that "reasonable accommodation" must be made to the infected employee. This may require light duty, special assignments, teaching versus more physically active work, etc. Whether the cause is injury or AIDS, the reasonable accommodation approach is generally cost effective and yields a "good image" for the organization.

Some agencies have a catastrophic illness program in place. This program may mandate specific forms, and allowance for other employees to donate sick time, vacation time, etc. to "fund" the affected individual's benefits. This permits others to feel they are helping in some way, and the process is confidential.

Sometimes debriefings are useful. This is where colleagues meet with a FOCUS psychologist and their supervisor to discuss their concerns, fears, feelings, and questions. This is necessary to honor and accommodate the team.

J. CATCH A FALLING STAR
LAW ENFORCEMENT ASSISTANCE PROGRAM
FOR OFFICERS AND THEIR FAMILIES, INC.
Cynthia L. Goss, President

Cynthia L. Goss is currently the president of Catch a Falling Star Law Enforcement Assistance Program for Officers and Their Families, Incorporated. Hired in 1987 by the County of Erie to reorganize their Employee Assistance Program for approximately 10,000 employees, her jurisdiction included the County's Sheriff's Department and Correctional Facility. Ms. Goss found they were doing well with all departments except the law enforcement agencies. This is what encouraged her to develop this specialized law enforcement assistance program for all law enforcement personnel in Western New York, which is available to officers including city, county, and state police agencies; international law enforcement agencies; correctional officers; probation/parole officers; college and university campus police; law enforcement retirees; and new recruits in training.

"Catch a Falling Star" has been cited by the Associated Press as one of America's most successful EAPs. Ms. Goss has served as a consultant to local and national television programs which have focused on law enforcement, numerous U.S. and Canadian law enforcement agencies, and has helped define the standards for law enforcement stress programs. Examples of her involvement include HBO's *Under Cover Series Program*, "Memphis P.D. War on the Streets," and a documentary developed by ABC's *Prime Time Live* on the topic of police suicide. She has been published in the "LEAA Advocate: Law Enforcement Alliance of America Magazine", Summer-Fall Issue 1997, and the "On Patrol Magazine" Fall Issue 1996.

Ms. Goss' specialized Law Enforcement Assistance Program stands as a model program for other law enforcement agencies in the United States as indicated by the National Institute for Justice in their publication released by Washington titled; "How to Develop Law Enforcement Assistance Programs for Officers and Their Families."

In conjunction with Doctor Grady Bray, a noted disaster psychologist, Ms. Goss has developed the Comprehensive Program for Law Enforcement Stress known as CPLES. The two have lectured internationally on the development of specialized law enforcement assistance programs, stress management programs for management and personnel, and the development of critical incident stress debriefing teams.

The logo "Catch A Falling Star" came out of a question Ms. Goss was often asked: "How do you save these guys?" Her response was: "You have to catch them before they fall!" The star signifies every and any law enforcement officer's badge. Her program is outlined below.

1. "CATCH A FALLING STAR"

Catch A Falling Star Law Enforcement Assistance Program for Officers and Their Families, Inc., offers a comprehensive array of services to officers and their family members with the focus on health, stability, and productivity. The objective of this program is to help officers cope with their personal problems that affect their workplace performance.

The foremost belief is that an officer is the single most important resource within any law enforcement agency. However, billions of dollars each year are lost due to rising costs of health care, on-the-job accidents, absenteeism, tardiness, personnel turnover, stress-related injuries, and excessive use of disability/compensation benefits.

"Catch a Falling Star" has been designed to counter these issues in an economical and efficient manner, thereby reducing these escalating costs. Issues addressed include, but are not limited to: alcohol/drug abuse, mental health related issues, physical fitness, financial/legal issues, domestic violence, marital discord, family related issues, health and nutrition, stress management, crisis intervention, critical incident stress, post-shooting trauma, and suicide.

The extensive experience of "Catch A Falling Star" has proven it is a confidential, professionally accountable organization that can easily assimilate varied client needs by providing the cohesive linkage between labor-management and employee concerns. The major purpose for the development of the program is to provide law enforcement officers with an objective and non-judgmental resource to which they can turn for advice and assistance in working out their personal problems. The problems the program is concerned with are job-related ones that decrease the officer's effectiveness or increase the likelihood of his or her being impaired or killed in the line of duty. No officer who sincerely seeks assistance with any problem will be turned away, regardless of the nature or magnitude of his or her problem. In fact, a major goal of the program is to help the officer learn to handle his or her problems before the problems reach the severity that loss of family and/or job may occur.

"Catch A Falling Star" has staff personnel who are motivated and highly experienced professionals having firsthand knowledge of all facets of employee assistance programming, human resources, labor-management, substance abuse counseling, and health care administration program evaluation. They maintain direct contact, helping to mold and modify program needs to best suit each individual's needs, thereby ensuring program efficiency. In coordination with the staff is a specific linkage network system composed of credentialed counselors, including psychiatrists, psychologists, licensed social workers, board certified alcoholism/substance abuse counselors, physicians, attorneys, and financial management consultants, to name a few.

The most successful EAPs consist of those whose management staff, employee (union) representatives, and employees fully understand and promote the utilization of all services provided. Therefore, the need to orientate on each organizational level becomes apparent.

Manager, Supervisor and Employee Representative Training

Introduction of program specifics are reviewed and are aimed at helping supervisors and employee representatives recognize and better understand problems on the job and how to utilize the EAP effectively. Problem employee identification is essential as early detection of behavioral manifestations can avoid costly deterioration of employee work performance. A supervisor's constant contact with officers can provide a vital link to the success of EAP. Areas covered in orientation include:

> How and when to refer to EAP.
> The importance of documentation.
> Signs and symptoms of problems.
> The importance of confidentiality.
> Voluntary vs. supervisory referral.
> Incorporation of disciplinary action.
> Topics/questions of concern, etc.

Employee Training

Introduction of program specifics are reviewed illustrating how the Employee Assistance Program relates to employees and their immediate family members. A unique aspect of this service is the stress placed on family involvement within the program with the belief that the health of the family unit is important to the health and well-being of the officer. Areas covered include:

> Who pays for it?
> Who can use the EAP?
> What services are available?
> Confidentiality.
> Voluntary vs. supervisory referral.
> Family and the EAP.
> Topics/questions of concern, etc.

Intake Procedure

Officers, their family members, employee representatives, and managerial staff can contact the EAP Monday through Friday from the hours of 9 a.m. to 5 p.m. Emergency calls are handled on an immediate basis through beeper contact 24 hours a day, 7 days a week. Each individual is eligible for unlimited use of the EAP services as needed. Upon contact, an appointment is scheduled within 72 hours for a face-to-face consultation with an EAP staff member to address the presenting problem(s).

Assessment

During the initial appointment, the EAP staff utilizes assessment instruments such as self-identification, supervisor's documentation, past medical and/or mental case history, and/or psychosocial assessments to determine the appropriate actions or interventions needed. Short-term counseling may continue within the EAP organization if appropriate, or, if necessary, a referral will be made to the level of specialized treatment required. EAP assessment of the problem before referral to treatment or rehabilitation can contain needless expensive or overly intensive treatment.

Case Management and Quality Assurance

The President of Catch A Falling Star Law Enforcement Assistance Program Inc., oversees counseling and training activities and develops basic guidelines of operation which ensure quality through a formal evaluation process, including peer review and supervisory feedback, questionnaire, and client-user program evaluation. In addition to a set of procedural guidelines for delivery of service, a staff member must develop individual service plans appropriate to a client's specific problems. In development of these plans, accurate, current and pertinent documentation must be made regarding all services provided. All activity is guided primarily by the principle of promoting human welfare and well-being.

Follow-Up Services

Clinical follow-up assessments are performed on all clients within the program. Tracking the well-being of problematic employees with careful current and future evaluations help to facilitate a permanent solution to their presenting problems.

Organizational Tracking

Bi-annual utilization reports are furnished upon request from any participating agency or department. Current quantitative statistics are provided along with areas of service usage while still allowing for the confidentiality of participants. Data collection is secured in locked files by EAP staff.

Program Awareness and Promotion

"Catch A Falling Star" actively promotes and builds awareness through promotional material developed to maintain program visibility. Materials include EAP brochures introducing the program, *Supervisor's Manual* guide, posters, business cards, and periodic payroll stuffers.

Areas of Service

- One-On-One counseling
- Information, assessment and referral
- Mental health issues
- Physical fitness
- Health and nutrition
- Financial/Legal issues
- Marital discord
- Family related issues
- Alcohol/Substance abuse
- Domestic violence
- Crisis management
- Stress management workshop
- Post-Traumatic stress syndrome
- Educational awareness seminars
- Suicide intervention/education
- Peer officer support program
- Self-Help support groups
- Spiritual guidance

Confidentiality Policy

It is the policy of the Program that a firm, absolute guarantee of confidentiality for all participants be maintained. No individual group, organization, department, City, or County official or agency shall have access to any information regarding any individual's participation in the Program. Neither the President or EAP staff members discuss any fact or aspect of an individual's participation unless specifically requested to do so in writing by the participant. All information shall be considered privileged and will not be available to any department or any other agency for disciplinary proceedings.

Anonymity

The President of the Program, Ms. Goss, maintains only those records of participation that are essential to the orderly administration of the Program. Further, she insures all records and files are kept confidential at all times. The record of an officer's participation is absolutely restricted to the officer, EAP staff member and the President. No exceptions!

Records

Records are necessary and important in a program such as this. Most staff members will be called upon to deal initially with a variety of social and emotional problems with limited expertise in mental health care. Their intake assessment of a participant's problem will be a crucial factor in the speed and effectiveness at which a problem is resolved.

By the maintenance of minimal, confidential, and anonymous records, the staff will be enabled to: monitor their own performance and critically assess their work through consultation and consulting professionals from the community; decrease the likelihood of oversights or judgment errors in recommended care; and provide a basis for which the Program can justify the need for supplies and funds for additional personnel.

Office Location

Catch A Falling Star Law Enforcement Assistance Program Inc., is centrally located and conducive to providing a professional and therapeutic setting away from all law enforcement agencies. All participants are pre-screened prior to admittance into the Program's office location or activities.

Professional Services and Referral Agencies

Various human service organizations and professionals are utilized for immediate, intermittent, and aftercare of officers as needed. Staff members carefully pre-screen these helping agencies and professionals to find key personnel who will best serve the needs of the LAW-EAP program. All referrals made to both inpatient and outpatient alcohol/substance abuse and psychiatric programs will be pre-screened and placed in specialized programs designed to address the unique stresses associated with law enforcement officers. Referrals are made based on each individual officer's health care benefit while matching those benefits to the agencies appropriate and taking into consideration the officer's geographic location.

Resource Staff

The Program has a resource program consisting of psychiatrists, psychologists, clergy members, and other professionals who are available to EAP staff members for emergency consultations when serious and/or difficult situations arise. These professionals are also available to provide training programs and seminars periodically to officers and their family members. All professionals associated with the LAW-EAP program are required to complete a training program to include the completion and certification of the Jeffrey Mitchell/Grady Bray Model on Critical Incident Stress Response and the CISD debriefing process.

Who Can Participate?

It is a safe assumption that if an officer is having problems at home, it is more likely it will effect his or her job performance. To preclude these problems from the Program's scope would be folly. Therefore, it is the policy of the "Catch A Falling Star" program that all officers and their family members have complete usage of the LAW-EAP as a resource.

The Program is available to officers including:
City, county and state police agencies;
Federal enforcement officers;
International law enforcement agencies;
Correctional officers;
Probation/Parole officers;
College and university campus police;
Law enforcement recruits; and
New recruits in training.

K. METRO-DADE POLICE DEPARTMENT COMPREHENSIVE PSYCHOLOGICAL SERVICES MIAMI, FLORIDA
Scott W. Allen, Ph.D.

1. PERSONAL PROFILE

Dr. Scott W. Allen is an accomplished scholar with degrees in many areas. He obtained a B.A. in Psychology from Notre Dame, an M.Ed. in Counseling Psychology from the University of Georgia, and a Ph.D. in Clinical and Counseling Psychology with supporting work in Rehabilitation Counseling from the University of North Carolina at Chapel Hill. His Graduate pre-doctoral internships were completed at the University of North Carolina and the Yale School of Medicine at the Veterans Administration Medical Center, West Haven, Connecticut. He is honored with 24 individual and unit commendations from the Metro-Dade Police Department, and has served as Chair for the American Psychological Association, and President for the Council on Police Psychological Services.

At present, not only does Dr. Allen have his own private practice in Coral Gables, Florida, but he is a consultant for the Bay Harbor Islands Police Department and the Golden Beach Police Department also located in Florida. He is the primary psychologist for the Critical Incident Program, United States Border Patrol, Detroit/Canada Sector, and a consultant for the U.S. Customs Service where his responsibilities include post-trauma intervention, stress reduction training, clinical referral, and consultation to departmental staff. He consults many Federal agencies, including the FBI, ATF, and Customs, in areas of hostage negotiation, anti-terrorism, post trauma, and psychological profiling of criminals.

Dr. Allen is a consultant and board member for the Advocates for Victim's Assistance, Governor's Task Force on Adolescent and Youth Suicide, and Safe-Net Task Force/Switchboard of Miami. He is a committee member and consultant for the Office of Minority Business, Psychological Pre-Screening of Police Applicants/Metro-Dade County, and the United Way Task Force on Youth Suicide, Miami, and script and technical consultant for Miami Vice Productions, Inc., Miami, Florida. Not only is he a published author, but Dr. Allen's extensive research produced papers discussing such topics as the role of the police psychologist, critical incident stress debriefing, and hostage negotiators and successful negotiation outcomes, to name a few.

As police psychologist for Health Services Section, Metro-Dade Police Department in Miami, Florida, Dr. Allen is responsible for the supervision of subordinate police health professionals, and for the application of professional psychological principles, theories, and techniques to a variety of problems and situations encountered in the provision of metropolitan area police services. His responsibilities include individual, marital, and family intervention and providing 24-hour consultation on behavioral approaches in dealing with disturbed and/or criminal personalities including hostage, barricaded, or suicidal subject situations. He is involved with anti-terrorism interventions, training and supervision of the Department's hostage negotiation team, psychological evaluation, wellness program, and police training programs.

Dr. Allen is also an expert witness in forensic psychology, providing advisory assistance in personnel management, referrals for departmental personnel and their families, crisis intervention, advising on stress management and police recruitment screening, and providing didactic experiences to the Police Academy and the in-service Training Bureau. The Comprehensive Psychological Services program which is utilized by the Metro-Dade Police Department in Miami, Florida, follows.

2. COMPREHENSIVE PSYCHOLOGICAL SERVICES PROGRAM

Background

Law enforcement involves a broad range of situations requiring understanding and control of human behavior. Emotional stability in the face of stressful situations is a prime requirement for effective police action. Comprehensive psychological services provide support for these tasks through the following approaches:

Applicant Screening: Screen out police applicants not considered psychologically suitable for the law enforcement occupation, and screen in those applicants desirable for the position.

Professional Assistance: Through voluntary or mandatory identification, provide short-term counseling and referral service to departmental employees experiencing stress-induced or other emotional problems.

Early Identification: Identify personnel with emotional or stress-related problems before performance is seriously affected.

Policy and Action

In order to maintain a stable and well-adjusted workforce and to provide the community with the best possible service, Metro-Dade Police Department (MDPD) commits to screening out police applicants who possess exclusionary traits considered excessive by psychological standards, assists departmental employees who experience stress-induced or other emotional problems, and evaluates employees with performance problems who may require assistance from the Psychological Services Program. A standard operating procedure titled Comprehensive Psychological Services has been established to reduce the incidence of emotional or stress-related problems among departmental employees by providing psychological testing of police applicants, professional counseling assistance, and in-service screening and training programs to personnel.

3. PSYCHOLOGICAL SCREENING AND TESTING REGULATIONS

General

Under the purview of the Personnel Management Bureau, psychological testing is utilized as a criterion for screening police applicants. The testing is conducted after a conditional offer of employment has been made.

Recruitment Phase

All phases of the screening and selection process are explained to applicants; *e.g.*, psychological testing, physical examination, and background investigation. Applicants are advised that psychological testing is an integral element of the screening and selection process. Testing is accomplished concurrently with the requirement for successfully passing the merit system examination, oral interview, physical examination, and background investigation.

Test Location
Psychological testing is conducted at a location which is convenient to applicants and the Department. The applicant is notified in writing by the Personnel Management Bureau of the date and location for taking the test.

Test Administration
Psychological tests are administered and evaluated under the direction of a licensed psychologist who is experienced in psychological testing.

Psychological Standards Criteria and Test Scoring
The screening process utilizes test batteries and evaluation procedures to identify and screen out individuals who possess certain mental conditions considered excessive by professionally accepted psychological standards. Raw test scores are evaluated by the testing psychologist, and a summary report is forwarded to the Personnel Management Bureau within two weeks where it is maintained on file.

Exclusionary Factors
Mental conditions considered excessive that are exclusionary include, but are not limited to, the following:

- Psychosis
- Character disorders
- Neurosis
- Mood disorders
- Poor impulse control
- Need for very high levels of excitement
- Tendency to be very passive or aggressive, especially during conflict
- Strong racial, religious, or ethnic prejudice

Continued Employment Consideration
Based on the psychologist's written report assessing exclusionary factors, the following actions will result:

1. The applicant's file is forwarded for background investigation if the report contains no exclusionary factors; or

2. The applicant will not be considered for employment if the report contains exclusionary factors.

Written notification by the Personnel Management Bureau informing the applicant that he or she is no longer being considered for employment is made within two weeks from receipt of the report. If requested, reasons for the decision will be provided.

Special Provisions

The Administrative Services Division Chief may require supplemental psychological testing pursuant to identified exclusionary factors, or additional background data as may be required to make a final determination of employment suitability. Appeals of decisions at all phases of the selection process are available to the applicant in accordance with established departmental procedures.

4. PSYCHOLOGICAL SERVICES PROGRAM

General

The Personnel Management Bureau's Health Services Section provides professional counseling on a voluntary basis, and referral assistance for management of stress-induced or substance abuse problems.

Program Functions

Health Services Section staff members provide the following services to departmental personnel:

- Short-term counseling of sworn and non-sworn personnel, referral to outside professional sources for extended counseling, or, upon request by the affected employee, referral to the Department's police chaplains for pastoral counseling.

- Availability on a 24-hour basis for emergencies such as on-scene response to shootings or other serious incidents involving police personnel. Personnel involved may voluntarily consult with program staff.

- Consultation concerning situations involving hostages, barricaded subjects, attempted suicides, and, when necessary, participation in the negotiation process.

- Consultation concerning crisis situations involving police personnel.

- Assistance to employees observed demonstrating uncharacteristic performance errors or a decline in job performance.

- Development of intradepartmental procedures required for program administration.

- Through consultation with appropriate supervisory personnel, assist them with behavior-related issues concerning their employees.

- Design or assist in the design of research programs which apply behavioral sciences to law enforcement and community needs, training, organizational development, and related areas.

- Consultation concerning the application of behavioral science to management, crisis intervention, investigation, and training.

- Instruction in various courses relating to the application of behavioral sciences.

- Assist Training Bureau with the design and implementation of training programs for sworn and non-sworn personnel.

- Assist in the design and development of specialized programs for departmental elements.

In coordination with the police academy, the Department provides recruit trainees access to psychological counseling services. This service is discussed during the first day of Basic Law Enforcement training by the training advisor.

Voluntary Participation

Employees are encouraged to seek professional consultation from Health Services Section to alleviate stress-induced, emotional, or relationship problems. Regarding voluntary participation in the Program:

1. The Department does not request or require Health Services Section staff to furnish information resulting from voluntary participation.

2. Health Services Section staff may advise the concerned supervisor of the contact only when permission has been given by the affected employee. Information concerning the diagnosis of treatment of any voluntary participant may not be requested by supervisors.

3. The Department does not initiate an investigation or complaint based on an employee request for professional assistance. However, such voluntary participation does not preclude prosecution or disciplinary action which may result from a related investigation or complaint.

4. At the request of an employee, the following may be provided:
   a. General information concerning psychological services.
   b. Short-term counseling regarding personal problems.
   c. Information regarding outside counseling service, costs, and insurance coverage.

5. When it becomes necessary for an employee to be absent from the workplace during duty hours, supervisors accept the

notification from Health Services Section staff as valid confirmation of the employee's expected availability for duty.

Conflict Resolution/Team Building

This voluntary service provides for mediation sessions or team building sessions between employees or the employee and the supervisor. The Health Services Section serves to clarify the problematical issues of the interpersonal conflict, elicit options, and contract a resolution. The concerned supervisor can approve this service.

This process is an alternative to other counseling solutions and is designed to assist with targeting optional resolutions. The conflict resolution/team building session is utilized to resolve personal differences concerning work-related matters. This process is not used to mediate issues which have resulted in litigation with the employee or the Department, a union action, or a Professional Compliance Bureau investigation.

Supervisory Intervention

Supervisors should remain alert for continued job performance problems, and encourage employees to maintain acceptable standards of performance. When a supervisor observes a continuing performance problem, he or she contacts Health Services Section for consultation concerning use of an intervention or other options to correct the problem.

The supervisory intervention services is a voluntary counseling session facilitated by the Health Services Section staff and is not utilized for psychological evaluation of the employee. The service is provided to assist the supervisor and the employee in the resolution of problems which may be symptomatic of underlying personal or interpersonal problems that are manifested in job performance. This service is considered by supervisors when all other means of counseling and performance discussions have proven unsuccessful. However, this is a separate issue and is not associated with disciplinary procedures or considered an alternative to discipline. It is used only to address less than satisfactory employee performance which is based solely on observable deficient or deteriorating job performance.

A Health Services Section staff member facilitates supervisory intervention sessions in order to:

1. Articulate the observable performance errors and the declining job performance in specific terms.

2. Outline expectancies for desired performance change.

3. Agree on a time frame for instituting the desired changes.

4. Clarify between the employee and the supervisor any other peripheral issues which may affect the desired outcome.

5. Agree upon the amount or degree of feedback provided to the supervisor during the interim period and appropriate supervisory feedback to the employee on his or her progress.

The supervisory counseling session is conducted utilizing informal counseling guidelines. If the supervisor does not see satisfactory improvement within agreed upon time limits, additional action must be considered.

Mandatory Referral

If, in the opinion of a supervisor, actions of an employee indicate that psychological or psychiatric evaluation is required in order to make a determination regarding the employee's fitness for duty, the concerned district or bureau commander, supervisor or an office reporting to the Director's Office, or higher departmental authority can direct the employee to submit to such evaluation. The employee must answer all questions directed to him or her, and provide complete information and documents requested by Health Services Section or an outside consultant to whom the employee is referred. The employee must submit to all examinations considered necessary by Health Services Section or an outside consultant, and sign any waivers granting access to records and reports that may be prepared or generated by Health Services Section or an outside consultant.

The directing authority consults with Health Services Section staff and determines the appropriateness of mandatory referral into the program. If mandatory referral is deemed appropriate, the directing authority advises the employee via memorandum of the general circumstances that prompted the action and the appointment date, time, and location.

When deemed necessary, Health Services Staff arranges for outside psychological testing and evaluation consultation. Evaluation results, opinions, and recommendations made by an outside consultant are forwarded to the appropriate Health Services Section staff member. The staff member interprets the results and contacts the directing authority. The directing authority, upon the advice of the Health Services Section staff member, may initiate appropriate action predicated on the recommendations.

When deemed necessary by Health Services Section staff or outside consultants to whom the employee was referred, the directing authority may request the employee to attend and successfully complete a therapeutic or counseling program approved by Health Services Section staff. Failure to attend and successfully complete the program is considered in determination of personnel action.

Metro-Dade Police Dept. **Programs**

Communications between affected employees and Health Services Section staff or outside consultants, test results, written opinions and recommendations, notes, reports, and actions taken, are not privileged and become departmental records. These documents are distributed and maintained as follows:

1. Originals go to the concerned program administrator.

2. Copies go to the concerned employee upon a verbal request to program administrators.

3. Requests for information, as part of official departmental investigations, are directed to the Personnel Management Bureau Commander.

Temporary relief from duty with pay, reassignment, or return to duty after temporary relief is decided by the concerned commander/supervisor based on consultation with Health Services Section staff.

Post-Shooting or Other Traumatic Incident Counseling

1. An on-call member of the Health Services Section is included as part of the Homicide Bureau Police Shooting Team and responds to the scene for the benefit of involved officers. This service exists solely for the benefit of the concerned employee.

2. All efforts to provide for the emotional well-being of the involved officer is made without jeopardizing the crime scene or investigation. The responsibility of balancing the urgency of the concerned officer's immediate needs with investigative requirements rests with the Police Shooting Team Command Officer. A decision concerning these issues is rendered following a conference between the Police Shooting Team Command Officer and the Health Services Section staff member.

3. Health Services Section staff is available for officers and their immediate family as may be needed following the initial contact.

4. Health Services Section staff is advised of significant changes in the case prior to notification of the officer; *i.e.*, death of injured subject, or identification of shooting officer when multiple shooters are involved.

5. The concerned commander may temporarily reassign the employee to administrative duties based upon the commander's assessment of the situation, at the request of the affected employee, or at the advice of the Health Services Section staff member.

6. When an employee is involved in other job-related incidents of a severe nature or exposed to an extreme emotionally debilitating event, as soon as circumstances permit, the concerned

commander advises Health Services Section staff of the incident; *i.e.*, serious physical injury, officer is fired upon, severe accident, or significant physical contact or trauma. It is the concerned commander's decision whether or not to temporarily reassign the employee to administrative duties.

Health Services Section staff provides assistance which may be required by the employee due to stress-induced problems resulting from the incident. If the employee requires hospitalization, Health Services Section staff coordinates with the hospital staff to provide an environment most conducive to the employee's recovery.

Management Consultation
Supervisors, commanders, and higher departmental authorities may request technical assistance relative to: personal management style and its impact on subordinates; personnel management problems existing in their respective command area; and other problems related to their respective duties and functions.

Confidentiality
Health Services Section staff and/or any person participating in the diagnosis or treatment under their direction, maintain in confidence communication made by a client in the context of such services, except by a written permission or in the face of a clear and immediate probability of bodily harm to the client or others.

5. INTRADEPARTMENTAL STRESS OR PERFORMANCE-RELATED PROGRAMS

General
Ad hoc programs have been developed by departmental elements to identify stress-induced or performance problems and to provide assistance through resources available from the Psychological Services Program. These programs work in conjunction with, but are not within the purview of, the Psychological Services Program.

Early Identification System
Established under the purview of the Professional Compliance Bureau (PCB), the System provides a systematic review of complaints and Use of Force incidents among departmental employees. Utilized in conjunction with other criteria, the determination of problems that may or may not be stress or performance related is accomplished.

Employee Profile System
Instituted and operated by PCB, the system establishes a data collection source profiling departmental employees to identify patterns of stress-induced or performance problems. Profile criteria include: complaints, Use of Force incidents, commendations, correctional action, and promotional status change.

Metro-Dade Police Dept. **Programs**

Profile reports are reviewed by immediate supervisors as deemed necessary. The concerned commander or designee reviews profile reports annually, in conjunction with other criteria, to identify problems.

Action Alternatives
Based on profile reports and relevant data, the following results:

1. Referral to the Psychological Services Program for counseling or referral assistance.

2. Participation in the Stress Abatement Program for training assistance.

3. Correctional action.

4. Assessment that no problem exists, terminating further action.

Stress Abatement Program
Under the purview of the Training Bureau, the program consists of a 40-hour block of courses designed to provide educational resources to departmental employees for assistance in effective stress management. Program emphasis includes a comprehensive overview of approaches to stress management and the nature of police stress. Employees participate voluntarily or may be requested to attend by immediate supervisors.

L. FEDERAL BUREAU OF INVESTIGATION

1. BACKGROUND
Fidelity, Bravery, Integrity. The three words that form the foundation upon which the men and women of the FBI strive for excellence and perfection in their pursuit of investigative responsibilities. It is this standard and the commitment to excellence and professionalism that defines the FBI. But, it is not without a price. The only true asset, the only thing of value within the FBI, is its people. For it is the people who are the FBI, who everyday willingly go in harm's way to protect our nation's way of life and its citizens. And, it is because of the men and women of the FBI who do the living, working, and dying, that the current Employee Assistance, Peer Support, Critical Incident Debriefing, and Chaplain's Program exist. But that was not always the case. An old Bureau axiom said that, "we do our best work on each other, we eat our young, and after a critical incident, we send out the goons to bayonet the survivors." Many on the job today think back over the past 20 some odd years and recall individuals that they have known who have encountered organizational and managerial insensitivity to real life problems that impacted an individual's job performance and, sometimes, shortened their career. Supervisory Special Agent Chuck McCormick is one of those individuals with such memories.

In 1982, while assigned to the New York City Office of the FBI, then Special Agent (SA) McCormick made a commitment, based on personal observation and experience, to ensure that something was done to take care of their own. As an organization, the FBI was accomplishing the one thing that the KGB, the Mafia, the street gangs, and killers could never accomplish, and that was to destroy the will to work. Individuals were treated with indifference and insensitivity regarding catastrophic life experiences impacting their lives. Very dedicated and talented individuals were being punished for situations that were beyond their control. Granted, conduct and behavior are components of judgment, and there are many instances where FBI Agents have demonstrated atrocious judgment, but the acknowledgment of human fallibility was not part of the Bureau disciplinary system.

One such area of disinterest was alcohol-related accidents and misconduct. The consistent response to this type of situation usually involved some form of administrative sanction or punishment, but rarely, if ever, was the underlying root cause of the infraction probed. In 1982, SA McCormick joined a very few, but dedicated, individuals who had a problem with alcohol, and whose lives had become unmanageable. It became the defining moment of SA McCormick's FBI career. By 1988, SA McCormick had transferred to Los Angeles. With a directive from the Department of Justice to create an Employee Assistance Program, SA McCormick became a pioneer in the FBI's program, participating in the original policy writing and becoming the first full-time EAP Coordinator in an FBI field office. Subsequently, SA McCormick returned to UCLA Graduate School where he completed a postgraduate program as a Certified Alcohol and Drug Counselor (CADA) and subsequently attained the internationally recognized credential as a Certified Employee Assistance Professional (CEAP). Working diligently with other members of the EAP throughout the FBI, as well as the renowned Behavioral Science Unit at the FBI Academy, SA McCormick combined his skills and counseling with those of the Critical Incident Debriefing Program, and became the only field agent selected to be on the Chaplain's Program Advisory Board at the time of its inception.

In November 1993, SA McCormick was selected by his peers from the EAP Advisory Group to make a presentation to newly appointed FBI Director Louie Freeh. Following this presentation, Director Freeh selected SA McCormick to be the first EAP Administrator and Chief of the soon-to-be-created Employee Assistance Unit. Director Freeh gave Unit Chief McCormick the order to: "Do whatever it takes to take care of our own." Empowered by Director Freeh with direct and immediate access as necessary, Unit Chief McCormick went about the task of designing and implementing a global Employee Assistance Program comprised of the integration of EAP, Critical Incident Stress Debriefing, Peer Support, and the Chaplain's Program. This program was accessible and responsive to all 25,000 employees and their immediate family members, which total 100,000 people, assigned to all 50 states and 33 foreign countries. This program, which began as a personal commitment on the part of SA McCormick and a few other very dedicated individuals to "take care of our wounded," is now recognized by the Department of Justice as the premier law enforcement Employee Assistance Program and has become the model after which other federal law enforcement agencies fashion their programs.

After 28 years in the FBI, SA McCormick's investigative experience, as well as his commitment and dedication to the FBI family, have been rewarded with his current assignment as the Supervisory Special Agent in Austin, Texas, in charge of violent crime, drug, and counter-terrorism investigations. SSA McCormick continues to play an integral role in the FBI's Program by teaching and training personnel who volunteer to be a part of this program, as a means of giving something back to the organization and its people. The basic commandments of leadership which SA McCormick learned as a 20 year old squad leader in the United States Army Infantry—"accomplish the mission no matter what, take care of your wounded, and leave no one behind"—continue to be the driving force for which he continues to teach and train executives, managers, and employees regarding the techniques of psychological survival necessary in today's law enforcement vocation.

2. PROGRAM PROGRESSION

"I Get By With A Little Help From My Friends (At The EAP)" was published in *The Investigator* reporting FBI News. It states the first FBI Employee Assistance Program in-service was held 10 years ago. It was attended by 36 employees from the field who had volunteered or been selected to serve as EAP coordinators within their offices. At that time, the EAP, although very well intentioned, lacked focus. EAP services were not altogether consistent because EAP coordinators, Bureau supervisors, and management were not given adequate training.

In 1994, the EAP experienced major changes. It became re-energized. Shortly after taking office in late 1993, Director Freeh recognized the potential of employee assistance programs, particularly in an organization with nearly 25,000 employees who had about 75,000 immediate family members. He elevated the importance of the Employee Assistance Program, making it a high priority within the Bureau. The Employee Assistance Program, previously a sub-program of the Health Care Programs Unit, became the self-contained Employee Assistance Unit. The new unit also became responsible for the Critical Incident Stress Debriefing Program, Peer Support Program, and the Chaplain's Program, formerly administered by the Behavioral Science Unit at Quantico. SA Chuck McCormick became the first chief of the newly created unit.

Since then, the EAP has evolved into a major component for FBI members and their families. Today, there are more than 300 EAP counselors and coordinators—agent and professional support—located throughout the field and at Headquarters, ready at a moments notice to help members cope with a problem.

Today's EAP is a peer based program. The counselors and coordinators are well trained. Some have advanced degrees or certification in a variety of professional fields. They are mandated to participate in annual training on a wide variety of subjects, including depression and suicide awareness, workplace violence and crisis intervention, death notification, stress management, the effects of various medications, financial counseling, resolution of traumatic experiences, and issues concerning the use of alcohol, drugs, and other addictions.

The EAP also provides training for Bureau supervisors and management and educational instruction for employees when requested. It provides assessment, short-term counseling, referral to a mental health professional within the member's insurance plan or to community resources. It also provides follow-up services.

To enhance EAP training in the field, SA Vincent McNally, current head of the Employee Assistance Unit, hired regional managers who will serve a five-year term and be responsible for the training of EAP coordinators, along with supervisors and managers in the field. EAP now includes a full-time clinical psychologist, Dr. Nancy Davis, and psychiatrist, Dr. Dickson Diamond. Before these professionals joined the staff, EAP used to contract mental health professionals.

Dr. Davis, as Chief of Counseling Services for the EAP, provides oversight and guidance to the Employee Assistance Unit's five full-time counselors. She also offers guidance to, and consults with, EAP counselors and coordinators in the field. Dr. Diamond is the medical consultant to the unit and its four programs.

The EAP gets its business from several different sources. If a member has problems or feels overwhelmed with what is taking place in his or her life, the member can contact the EAP counselors directly, or a concerned family member may do it for him or her. If the problem is adversely impacting a member's work, his or her supervisor—after first letting EAP know that he or she is taking that step—may refer the member to the EAP, although actual contact is left totally up to the individual. A member may contact EAP if he or she feels a family member is in need of assistance.

3. PROGRAMS

Employee Assistance Program

The Employee Assistance Program offers help in a variety of ways. It provides counseling and referral services (immediately if it is a crisis situation) for employees and family members going through personal, family, job, substance abuse, or financial difficulties. Sometimes, just by talking with someone else, a person can get a handle on his or her problem and move on from there. But, sometimes one can't, and if the EAP coordinator or counselor feels the person would be better served by an outside resource within the community, the coordinator or counselor will refer that person there, working out the best affordable care.

In other areas, EAP offers assistance to supervisors who feel the need to refer an employee whose personal problems are affecting job performance or negatively impacting the workplace. EAP offers training for supervisors and employees in the use of EAP and EAP issues. EAP conducts periodic workshops, both at FBI Headquarters and in the field, and offers resource materials on a variety of individual, family, substance abuse, and financial issues.

The EAP is confidential. EAP records do not become part of an employee's security or personnel file, and are destroyed after three years. Also, FBI policy states that job security, promotional opportunity, and career assignments are not jeopardized simply because an employee has sought EAP services. Confidentiality is breached only in criminal matters, or matters involving national security, child abuse, or if an employee is suicidal or threatens the life or well-being of someone else.

Chaplain Program

This all-volunteer army of 100 plus chaplains puts in more than 20,000 hours annually working with FBI employees and their families during times of need. Each chaplain has passed a full background investigation and has a "Top-Secret" security clearance. They all understand the unique situations and problems faced by law enforcement employees and their families, as well as the universal problems encountered by people everywhere.

Critical Incident Stress Debriefing (CISD) Program

The CISD Program can help those who have been involved in, or exposed to, a sudden, intense, or life-threatening event such as a shooting incident. The CISD Program can also help employees who have lost a spouse or child (by natural death, suicide, or homicide); been involved in an investigation involving multiple fatalities; been in a natural disaster; or been suspended from their job or threatened with dismissal.

In 1995, the FBI created four CISD teams, assigned to different areas of the country, to respond immediately in the event of a critical incident. Team members came from the EAP Unit, FBI Peer Support Team, FBI Chaplains, and mental health professions with experience in police psychology and trauma. CISD teams worked with those involved in the TWA 800 investigation and the Oklahoma Bombing case. They worked with the employee and other affected employees and, if necessary, family members, to help everyone involved come to terms with what happened.

Sometimes a critical incident—especially one involving the death or injury of a co-worker—can impact an entire office. In such cases, the

CISD team helps office managers in that office understand how they can be supportive in the emotional aftermath of an incident.

Another aspect of the CISD Program is the Post Critical Incident Seminars. All FBI employees who have experienced a critical incident or personal trauma are invited, along with their spouses in some cases, to this four-day seminar to discuss their reactions in a safe and confidential environment. EAP counselors, mental health professionals, and FBI Chaplains are available for one-on-one meetings with any employee. Attendance at the seminars is totally voluntary.

Peer Support Program
Many employees and spouses who complete the Post Critical Incident Seminars volunteer to take part in this program, which is all about linking people who have experienced a traumatic event with someone else who has gone through a similar situation. Who better to offer emotional support and understanding to someone who just lost a spouse than another employee who lost a spouse a year ago? The support could be in the form of a phone call, a note, an informal get-together, or even meeting during a Post Critical Incident Seminar.

The FBI is not interested in becoming involved in the personal lives of its employees. The FBI is interested in seeing that employees get the help they need to maintain a satisfactory job performance. While the Employee Assistance Unit administers four separate programs, all four programs have one goal; to help employees overcome problems that are hindering their ability to do their job.

CLOSING

Managing stress and combating trauma in law enforcement require three major elements: knowledge, prevention and program installation. By providing avenues for police officers to realize a problem exists and to talk of solutions, programs must be made readily available. For more information on any of the listed programs, contact the program directors, law enforcement personnel, or agencies.

This page intentionally left blank.

INDEX

ALBRECHT, STEVE (ARTICLES)
Keeping It in Balance - 40
The Police Officer's Companion: Pain & Grief - 37
Running Out of Gas: Police Officers and Compassion Fatigue - 34

BOSTON POLICE DEPARTMENT
Boston Police Critical Incident Support Team - 141, 142
Officer profile - 141

BURNOUT - 65
Causes/Recommendations - 65
Stress management - 66–68

CATCH A FALLING STAR LAW ENFORCEMENT ASSISTANCE PROGRAM - 6, 170–176

CHICAGO POLICE DEPARTMENT
Alcoholism and Other Addictions Services Unit - 140
Behavioral Intervention System - 138
Personnel Concerns Program - 135–137
Personnel Division - 138
Professional Counseling Service/Employee Assistance Program - 139
Traumatic Incident Debriefing Program - 140

CLEVELAND POLICE DEPARTMENT
Tenerowicz, Carolyn Ph.D. - 115
Program - 116, 117

CRITICAL INCIDENT DEBRIEFING - 45, 100, 163

DEPARTMENT PREVENTIVE MEASURES - 44
Helpline - 46
Psychological services - 45
Training and supervision - 44

DEPRESSION - 5, 46, 162, 163

DISCIPLINE
Negative - 14
Positive - 13

EMOTIONAL HARDENING
Defense mechanism - 24, 36
Examples - 25–29

EMPLOYEE ASSISTANCE PROGRAM(EAP) - 6
Catch A Falling Star Law Enforcement Assistance Program - 6, 170–176
Cleveland Police Department - 117
Federal Bureau of Investigation - 188–191
LVMPD Police Employee Assistance Program - 124
Membership Assistance Program/NYPD - 111
Personnel Concerns Program/Chicago - 135–137
Professional Counseling Service/Employee Assistance Program/Chicago - 139
Psychological Services Program/Metro-Dade - 180–185
San Francisco Police Department - 119
Trauma Counseling and Response Program/NYPD - 112

FEDERAL BUREAU OF INVESTIGATION
Background - 186–188
Programs - 189–191

INTERVIEWS
Goss, Cynthia - 6
Greco, Janet - 2
McKenny, Carol - 3
Police officers, anonymous - 20–22, 25–29
Symonds, Martin Dr. - 86

LAS VEGAS METROPOLITAN POLICE DEPARTMENT
LVMPD Police Employee Assistance Program - 124
    Supervisor's Guide - 125–135
Officer profiles - 122–124

LOS ANGELES POLICE DEPARTMENT
LAPD Behavioral Sciences Services - 113–115
LAPD Mental Evaluation Unit - 115
Systemwide Mental Assessment Response Team - 115

METRO-DADE POLICE DEPARTMENT
Comprehensive Psychological Services Program - 178
Intradepartmental stress or performance-related programs - 185, 186
Personal profile - 176, 177

Index — Stress Management for Law Enforcement

Psychological screening/testing regulations - 178–180
Psychological Services Program/Metro-Dade - 180–185

NEW YORK POLICE DEPARTMENT
Helpline - 46
Membership Assistance Program - 111
NYPD Psychological Services Unit - 45, 86
Suicide Investigations Unit - 45
Symonds, Martin Dr. - 86
Trauma Counseling and Response Program - 112
Trauma Counseling Team - 113

OKLAHOMA CITY POLICE DEPARTMENT
Critical incident workshops - 144–146
Officer profiles - 142–144

PHASES OF POLICE LIFE - 31

POST TRAUMA
Compassion stress - 35
Defined - 34
Healing - 92
    Co-Worker support - 96–98
    Family support - 95, 96
    Meaning - 94, 95
    Physical health - 92
    Process - 93, 94
McMains Study - 80
Reactions
    Combat stress reactions - 82
    Countertransference - 35
    Emotional hardening - 24, 36
    Neurosis - 74, 75
    Post-Shooting stress reactions - 82
Post-Traumatic stress disorder - 34

PROFESSIONAL/PEER SUPPORT SYSTEM - 84, 120
Debriefing/Counseling - 84
Symonds, Martin Dr. - 86, 87
Units - 101–103

SAN DIEGO POLICE DEPARTMENT
Albrecht, Steve - 34, 37, 40
FOCUS Psychological Services Program - 146, 147
    Description - 151–154
    Personnel - 147–151
    Supervisor/Management Guide - 162–170
    Trauma treatment and crisis intervention/Proposed program - 154–162

SAN FRANCISCO POLICE DEPARTMENT
Behavioral Science Unit - 117, 118
Programs - 119–121

SEXUAL HARASSMENT - 168–170

SPECIALIZED FIELD/TESTING UNITS - 99
Critical incident debriefing teams - 100
Peer support units - 101–103
Psychological screening/testing regulations/Metro-Dade - 178–180
Psychological testing units - 104
    Assessment center - 105, 106
    Police recruits - 104
    Screening - 105
    Tests - 105

STRESS
Adaptation - 24
Coping techniques - 37, 39, 40
General sources - 10
Police work - 11
    Discipline - 13, 14
    Extremes - 11
    Fear of death - 12
    High crime - 12
    Mistrust - 17
    Police brutality - 18
    Promotion - 14
    Schedules - 11
    Women officers - 19
Problems - 29, 38
    Combat team syndrome - 29
    Phases of police life - 31
    Sexual harassment - 168–170
    Spouse and family - 30
    Substance abuse - 30
Traumatic incidents - 75–77
Warning signs - 164

STRESS MANAGEMENT - 47
Alcoholic thinking - 57
Anger management - 54
Assertiveness training - 58
Burnout - 65
Commitment - 49
Communication skills - 51
Coping with panic - 56
Exercises - 48, 49, 50, 54, 61
Fair fighting - 69–72
General tips - 52–54
Managing distorted thinking - 55

Marriage and affairs - 63
Pacing - 49
Personal planning - 48
Sleep management - 50
Time use - 49
Valuing skills - 47

SUBSTANCE ABUSE - 30
Absenteeism - 166, 167
Abuse/addiction - 140
Alcoholic thinking - 57
Alcoholism and Other Addictions Services Unit/Chicago - 140
Denial - 126
Job behavior - 129-131, 165, 166

SUICIDE
Masked - 24
Officer's - 3

SUPERVISORS
Alcoholism and Other Addictions Services Unit/Chicago - 140
Arrest teams - 29, 30
Assessing job performance - 125, 129, 132-135, 162
Behavioral Intervention System/Chicago - 138, 139
Catastrophic illness - 170

CATCH A FALLING STAR LAW ENFORCEMENT ASSISTANCE PROGRAM - 6, 170-176
Confrontation - 131, 167, 168
Dealing with denial - 126-129
Debriefing/Counseling program - 84-86
Discipline - 13, 14
FOCUS Psychological Services Supervisor/Management Guide - 162-170
McMains Study - 80-82
Peer support - 101-104
Personnel Concerns Program/Chicago - 135-137
Preventive measures - 44, 45
Promotion - 14-17
Sexual harassment - 168-170
Women as - 20

TRAUMA - 74
Emotional - 76, 77
Management - 83, 84
Neurosis - 74
Response - 90, 164, 165
   Coping - 91, 92
   Hyperarousal - 90
   Numbness - 90
   Signs and symptoms - 90, 91, 164, 165
   Walling off pain - 90

VASOACTIVE SUBSTANCES - 68
Sympathomimetics - 68

CD-ROMS to HELP YOU

The only publications of their kind available on the market!
Immediate, inexpensive and user-friendly access to all 50 States and Federal Laws, updated by Gould's editorial staff with all changes enacted

Gould's DRUG LAWS on CD-ROM*

Includes Criminal Violations, Misdemeanors, and Felonies of drug-related offenses. The single-user subscription price per year, including updated discs, is only $249. Multiple-user/network pricing is available as follows-$249 for the first user plus; $99 each per user for more than 99 users; $129 each per user for 50 to 99 users; $149 each per user for 2 to 49 users. **ONLY $249**

Gould's FIREARMS LAWS on CD-ROM*

Includes Weapons, Arms, Crimes, Devices, and Ammunition. The single-user subscription price per year, including updated discs, is only $349. Multiple-user/network pricing is available as follows-$349 for the first user plus: $129 each per user for more than 99 users; $179 each per user for 50 to 99 users; $199 each per user for 2 to 49 users. **ONLY $349**

Gould's VEHICLE LAWS on CD-ROM*

Includes Traffic, Transportation, Vessels, and Motor Vehicles. The single-user subscription price per year, including updated discs, is only $499. Multiple-user/network pricing is available as follows-$499 for the first user plus: $199 each per user for more than 99 users; $250 each per user for 50 to 99 users; $350 each per user for 2 to 49 users. **ONLY $499**

Gould's CRIMINAL LAWS & PROCEDURE on CD-ROM*

Includes Penal, Crimes, and Criminal Procedure. The single-user subscription price per year, including updated discs, is only $499. Multiple-user/network pricing is available as follows-$499 for the first user plus: $199 each per user for more than 99 users; $250 each per user for 50 to 99 users; $350 each per user for 2 to 49 users. **ONLY $499**

Gould's U.S. CODE UNANNOTATED (USCU™) on CD-ROM*

Includes all 50 titles and appendices of the Federal statutes unannotated. The single-user subscription price per year, including updated discs, is only $99. Multiple-user/network pricing is available as follows-$99 for the first user plus; $20 each per user for more than 99 users; $25 each per user for 50 to 99 users; $35 each per user for 2 to 49 users. **ONLY $99**

*For use with Windows® 3.1, 95/98, or NT • All Gould products are Y2K Compliant

Customize Your Own Local City/County Ordinances, Policies and Procedures!

If you need quick reference to local ordinances, policies, and procedures, Gould is the way to go. Whether you've got old, typewritten pages, or a meticulously prepared version on computer disk, we can add them to our compilation of your state's **Criminal and Motor Vehicle Laws & Related Statutes** —Available in Softcover, Diskette, or CD-ROM.

We can create anything you need on demand ... from on-line via the Internet to computer disk, CD-ROM, softcover, saddlestitch, or looseleaf publication with your logo, seal or emblem on the splash screen or front cover. You can have your materials added to any of our publications, or we can combine different parts of various publications for your particular requirements. Gould writes, edits, typesets, prints, binds, packages, ships, replicates disks and CD-ROMS—all in house. **Send in your specifications ... We can fulfill your needs.**

GOULD PUBLICATIONS • (800) 847-6502 • E-mail — info@gouldlaw.com

Want more information? Point your browser to www.gouldlaw.com
Sample software and Search Engine • Complete Catalog • Table of Contents for each publication • Links and Legal Resources
For Quick Credit Card Purchases, try our Internet Shopping Cart.

GouldLaw™—*We give you the Law, You Choose the Medium*℠

ENGLISH ~ SPANISH
BILINGUAL GUIDES TO HELP YOU!

Spanish for Law Enforcement Field & Reference FlipCode™
(with cassette tape)
•••••
Virginia Benmaman

Provides the means to communicate critical information to Spanish-speaking subjects in a variety of situations. Also presents statements and questions in English and Spanish with a phonetic representation of the Spanish pronunciation. Accompanied by an audio cassette of the scripts for every situation presented.
POCKET FLIPCODE™ - Approx. 88 sides. $29.95

Criminal Justice Terms
BILINGUAL DICTIONARY (Second Edition)
•••••
Virginia Benmaman, Norma Connolly, and Scott Loos

A current, comprehensive collection defined in both English and Spanish. Reflects significant Penal Code offenses and Criminal Procedure terms. Also includes flow charts of criminal justice procedure, 11 penal offense charts of the major categories of penal offenses and the corresponding offenses within each category.
SOFTCOVER
Approx. 270 pgs. $24.95

Juvenile & Domestic Relations Terms
BILINGUAL DICTIONARY
•••••
Norma Connolly

A comprehensive collection of significant procedural and substantive family law and juvenile justice terms defined in Spanish and English. Also includes flow charts of juvenile justice procedures from the commission of the offense to disposition, as well as a Spanish-English index.
SOFTCOVER
Approx. 185 pgs. $24.95

Immigration Terms
BILINGUAL DICTIONARY
•••••
Norma Connolly

A current, comprehensive compilation of significant procedural and substantive immigration terms and concepts defined in Spanish and English. Also includes flow charts of immigration procedures such as visa application, deportation and exclusion, as well as a Spanish-English index.
SOFTCOVER
Approx. 120 pgs. $24.95

Please send me the following as quickly as possible:

.... Spanish for Law Enforcement *Field & Reference FlipCode*™ (with Cassette Tape) .... @ $29.95 $ ....
.... Criminal Justice Terms—Bilingual Dictionary (2nd Edition) [Softcover] .... @ $24.95 $ ....
.... Juvenile & Domestic Relations Terms—Bilingual Dictionary [Softcover] .... @ $24.95 $ ....
.... Immigration Terms—Bilingual Dictionary [Softcover] .... @ $24.95 $ ....
                                                                                                    Subtotal $ ....
Add shipping & handling ($5 for the 1st item, $4 for the 2nd item, and $3 for each additional item) $ ....
                          Add Florida, New York, or Texas sales tax where applicable $ ....
                                                                                                      Total $ ....

Quantity discounts available • Prices subject to change without notice • Minimum required for Billing or Charging is $15.00

☐ We have enclosed our check or money order in the amount of $ _____, including sales tax (where applicable) and shipping.
☐ Please send us a catalog and price listing for future ordering.   ☐ Please send us information on GouldLaw™ via the Internet.
Charge to (circle one): **MasterCard   VISA   AmEx**   Authorized Signature (REQUIRED) _____

Card #   Exp. Date
Tel. Number   Department/Agency
Name (Please print)
Street Address (No P.O. Boxes, please)   Apt./Suite #
City   State   Zip Code
e-mail address

Please return this order form with your check or money order to:

GOULD PUBLICATIONS, INC. — GOULDLAW™
1333 North US Highway 17-92, Longwood, FL 32750-3724   Fax: (407) 695-2906   Tel: (800) 717-7917
World Wide Web—http://www.gouldlaw.com   E-mail—info@gouldlaw.com

Want more information? Point your browser to www.gouldlaw.com
Sample software and Search Engine • Complete Catalog • Table of Contents for each publication • Links and Legal Resources
For Quick Credit Card Purchases, try our Internet Shopping Cart.

GouldLaw™—*We give you the Law, You Choose the Medium℠*   Prices effective 1/1/2001

ESSENTIAL GUIDES FOR YOU!

Drugs and the Law—Detection, Recognition, & Investigation (2nd Edition)

Gary J. Miller • A new, updated edition of the publication for anyone involved with the problem of Drug Abuse. Includes: Current Patterns of Drug Use; Crime, Behavior, and Violence; Drug Addiction and Behavior, Central Nervous System Depressants; Alcohol; Heroin Influence; Designer Drugs; Anabolic Steroids; Cannabis (Marijuana); Volatile Inhalants and Poisonous Substances; Rehabilitation, and more. Softcover (7" x 10"), approximately 770 pages. ONLY $44.95

School Violence: Law Enforcement Use of Force (Reasonable and Deadly)

Sheila A. Bolin, Fanchon F. Funk, Richard A. Flesch, and William G. Osborne • Find out what is "reasonable or deadly" force in today's educational institutions, and when it can be used. The authors have provided in-depth examination of self-defense and use of force, including legal definitions covered under official Statutes—*must-have* reading for anyone exposed to the threat of violence in our schools. Chock full of charts, diagrams, graphs, and photos. Softcover, approximately 150 pages. ONLY $24.95

Stress Management for Law Enforcement
(Behind the Shield: Combating Trauma)

Peter and Rachela Pranzo • This vital handbook covers stress and trauma associated with the law enforcement and criminal justice professional. Includes: Anatomy of a Breaking Point; From Stress to Burn Out; Learning to Cope; Post Trauma; Cures, Rehabilitation and Treatment; and Psychological Testing for Police Recruits in addition to related topics dealing with this growing problem. Approximately 200 pages. Softcover edition. ONLY$ 24.95

Disabled Offenders
(Stop, Search and Arrest)

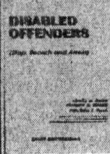

Sheila A. Bolin, Richard A. Flesch, and Fanchon F. Funk • Presents proper awareness and suggested procedures for law enforcement officers dealing with offenders with disabilities. Also includes related materials from Title 42, Chapter 126 of the United States Code, the Code of Federal Regulations, selected state statutes and relevant cases. Softcover, 8½" x 11", approximately 200 pages. ONLY $29.95

Investigative and Operational Report Writing (3rd Edition)

Larry E. Holtz • Offers a set of guidelines to aid in official reporting. Includes examples and step-by-step procedures on how to prepare incident, operations, investigations, and supplementary reports. Softcover, Approximately 60 pages. ONLY $11.95

Use of Force for Law Enforcement Field & Reference FlipCode™

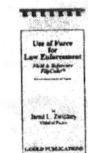

Jared L. Zwickey • An indispensable source for Peace Officers and Supervisors, this "FlipCode™" booklet can be reviewed when conducting preliminary investigations and other critical incidents, or documenting the facts and circumstances concerning Use of Force. Includes supervisors' checklists for "Use of Force," and "Critical Incidents." Also provided are representative government provisions covering the rights of peace officers, and a glossary of terms commonly associated with Use of Force incidents. 4¼" x 8½", approximately 38 sides. ONLY $15.95

The Official License Plate Book — PlateTracer (Quick Reference Version on CD-ROM)

Thomson C. Murray • Learn how to read and decode current U.S., Canadian, and Mexican license plates with **The Official License Plate Book**. This handy reference guide contains a registry of over 1,000 FULL-COLOR ILLUSTRATIONS, including plate validations with month and year for expiration. This year's edition also displays sample drivers licenses for all 50 States, Canada and Mexico. Discover how states and provinces code their plates, and the hidden meanings behind them.

If a quick visual reference is what you're looking for, then **PlateTracer** is the way to go. With this CD-ROM's powerful search engine, you can retrieve a full-color example of any U.S., Canadian, or Mexican license plate within seconds. View them one at a time in "Detail" mode, or start with a broad category search, such as all license plates for "Trucks" in "Florida". With **PlateTracer**, virtually any information you need about license plates is only a mouse-click away! Softcover $16.95 CD-ROM $49.95 ea. for a single user, plus: $19.95 per user for 2-49 users; $15.95 per user for 50-99 users; and $12.95 per user for over 99 users.

GOULD PUBLICATIONS • (800) 717-7917 • E-mail — info@gouldlaw.com

---

Want more information? Point your browser to **www.gouldlaw.com**
Sample software and Search Engine • Complete Catalog • Table of Contents for each publication • Links and Legal Resources
For Quick Credit Card Purchases, try our Internet Shopping Cart • Quantity Discounts Available.

GouldLaw™—*We give you the Law, You Choose the Medium*℠   Prices effective 1/1/2001